Boots & Roots

Boots & Roots

Anthea Elston

Boots & Roots
Anthea Elston

Published by Aspect Design, 2023

Designed, printed and bound by Aspect Design
89 Newtown Road, Malvern, Worcs. WR14 1PD
United Kingdom
Tel: 01684 561567
E-mail: allan@aspect-design.net
Website: www.aspect-design.net

ISBN 978–1-916919-03-7

This book is dedicated to my husband,
Mike Elston, route finder extraordinaire.

With huge thanks for his constant help, support and encouragement,
without which none of this would have been possible.

Contents

Illustrations

Prologue

May 2001

The church was silent. Really silent. You could have heard the proverbial pin drop. I stood in the pulpit, looking out at a sea of faces, so many people, most of whom I didn't know, would never know. The two coffins on their stretchers lay below. I took a deep breath and began to read.

Dear friends,

I hope I was able to say 'goodbye' to you in life and that you are left with only pleasant memories of me. If not, please blame the disease, not me, as I never wanted to hurt anyone I loved.

I always intended to achieve great things with my life – but it never happened. I enjoyed my life, however, and made some wonderful friends and it is through you that I shall be remembered. As a token of that remembrance, I ask each of you to plant a rose in my memory – it may not make the world a better place but it will make it brighter. I ask also that each of you reflect on your own lives and consider whether you are achieving your dreams and ambitions.

I hope that today's mass will bring peace to you. I pray that we will meet again and that this isn't really 'goodbye' but only 'farewell'.

As I read, part of my brain was aware of sniffs and sobs coming from the congregation, and no wonder. These were powerful, generous, moving words, written by one of the women lying dead in the coffin below, Marianna, my best friend. I made it through to the end of the reading, walked down the pulpit steps and back to my seat in the pew.

I didn't know it then, but the experience of walking the last six months of her life with Marianna had changed me. And her words, especially the injunction to reflect upon our own lives and consider whether we were achieving our dreams and ambitions planted a seed which has germinated in many different ways, taking my life off in many different directions, all of them challenging, life changing and enjoyable. All of them down to my friend Marianna

This book you are holding in your hands is the latest part of her legacy to me. I hope you enjoy reading it as much as I enjoyed living it.

Anthea Elston

June 2023

Part One
Genesis

A Boot Up the Backside

It was the walking boots on the coffin which pushed me over the edge. They turned a madcap scheme, the crazy idea of walking 150 miles, from a 'maybe someday' to a 'definitely this year'. Perhaps it was the speed at which ovarian cancer had taken our friend Ann, perhaps it was the fact that this was the third funeral of a friend at or about our age in the last six months. Whatever it was, something had shifted and made me decide that 2019 was when my epic challenge had to be done.

It had taken a while for that seed sown in May 2001 to germinate into active growth. It was now the beginning of 2019, and the scene had shifted from Our Lady and St Michael's Catholic Church in Abergavenny to Shrewsbury Crematorium, where we'd come together for the celebration of Ann's life. Most of us have a tendency to live life as if we are immortal, as if there will always be time to do those things we dream of doing someday, when the time is right, when all the planets align. It often takes the deaths of those close to us, at a relatively young age, to make us realise that time is finite and that we just need to get on and do rather than dream. Ann and Matthew and Benny were three important and significant people in our lives, who had all died in the past six months. Matthew was Reverend Matthew Baynes, my spiritual director, so go to guy for priestly problems. He had received a kidney transplant from his wife, Briony, and then been struck down by the liver cancer which had taken his life. I'd never been at a funeral with so many people, such amazing singing, and a life-sized model of a giraffe. Benny, aka Reverend Benny Hazlehurst had been our best man, and the reason we'd waited to get married until he returned from working with Jackie Pullinger in Hong Kong. He died of prostate cancer in early 2019, having been carer for his wife, Mel, for many years after she was badly injured in a road traffic accident. He'd neglected to follow up on his own symptoms until it was too late. Again, a packed church and the most forensic and loving funeral sermon from Reverend Jeffrey John, our old college chaplain, plus a solo of inspiring and tear-inducing magnitude from an old friend of Benny's, who had flown in from America. Three funerals of people of around my age, three lives cut short when they all had so much left to do and to give. That turned out to be the wakeup call I needed. As I sat and listened as the celebrant talked about what a wonderful woman Ann was – and she was, she really was – all I could think of was how much she would have loved nothing better than to put on her walking boots and her walking hat and stride off on yet another adventure with her beloved husband, Dave. And that she couldn't and wouldn't be able to ever again in this world – but I could, and, finally, I would.

The seed of the idea of doing a long walk to raise money for Macmillan Cancer Support was sown back when Marianna died from breast cancer, and she, and we, her family and friends, received such great support from the Macmillan nurses. I'd wanted to do something to give a little back in return. It had taken all this time for that seed to finally germinate into reality, partly due to the general busyness of life, but mainly because I didn't think I'd be physically fit enough to complete a walk of any great length.

But then I hit my fifties, that time of life when many of us start looking backwards at where we've come from and forwards at what might lie ahead and asking ourselves a few awkward questions as to where it's all gone wrong – or right. I'd been through a number of careers since leaving university – civil servant, technical author, managing editor at a computer book publishing firm, and now garden designer/gardener and part time priest. The major change from employed office-based job to gardening was a response to Marianna's death at the age of thirty-seven. She had wanted to change career and never had the chance to make that leap, so I used a legacy she left me to do it in her memory, and I loved it. One of the major benefits for me was that it meant I spent a fair amount of time in the great outdoors doing a physical job, rather than stuck in an office behind a computer screen for hours on end and in a car on the motorway commuting. However, even having made that shift, it still felt like there was a great disconnect between brain and body. It struck me that I only really thought of my body as a carrier for my brain, rather than appreciating it for the amazing piece of design and engineering it is. Like many women, I struggled with my weight and my self-image, uncomfortable with any compliments which came my way, hiding behind a jeans and baggy t-shirt uniform which I'd lived in for years. I had amazed myself a few years earlier by doing the Couch to 5K programme and becoming a runner, even completing a 5K race, organized as a fundraiser by a local school. But I did wonder what my body might be capable of if I started to think of it as something to be used and enjoyed, rather than something to be looked at, found wanting and cunningly concealed. What if I started living from the inside out, appreciating my body for what it could do rather than what it looked like? What if I was able to become embodied, finally comfortable in my own skin, how would that feel and how would it change me?

But before any of that could unfold, there was a much more basic question to be answered – where would I walk to and why? There had to be some sort of purpose to it all and a direction over and above simply raising money for a good cause. Such a vague and generic aim wasn't going to pin me down enough, wasn't going to make me actually get off my backside and do this thing.

Then I realised that the 150th anniversary of the building of All Saints, Hollybush, fell in 2019. This was the little church on the Common where my maternal grandparents and great grandparents are buried, where I was baptised and where I am the part time, unpaid, improper vicar – or non-stipendiary priest if you prefer – as opposed to the full time, paid incumbent – church speak, impenetrable! I have a great fondness for and sense of belonging to this beautiful little church, created by the drive and vision of one woman, Mary Selwyn – one of a number of strong women who emerge in the course of my story. So why not walk 150 miles to celebrate the 150th anniversary of this gem of a church, and raise money to install toilet facilities and bring it into the twentieth if not quite the twenty-first century? It could be a circular walk, starting and ending at Hollybush. Now all we needed was a 150-mile route taking in . . . some other landmarks?

The other thing you need to know is that I was born and bred in these parts, the borderlands where the three counties of Herefordshire, Worcestershire and Gloucestershire meet – in fact the border between Herefordshire and Worcestershire lies along the ridge of the Malvern Hills. Most of my life has been spent in either Herefordshire or Worcestershire and both maternal and paternal families originate in either one or the other – or both. What if I turned this journey into a songlines pilgrimage – walk the way of the ancestors, visit their graves and the places they knew and loved to try to find my roots, go back to discover where and who I'd come from in order to find the way forward – to put out new shoots, in gardening terms. I've always had quite an obsessive interest in my great uncle Clarence. He was a bit of a maverick, the kind of man who did his own thing, regardless of what anyone else said or thought. As this was the polar opposite of how I'd lived my adult life, maybe that was why he intrigued me so much. A dim memory stirred of thinking that I'd walk to Hay-on-Wye, where he went to live the life of a hermit – albeit a sociable one – and back. Even at that time it seemed impossible, and I was younger and fitter then. Now it seemed laughably ambitious, and yet, and yet, it turned out that there was a route which covered all these bases. If I started at Hollybush, I could head out across the Malvern Hills, overlooking Colwall, place of my birth where it all began. Then I could turn into Herefordshire and go via Bromyard to Leominster where my aunty Pat now lives and on out into Monkland where my paternal grandparents came from, visiting their grave in Monkland churchyard. I could then cross the English/Welsh border and head into Powys via Kington and the wonderful Offa's Dyke Path to arrive at Hay-on-Wye, the furthest point of my journey. My return journey would begin via Gospel Pass and Capel-y-Ffin where Clarence was buried, Monmouth where I'd been at school and first met Marianna, Walford where I'd done most of my growing up and where my parents still live, ending up back at Hollybush. Amazingly this route worked out at round about 150 miles, give or take. One of the many spooky coincidences – or perhaps non-coincidences – which would crop up periodically throughout this trip.

In a way I'd be walking the story of my life as well as theirs, which was quite a thought. Classically a pilgrimage is travelling from one site of religious significance or veneration to another. A chance to step out of the busyness and distractions of everyday life and focus in on faith, or the issues of life which get pushed aside in the hurly burly of living, but which will swim to the surface and cannot be ignored whilst walking. *Solvitur ambulando* – 'it is solved by walking'. Quite what would be solved by walking remained to be seen, but one of the questions gnawing away at me was what had happened to the confident, fearless, tree-climbing tomboy I'd been as a child? Where did she disappear to and why did this diffident, fearful, people-pleasing placator take her place? And, more importantly, could I get back in touch with her – was she still there, buried deep within, waiting for a chance to break free of the restraints I'd placed on her for so many years? As part of the process of planning this walk, I was to discover that the limits we impose on ourselves because of the fears in our heads are often not based in any sort of reality at all. Our prehistoric brains do such a good job of being on high alert for any sort of danger to life and limb that they can guide us into a risk-free, yet also challenge- and stimulus-free existence without us even knowing it.

So, a songlines pilgrimage it would be. I'd pay my respects to the ancestors and remind myself of where I'd come from in an attempt to work out where I was going. What should I be doing with however many years I might have left on this earth. Along the way, I'd walk through some of the most beautiful countryside this country has to offer – and yes, I'm biased! I'd learn a whole new set of skills – map reading being the prime one, courtesy of Ann's Dave. I'd walk sometimes alone and sometimes with friends old and new and get to know them better. I'd visit many rural churches along the way and muse about the place they have in our modern-day society, and how much longer the Christian faith may or may not survive in rural communities. Most of all, I'd learn a lot about myself, what I was capable of physically, mentally and spiritually, what my history meant to me, how grief expressed itself through the act of walking, and how doing this madcap project changed me – for better or for worse.

And talking of for better or for worse, I should also begin by paying tribute to my long-suffering husband, Mike, who will crop up regularly over the course of the narrative. He was the one who took the rough idea of the walk, and turned it into a real live route, painstakingly breaking 150 miles down into walkable chunks with suitable drop off/pick up points at the beginning and end of each leg – a truly Herculean task. Or maybe he just fancied having three weeks of peace and quiet while I did the walk? If this was his motivation, he was sadly mistaken – it turned out he'd be a very busy boy driving to and fro, cooking meals when I got in, making sure stocks of ice were at hand to cool my aching feet – and generally being the hero he always is. Quite literally I couldn't have done any of this without him. In fact, in another coincidence it was the fact that he was being made redundant from one of his many jobs on 30 June 2019, my fifty-fifth birthday, that enabled him to be free to be chauffeur, chef and so much else. The date was set. On 1 July 2019, I would depart from All Saints Hollybush to walk in a 150-mile circle, ending up back where I had started three weeks later. I would walk on weekdays only, coming home each night apart from a couple of overnight stays at Hay and Capel-y-Ffin where distances made it impractical.

This book is the story of the walk and all that I learned, and continue to learn, as a result of it. It was a truly life-changing experience for me and the writing of this book is one of many changes and promises to myself that I'm keeping as a result of doing it. I hope it will encourage you if you have a dream to dare to get on and take action to pursue it. Because one day, it will be you in that coffin, and then it will be too late. So carpe diem, seize the day, and walk with me the story of my life – then go and do whatever it is that scares you, challenges you but also makes you feel truly alive.

Boots on the Ground

My grandad Lewis always advised that you should spend a penny on the plant and a pound on the hole, meaning that preparing the ground to be as welcoming and full of nutrient ready for the plant would give it the best chance of thriving. In the context of the walk, I realised that having decided to embark on this foolish but wonderful thing, I now needed to put in the time and effort to prepare properly for the challenge. It wasn't just the fitness side of it, trying to prepare my body to walk a lot more distance than it was used to on consecutive days, it was logistics, kit, publicity, mindset – there was a lot to do! The thought that I might well have bitten off way more than I could possibly chew crossed my mind frequently.

Originally, I'd thought, it's just walking, how hard can it be? You just carry on putting one foot in front of the other – right? But even though I was pretty sure that I'd be able to walk for say ten miles one day, and maybe the next one too, could I really do that for five, then another five, then a final five consecutive days? It seemed like a pretty tall order, and a literal step into the unknown. Preparation Part One was to start walking some longer walks, fitting that in with work, church, etc. In fact, the preparation had begun way back in February when Mike and I were on holiday in Dorset and I first ran the whole idea past him. We decided to road test it by seeing if I could cope with a walk of ten miles, a circuit starting from The Hive near Bridport and ending back there by walking out into the countryside and then back along the famous Chesil Beach. In the end the walk turned out to be only – only! – 8.5 miles in fabulous weather, but I coped with the distance – even coped with climbing over various electric fences which blocked our way and under fences where there should have been stiles – a taste of things to come.

Back home, my first major test was to walk to Malvern. Already this sounded impossible and would mean walking much further along the Hills than I'd ever managed before. Normally I stuck to a fairly local beat of Midsummer and Hangman's Hills, going on to Broadoak Downs, across to British Camp and home via the reservoir. Doing the full route would mean going as far as the Worcestershire Beacon, a distance of almost seven miles but very up and down. The Malverns form a ridge, like a giant dinosaur back, rearing up between two flat plains with Herefordshire on one side and Worcestershire on the other. You get the most fantastic views as far as Wales on one side, and Gloucestershire and the Cotswolds on the other. So, although a shorter distance than I'd already walked in Dorset, it was much hillier, physically more challenging, and psychologically the idea of walking from home into the centre of Malvern was a big mental barrier for me to conquer, but a morale booster if I succeeded. This particular Friday afternoon, Mike was playing golf so we arranged I'd head off from home and he would pick me up in the centre of town once he'd played golf and picked up the Waitrose click and collect – could you imagine a more middle-class set of circumstances? I was also going to start using my smartphone as a map aid and a way of staying in contact. Now I am pretty allergic to mobile phones. I'm not a Luddite as such, I've worked with computers for a long time – going way back to the days of floppy disks and desktop computers. I even worked in the industry peripherally during my time as managing editor of a computer book publishers back in the 1990s, managing to get an invite out to the Microsoft campus in Seattle and go on a boat trip on the lake where they pointed out Bill Gates' mansion- nerdvarna indeed. I'm fine with computers – I'm writing this on one for heaven's sake – but the thing with a computer is when you're done, you're done. You shut it down and go off and do something more interesting instead. The problem with mobile phones is that they are a constant distraction if you use them as most people do. They are attention thieves. You are never quite present, not 100 per cent, your ears hyper tuned to the text or email alert going off on your phone, not wanting to miss out. There's even an acronym for it now – FOMO, fear of missing out. And, of course, you are permanently contactable – on the train, at the theatre, at the match, in the bathroom – nowhere is private anymore, nowhere is off limits – unless, as I do, you keep the damn thing turned off 99 per cent of the time and refuse to have email and browsing capacity activated on it.

I've always liked being alone. The small child I was trying to get back in touch with spent many happy hours on her own, climbing trees, building dens, reading books, listening to music, watching TV when she was allowed to and listening to classic radio comedy – still a great love of mine. As an only child I was very happy with my own company, and I'd grown up to be a pretty private person. The idea of being permanently contactable was an anathema to me, and up until a few months before I'd had an old-style Nokia phone which was just a phone and rarely, if ever, turned on. Then my friend Mel had grown so fed up with this elderly piece of technology that she gave me a Samsung Galaxy Smartphone – one that had sat in her drawer from a couple of upgrades back. This was incredibly kind and generous of her – typical of the woman herself – and was another thread in the tapestry of the walk preparations. I was to benefit from the kindness of friends and strangers a lot over the next few months – it was one of many learning points from taking on this whole adventure and it was hugely humbling. And it also taught me that for all my liking to see myself as a loner, we all need people, we all need help and love and support to function as fully alive human beings and I'm so lucky to have other people in my life who give me that in spades.

So, back to the walk and the phone. Mike downloaded Viewranger mapping software onto my new-to-me phone, so that I could track where I went. This meant we should have an accurate record of my route and how far I'd walked, provided I remembered to turn the phone on. My practice walks were also practise for using the phone and a learning curve for both of us on how to work the drop off/ pick up part of the walk. Each track was saved, which is how I can tell you that this walk was done on Friday 1 March, the distance covered was 6.73 miles which took me three hours twenty-one minutes and thirty-eight seconds at an average speed of two miles per hour. Because that was the other point of doing these practice walks – to work out my average speed so that Mike would have some idea of when I was likely to complete each leg of the walk. Of course, what we didn't consider was that walking the Malverns was easy from a route-finding point of view. First, because I knew most of the hills pretty well after years of walking them and second because once you were up it was pretty much just keep going – the hardest part, as I discovered on that first training walk, was working out how to get down and one of my distinct memories from the walk was the pain in my knees at coming down via St Ann's Well, which is steep! I was very glad of my walking pole, and even gladder to see Mike waiting for me outside the post office in the Landrover – although clearly less glad when I realised I was going to have to heave my aching limbs up into its welcoming bucket seat. From my perspective now, that walk seems incredibly short, and easy – no field margins to battle with, no mapreading/route finding to go wrong, and only just over three hours duration. But at the time it felt like a real breakthrough, an epiphany. I had walked from home into the middle of Malvern. That felt epic. Didn't feel like the sort of thing that unfit middle-aged women like me did at all. Didn't really seem possible, yet I had done it. Now I look back and feel that the practice walks weren't so much about getting my body fit and ready for the distances – but more about building my confidence, convincing my brain that this was actually possible. Because it turns out it's your brain that holds you back, whispering all sorts of negativity into your mind, whereas your good old dependable body just keeps going, if you let it. All down to a group of cells in the brain called the amygdala, which governs our fight or flight responses – also known to me as 'the lizard brain' – there to keep our ancestors from being eaten by wolves – or Nagging Norah, the negative voice in my head. Nowadays, we don't need that level of self-protection, but nobody's told the amygdala, or good old Nagging Norah as I've nicknamed my own personal voice of doom and gloom. That self-conscious, self-limiting conforming voice had begun to make its presence known in my teenage years and had been growing in power and influence ever since. Having read Caroline William's wonderful book, 'Move!', which I commend to you, I now realise there's a scientific reason why this happens. She explains that the prefrontal cortex, the impulse control, logical, thinking part of the brain doesn't get fully wired into the rest of the brain until early adulthood, which explains the fearlessness and amazing creativity of children, but also means we can get trapped and restricted in a fear bounded, logic dominant box of our own making as adults, unless we're determined to break out of it and try something new, creative and daring. This was it for me! Time to put Nagging Norah firmly in her place and reclaim that fearless tomboy with the can do attitude from my childhood – I just knew she was still in there somewhere if only I could find a way to release her – hopefully this 150 mile challenge would be the key to unlock that prison door and set her free, free to be me, the real me once more.

The most common question I was asked before I set out was – 'You're not going to walk on your own, are you?' And it kind of wasn't even a question, more an assumption that it somehow wasn't safe for a middle aged woman to go walking in broad daylight in the English and Welsh countryside on her own. What is that all about? There was even an item on *Woman's Hour* about solo female walking during the build up to my walk – obviously being positive about it and making sensible suggestions – but still. At first, I was surprised by it and then slightly irritated. Most of my walking was done alone. When Mike and I were on holiday we went for walks together – well, I say together, normally he was at least ten yards ahead of me – but at home, I'd go for long walks on my own. I enjoy my own company and find that walking is a great way to restore sanity. Walking alone is part of that for me. You're in your own head, don't have to make polite conversation and can plug yourself into your iPod if you want to without being rude. In the end I was lucky enough to have some lovely people accompany me on parts of the walk and that was great. In fact it proved vital in any number of ways. But I also did quite a bit of the walk alone, and that was fine too, more than fine in fact, it was fab.

But to return to my preparation, my phone tells me that after this initial training walk on 1 March, my next walk was 7.48 miles long and I kept at it, building the distance up gradually, walk by walk, until by 23 June I was able to walk twelve miles continuously. The calculator on my phone tells me that this means I did a total of 90.18 miles in training to walk 150 miles – which even now doesn't seem enough. My ultimate goal before setting out had been to cover twelve miles in a single walk, which I achieved a week before I was to set off. This was the furthest I would have to walk during what we were now calling 'Anthea's Amble', according to the schedule Mike had devised. Although to be fair he did mention that, although that twelve-mile walk would get me to the outskirts of Hay, it would be much better if I could then walk just a bit further to the centre of Hay – a bit in this case turning out to be another four miles. However, that was way off in the future. For now, having proved to myself that I could walk twelve miles in just five hours thirty minutes at an average speed of 2.2 miles per hour, I was as confident as I was ever going to be that I could do this thing. Or at least that I could do the first day of it – after that it was anybody's guess as to how long my brain and body could keep going.

However, as time ticked inexorably by towards my 1 July start date, it occurred to me that there were other things that I could do to help myself, other forms of preparation over and above just walking. First of all, the inspiration. I'm a bit of an addict for books in general, but books on walking and people who had done big walks became part of the preparation. *Wanderers – A History of Women Walking* by Kerri Andrews and *Windswept – Walking in the Footsteps of Remarkable Women* by Annabel Abbs were both very inspirational and I commend them to you. An unexpected side effect of the walk was that it reawakened my feminist side, which again had lain dormant for way too long! I'm also lucky enough to know other people who have done big walks, and they were incredibly helpful. You'll meet Dave later in the book, a veteran of many long-distance walking adventures, then there was our friend Paul, now a runner as well as a walker, and of course Nick who would be doing the Camino de Santiago at the same time as I was attempting the Amble.

Then there was the vital matter of acquiring the right kit for the journey. My trusty walking boots were not in the first flush of youth. I'd bought them a few years previously in an outdoor shop in Brecon just before we headed off for our first walking holiday abroad – Tuscany in July. They were more lightweight boots, suitable for those conditions, and had been great on that and subsequent trips abroad. But they were starting to show signs of wear and tear, so I thought I'd better invest in another pair and start to wear them in before the walk, just in case my old pair fell apart as our friend Paul's had, just before he was due to do a massive, through the night organized walk. I started by asking my brother-in-law, Colin, for recommendations as he's a proper professional outdoorsy mountain climbing, mountain biking instructor, professional outdoorsman. Also, he's a pastor and a generally all-round lovely man. The only problem was that he recommended the sort of boots which turned out to only be available in Italy, or online, or not in stock when we went to the outlet store in Gloucester Quays. So we headed for Hereford, to the wonderful Trekitt outdoor shop, where the frankly heroic sales assistant spent an hour and a half helping me to buy pretty much the same sort of boot I always end up with and not the much more modern, trainer-type boot Col had recommended. BUT – and this was very much the sales assistant's point – they fitted. In fact, when I suggested I might buy the pair that didn't quite fit but were more lightweight and less clumpy, he told me he would have refused to sell them to me – that's how committed these guys are! At the same time, I bought the socks which Teresa, my boss at work, had recommended – which again proved vital. We left the shop with me clutching my Meindl boots and Bridgedale socks and having also purchased a rucksack with fitted Camelbak water-carrying and supply system in it. I felt well equipped and started to get the Meindls broken in on my training walks. Mike wasn't convinced the Camelbak was big enough to carry all the water I'd need as we'd both still got vivid memories of the time I got heatstroke on day one of our Tuscany holiday because I'd been waiting until I was thirsty to have a drink rather than sipping all the time as I went along. Heatstroke wasn't pleasant and not an experience I was keen to repeat.

Luckily, Dave Galloway, Ann's husband, came to stay a couple of times during the build up to the walk. He was filling in time doing some long-distance walking and had decided to walk the Geopark Way, a 109-mile walking trail through the Abberley and Malvern Hills Geopark, which runs relatively close to our house. He stayed overnight twice within a couple of weeks, which gave me time to pick his brains on equipment and preparation in general, and to book him in to walk a couple of days with me during the Amble. This proved so important that I truly believe I wouldn't have completed the walk without it, but I was blissfully unaware of this at the time. I got Dave to take a look at my old boots, and his verdict was that he didn't think they had 150 miles left in them – but he suggested that I alternate old boots with new boots, thus cutting down on the risk that the old boots would disintegrate but not putting all my eggs into one boot. I'd realised that the heavy cotton T-shirts which I normally wore to walk in weren't the best kit because they grew wet and heavy with sweat. Dave confirmed that what I really needed were base layer T-shirts in a wicking material to take the sweat away from the skin. I also queried with him whether I should get a second walking pole. Other people, who I respected and knew had experience of doing long walks, had suggested this, but I wasn't sure. I was very used to walking with just the one pole to give me added security and stability on steep descents and I liked having the other hand free to blow my nose, change tracks on the iPod, hold my hat on, etc. Dave listened and confirmed that I was okay to stick with the one pole. He explained that had I been walking continuously, camping out rather than coming home each evening, I would have needed to carry a much heavier rucksack, and two poles would have been necessary to help take the weight of the rucksack and keep the strain off my knees. As it was, my rucksack would be fairly light, carrying a couple of litres of water max, so one pole for balance would be fine. He also advised me on how to walk distances, and the importance of taking regular breaks. Every two hours, whether hungry or not, he said, you need to stop, take a break, even if it's only five minutes, eat something and take a drink.

This rang true because the Sunday before, I'd done a mega practice walk which had been really enjoyable, right up to the point where I completely ran out of energy at the bottom of the path up to the Eastnor Obelisk. By then, I'd been walking for about four and a half hours without taking a break and that was clearly just too far. Luckily, I had the sense to stop – I didn't have a lot of choice about that, actually, as my body decided it really wasn't going any further – and take onboard some nutrition and more water. Unfortunately, the nutrition was a bar left behind by my marathon running friend Paul the previous weekend, highly recommended by him, but way too sweet for me. Anyhow, it did the trick and, slowly but surely, I climbed the hill to the obelisk, from where it was all downhill to home. But, lesson learned, keep your body fuelled up or it won't be able to carry on functioning.

Above all Dave inspired confidence. He was calm, practical – and funny, with a wry sense of humour and a bucket load of experience and common sense. This was a man who had led expeditions to Outer Mongolia – Herefordshire wasn't going to provide much of a challenge for him – although my poor map reading skills just might . . .

Of course, there were things I didn't feel I could ask Dave about

– like underwear. Probably he would have had knowledge of even this to share, but I took matters into my own hands and bought a job lot of sports bras from Amazon and some posh running knickers, with more wicking ability. As I worried away at all the possible things that could go wrong, having underwear which rubbed and chafed was something I wanted to avoid if at all possible.

Then people started suggesting I would need massage to ease my aching limbs, so I did a bit of research on the benefits of sports massage and came across magical Michaela, a dynamo of a woman with healing hands, who came to the house and gave me three sports massages which really loosened up my muscles. It was little short of miraculous because after the third session she told me I didn't need any more, I was clearly one of those people who responded well to massage. It was another new experience, and one I didn't think I'd ever have, but it was great to chat about podcasts and politics, veganism and walking. She made great suggestions for how I could look after my body during the walk – drink lots of water, ice my feet when I got in to remove the inflammation and use Epsom salts in the bath. Michaela was a real tonic and an inspiration, and a complete stranger who didn't think that what I was proposing to do was outlandish or impossible. In fact, at one point, she told me I had strong legs – a mantra I returned to when the going got tough. She was also just a lovely person to spend time with – so many thanks to Michaela.

In summary, I'd done the practice walks, I'd got the kit, I'd learned about the importance of taking regular pitstops to take fuel and water onboard and I'd learned how to follow a route using the maps on my phone. Mike and I thought that would be my primary method of route finding, along with waymarks. Experience would show that was not the case, but the phone route did still have a part to play. But let's focus on the route for a while. I had absolutely nothing to do with working this out, apart from saying that it needed to start and finish at Hollybush, that Capel-y-Ffin should be the furthest point and that if we could also go via Monkland on the way out and Monmouth and Ross on the way back, that would be grand. Mike then did all the hard work of turning these rough ideas into a 150-mile walk, using waymarked public footpaths. It's exactly the kind of task at which he excels, with his map reading skills and precise attention to detail. And can I just say that he did a brilliant job. The fact that some of the footpaths were not as well kept or waymarked as I might have wished doesn't change his achievement in knitting together a disparate group of paths into a 150-mile circular walk. He tried in the main to stick to the bigger and more well-known, and therefore hopefully well-walked paths – the Worcestershire Way, the Three Choirs Way, the Herefordshire Trail, Offa's Dyke and the Wye Valley Walk. Where these didn't quite mesh together, he fell back on more niche walks like the Black and White Village Trail, and in one case just used various public footpaths to get me from the Worcestershire Way to the Three Choirs Way. But that's not all. As well as sorting out the overall route, he had to break it up into relatively even walkable chunks of approximately ten miles, but which began and ended at landmarks or places where it was easy to pick me up or drop me off. Churches and pubs were popular options, even though one of the pubs was currently being turned into a private home, but laybys, car parks and telephone boxes also played their part. He did an amazing job, and it all worked perfectly – allowing for the odd operator error on my part from time to time. Without Mike working out the route and being prepared to drive over a thousand miles and give up large chunks of time to drop me off and pick me up, the walk just wouldn't have happened.

And finally, the preparations included the ultimate way

of ensuring that I didn't back out and give up on the whole idea – publicity and fundraising. I hated this. I hated telling people what I was going to do, so I wimped out and did a parish magazine article to avoid actually having to give voice to such a mad plan. This led to me receiving one of the nicest and most encouraging emails from Tim, the grandad of a couple of babies I had baptised, and someone who gives up lots of time to keep one of our churchyards looking good. He emailed wishing me luck and giving me loads of good advice. He'd attempted to walk the length of a canal to raise money for the Bristol heart unit which had saved his life – but it had been during 2018, in that really prolonged hot weather, and he'd run out of water. He'd assumed, not unreasonably, that being by a canal there would be water available, but as we'd learned on a canal boat holiday, the water taps are pretty spread out. He'd been forced to call it a day, return home and then go again when he'd recovered. He'd completed his walk and raised a load of money for the Bristol unit and was a real inspiration and encouragement for me.

Mike prepared and printed off some leaflets for me, which we gave out at the Hollybush Plant Sale and the Hollybush Flower Festival, held to mark the 150th anniversary. This had an unexpected result. At the Plant Sale, a man called Simon introduced himself to me, along with his partner Vanessa, and said he'd like to do some of the walk with me, specifically the first day. This took me aback a little, but I was very impressed and touched by his offer, and glad to accept it. Part of me also thought it might not materialise, purely on the basis that people live busy lives and something else might come up – but I underestimated Simon. The week before I was due to start, he phoned to check the start time and location, and, sure enough, there he, Vanessa and Sparky the dog were on the morning of 1 July ready to head for the Hills. I also set up a couple of JustGiving pages, one for each cause, and publicised them via more parish magazine articles and the strap line under the signature on every email I sent out, encouraging parishioners, wedding couples and friends and family to give generously. The response exceeded my wildest dreams. In addition, Mike set up a blog for me to be able to keep everyone updated on how I was doing, and later sections of this book are based on those blog posts.

Everything was coming together nicely, all the hard preparatory work had been done, and we were fast approaching the point of no return where I'd have to put my best foot forward and walk the walk after talking the talk for so many months.

To Be a Pilgrim

I've covered some of the physical and mental challenges I faced and preparations I made in the previous chapter, what about the spiritual side of the walk? As an Anglican priest, where did my Christian faith come in all this? It was partly inspired by friends who had also been priests, and partly in aid of the church where I was baptised, and my grandparents and great-grandparents were buried. But equally it was partly inspired by a friend who was not a person of faith, and also in aid of a cancer charity. So, was it a pilgrimage? I'd deliberately stayed away from the *p*-word, currently becoming fashionable again as a secular as well as a religious thing, because it seemed a bit churchy and I didn't want to put people off supporting the charity part. However, I do think it became a form of pilgrimage for me.

Traditionally, pilgrimages were made to shrines of the saints or places of great religious significance – Chaucer's pilgrims made for Canterbury and the shrine of St Thomas à Becket. Our friend Benny was conceived as a result of a pilgrimage to Walsingham. My friend Nick was doing the Camino de Santiago at the same time as I was doing my amble, and our niece Lydia had done part of it the year before. Mike and I had done part of the Via Francigena – the old pilgrims' route from Canterbury to Rome – as part of our Tuscan walking holiday and I had returned from Tuscany with a drawing of the route and a dream of one day doing the whole thing.

A dream which had seemed totally unrealistic, but if I could manage 150 miles . . . who knows? The drawing of the route is laminated and still stuck to the wall of my office. Maybe that's what the next book will be about. . . .

What is a pilgrimage? To me it's a time out, to be alone in nature, walking, processing, being with God. It heightens your awareness of the natural world, of creation, and of all that is going on around you. These days, walking is not our usual way of getting from A to B – too slow, too much effort – and so we lose awareness of the countryside, the seasons, the wildlife, even the weather happening all around us. To be a pilgrim is to reconnect with the world around us but also to reconnect with your own inner world, because walking does take time, and concentration, but there are also times when your mind can float free and, freed from the obligations of everyday life, you can think and imagine and just be. This reconnection doesn't need to involve a long walk. Once a month, I schedule in a Quiet Day, like a mini retreat, something all priests are advised to do. I'm lucky enough to be able to go to a very special one-off small retreat centre in rural Herefordshire, beyond Orcop, the home of my good friends, Tina and Nick. You can find them at https://www.sanctumretreats.org. They have a very lovely cabin, called The Fold, where you can go to be alone, be quiet, sit and pray and think, and it's set on the edge of a field. I have taken to walking around this field barefoot every time I visit. It's not a massive field, but when you take time to walk round it, connecting to the earth, being aware of each blade of grass and potential thistle, you take care, you place your foot, you connect to the earth beneath you, you feel your way, you feel the wind and the sun, you see the birds, the leaves, the sky – it's not necessarily quantity of time, but quality of time and awareness that can make a difference.

The weekend before the walk was a classic example of priestly busyness, which is one of the things which stops us from having that quality of time and awareness necessary to draw near to God, to rekindle the flame of faith and love in our hearts. Priests are definitely not immune to a dulling of the light of faith. In some ways, they are more prone to it. Indeed, it can become a dangerous badge of honour among the clergy to proclaim our non-stop busyness. And then the danger is that a priestly calling becomes a job rather than a vocation. Something routine, something we just do week in and week out, part of the daily grind, rather than a spirit-filled vocation. When that happens it can be dangerous, because our apathy or boredom is quickly and easily communicated to our congregations in ways we may well not even be aware of. I've never been particularly confident in my vocation – that is, I've never doubted God was calling me to be a priest, but I've always doubted my ability to fulfil that vocation adequately – which I guess is a bit sacrilegious – the equivalent of doubting that God knows what he's doing. Priesthood has always been a struggle for me, lacking confidence and doubting my abilities as I do. And I don't think I expected the walk to change that, but in some ways, which I'll explore later, it has.

I didn't undertake my walk expecting it to reinvigorate my faith, but I did welcome it as a break in the routine, and a chance to learn more about God, about prayer, about endurance and, as it turned out, about community. And I learned more about grief and grieving. Of the folk I walked with and encountered on the walk, a large proportion had been bereaved, losing their husband or wife years or months before. And as we walked I realised part of the walk was a chance for me to grieve – for friends like Marianna and Martin, Matthew, Benny and Ann, and for the parishioner friends like Susan and Rosemary whose funerals I had taken. The problem, and the joy, of being a parish priest is that while you are one of the few people who can do something practical and useful to help the bereaved family, when it's someone you know and care for, you can't grieve. It's not helpful, and it's not your role. Your role is to provide a safe sacred space so that others can grieve, but that can mean you become a receptacle for their grief without ever being able to express your own. God is gracious and takes that overflow from you, but during the walk I was often thinking of those I had loved and lost, and, in the walking, honouring their memories.

And I also considered it a visit to my ancestors, to remind myself of their wisdom and strength and the long journey they had made from rural working class to educated middle class in a couple of generations. To understand myself better, I needed to go back, to visit the places where my family was from, where I came from, my origins. To revisit the places where I grew up, went to school, got married, called home. To go back to where that seven-year-old had dreamed dreams of being a rebellious non-conformist like her great uncle and work out where it had all gone wrong – or right, depending on your point of view! And to remind myself that I was of that Herefordshire/Monmouthshire borderlands, neither quite one thing nor another. There's something very special about border country and this one had been fought over and disputed for thousands of years, evidenced by the castles and encampments I encountered along the way. So, it was a pilgrimage of sorts, a journey back through the story of my life, and my history, to see what light the past would shed upon the present and the future.

As it turned out, it also gave me a fresh insight into the importance of prayer. All priests are supposed to say morning and evening prayer every day. I have always been very bad at this – as a priest who also has a day job to pay the bills, you could maybe cut me some slack, but not really. Yet, during the walk, it felt really vital to say morning and evening prayer, to drench the walk in prayer. I have no idea why. I was also aware that other people were praying for me, for my safety and for my health and welfare, and that was a pretty amazing and inspiring feeling. Maybe the reason prayer become so vital was that I was so far out of my comfort zone. Despite all my preparation, I still had no idea whether I'd be able to cope and the fact that people had donated loads of money meant that I had to keep going no matter what. Launching out into the unknown like this made me aware of my total reliance and dependence upon God in a whole new way. I prayed because I needed to pray, because I was aware that I really couldn't do this on my own. Let's be clear – I didn't pray because I was holy or good, I prayed because I was keenly aware of all my failings and vulnerabilities and knew that only God could enable me to overcome them and make it to the end of the walk. Rowan Williams said that when he was too busy to pray, that's when he knew he needed to spend even more time praying. During the walk, I had every excuse I needed not to pray, yet it became part of my every day in a way it never had before – and it has stayed that way ever since. I've still not got the daily morning and evening thing totally sussed – but my heightened awareness means I know when I've missed and I know I need to put that right pronto. So maybe the pilgrimage did reconnect and revive my relationship with God after all.

So, back to that busy pre-walk weekend, which veered from the public to the private and back again. From a well-attended memorial service, with many of the local farming community turning out, to a smaller family gathering where part of the farmer's ashes were scattered on land he had farmed, his son now farmed and hopefully in due course his grandson or granddaughter would also farm. The ashes were scattered on a hilltop with 360 degree views, May Hill one way, the full range of the Malverns the other. It did not escape my notice that in a couple of days' time, I would be walking the length of that range. But in the meantime, it was a wonderful place to be laid to rest. The grandchildren participated as did the adults. It was sad and happy all at once, a fitting tribute and a return of a farmer to his land – earth to earth, ashes to ashes, dust to dust.

From that family gathering to one of the smallest, most intimate and in many ways, most important services which priests perform – the giving of home communion. Liz and Derek to whom I took home communion are such an impressive couple, smart in every way, devoted to each other, Liz fighting Derek's corner like a tiger to get help for his physical health problems, which are multiplying. She refuses to give up or be defeated, and with her nursing background and knowledge she is a formidable opponent for the unwary and arrogant consultant. But she is also hugely creative – as is Derek. Both artists, Liz now works in glass, stained and fused. I think her creativity keeps her sane. She is full of curiosity about the walk, updates me on the Archers and Megan Baker House, tells of her arrival in Herefordshire, which she thought was Hertfordshire, as a young nurse, the friendliness and the hospitality she received. I enjoy my time with them and always learn stuff – and always come away full of admiration and respect for them both. Part of the problem with most of our medieval buildings not having toilet facilities is that it excludes different groups of people from services, and Derek was one of my main inspirations for trying to get a toilet up at All Saints, Hollybush so it was highly appropriate that I got to spend time with him and with Liz in the final run up to the Amble. There is a real power in the short and simple service of home communion, partly because it is so concentrated, partly because you can make the prayers and reading very personal to the people you are visiting and partly because you know it really matters to them, that they find some sort of sustenance from it, some sort of reassurance that though prevented from attending regular church, they are still very much part of the body of Christ, part of the Christian community in this place.

And finally, I made it through to Sunday, the day before I was due to start walking. In some ways it was a quiet Sunday as I was only leading one service, but there was a lot to pack in – a baptism of baby Rose for a local family, two much loved members of our congregation celebrated eightieth birthdays and it was a communion service too, so lots going on. The baptism family arrived on time, which was good, and told me that baby Rose really hated water, which was bad. The choir were there practising when I arrived and sounded really good. They were there as a ruse to ensure the presence of our second eighty-year-old, unaware that her birthday was to be celebrated too. However, they added a lot to the service, so all was good. We began. I embarrassed both eighty-year-olds with my sermon, praising them to the skies as is right, proper and well deserved – they are an inspiration to anyone setting out on the Christian journey as baby Rose did that day. She screamed the place down during the baptism, and clearly hated every minute of it, but then we got to the candle lighting bit and I lit the candles of her two older sisters too and then encouraged all the children to join me in parading up and down the church with our candles while the choir sang 'This Little Light of Mine'. Corny I know, but the idea was to symbolize that they belong, that the Church is there for the children as much as for everyone else, that it's their place and they are welcome and we celebrated baby Rose becoming part of the Christian family by showing her to the Church and the church to her.

We continued with the communion part of the service. The choir sang magnificently during the distribution, it sounded lovely. At the end of the service it all degenerated into a wonderful chaos. Tea and coffee and squash were served, a celebration cake was presented to one eighty-year-old, a gorgeous bouquet of flowers to the other. Then, a surprise, Revd Julie called me to the front to be anointed and prayed for. Baby Rose was anointed with oil as she set out on her Christian journey, I was anointed with oil as I set out on my 150-mile journey. Partly for protection and partly to mark the start of something new, something big – kings and priests are anointed when they take up their roles. I was grateful, and thankful for Julie's prayers.

And it seemed to me that this was the perfect preparation. Birth, death and eucharist. We celebrated the beginning of life and faith, we mourned the loss of a beloved husband, father and grandfather, but celebrated his life and all that he had achieved and the legacy he left behind. And it all came together in the eucharist. Birth, life, death, the whole caboodle, but with resurrection hope and faith at the heart of it. And endurance. Endurance is a theme which keeps coming back. Liz and Derek are going through the toughest of tough times, yet they endure, they keep going, they keep their sense of humour and they keep the love alive. These three remain, hope, faith and love and the greatest of these is love. How many weddings have I heard these words of St Paul read at? Yet to see them lived out, painfully, joyously, relentlessly, that is something else again, something to be in awe of and to cherish. Life as a journey, the highs and the lows, hills and valleys, peaks and troughs, times when you're walking on air, times when you're laid low in a ditch, from birth to death it's a pilgrimage, we live and learn, and go again – at least that's the plan.

Finally I arrived home to enjoy the remains of my birthday. Mike bought me walk related gifts – a bigger rucksack and Camelbak, a dry sack and a new tool bag for my gardening kit. Not remotely romantic, but eminently practical – that's my boy and I love him for it. All is set fair. The weather forecast is good. All my clothes and equipment are ready to go – even my silly sun hat has received the Dave seal of approval. The preparations are over and done. Now the action begins.

Part Two
Exodus

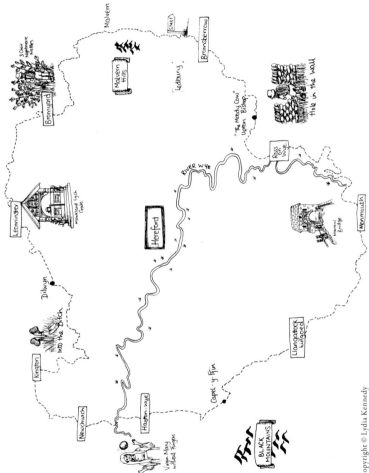

Malvern

3 Chair nightmare Nettles

Bromyard

Malvern Hills

Ledbury

START

Bromsberrow

"The Mardy Cow" Upton Bishop

Hole in the wall

Leominster

Monkland Irish Grate

RIVER WYE

Hereford

Ross on Wye

Dilwyn

Into the Bitch

Monmouth

Monnow Bridge

Kington

Newchurch

Hay-on-wye

Llangattock lingoed

Vegan Mary without fingers

Capel-y-Ffin

BLACK MOUNTAINS

Day One: First Steps
All Saints Hollybush to Storridge

1 July 2019

First steps are always really important. A baby's first steps are recorded and exulted over. First steps on a journey, first steps on a pilgrimage, first steps in a faith journey, daring to take the first step in any new venture is always the hardest part. So how did I get on with taking the first steps of my 150-mile journey?

The omens were good in that the day of departure dawned fair and bright, and we were up on time and ready to get going. My rucksack was packed with all the essentials which continued to help me throughout the trip. Water – at least 1.2 litres – in the Camelbak in the rucksack which came out via a non-decorative plastic pipe that I could suck on in a completely unladylike but very effective way as I walked. Food – I opted for a couple of oaty energy bars and a little pot of almonds and dried apricots. I didn't really want a lot of food to fill me up, just enough energy to keep my body fuelled. Map – hung round my neck in one of those poncy waterproof cases, which actually proved to be very handy. Phone – with map and route downloaded so that it could follow exactly where I was going and alert me when I got lost. iPod – which proved vital for providing a soundtrack to my solo walks. Notebook and pen – my good friend Tina gave me a small, thin, light notebook and pen to record my impressions as I walked. Waterproof – very light, running waterproof, carried tucked into the straps of the

rucksack – never needed. Compeed blister plasters – just in case
– never needed, thankfully.

Add to this my third arm of a walking pole and floppy floral
sun hat and I was good to go. We took the short car journey up
the Common and across the Roughs, where Great Uncle Clarence
used to go shooting rabbits, then down to All Saints Hollybush, the
little Church on the Common, where a small crowd had gathered.
Well, I say crowd – seven people and a dog! Cathy Powell-Chandler
arrived just as we were arriving. Cathy had volunteered to walk
with me on this first day, along with Simon who I'd bumped into
at the Hollybush plant sale. Let me give you a little background.
Cathy was another of my reasons for doing this walk. I had known
Cathy – and her late husband Richard – over many years. She was
a retired radiography consultant, who loved to walk, indeed had
founded a benefice walking group. Cathy had recently moved into
Ledbury, downsizing, but very much kept in touch with the benefice.
She is one of those amazing people who do so much for others you
wonder how she has any time for herself, particularly now she has
Rex, a large black Labrador to take care of. Thankfully, Rex was
not going to be joining us on the walk today as he tends to get a
little overexuberant from time to time. She is a friend, parishioner
and prayer partner, with what appears to be a permanently packed
schedule! However, she'd been forced to slow down a little by a
cancer diagnosis, which she took on the chin in her usual positive
and can-do way. She'd been through the treatment cycle and was,
by the time of the walk, well on the road to recovery, as was shown
by the fact that she was here to walk the whole of the first day with
Simon and me. And I suspect that for her, part of doing the walk
was to put two fingers up to cancer and show it and herself that she
was doing just fine. The other thing to say about Cathy is that she
has a certain reputation for lateness, or Powell-Chandler time as

it is known locally. If the Church door opens as you are doing the notices at the beginning of the service, it's either a wedding couple who've got lost in our country lanes, or Cathy. And yet, here she was, bang on time for the start of the walk. Also already there and dressed for walking was Simon with his cricket hat and day sack, plus partner Vanessa and dog Sparky who were to accompany us for the first part of the walk.

Why start from the church? Well, as I've already established, part of the reason I was doing the walk was to celebrate the 150th anniversary of the opening of this beautiful building and to fundraise for a toilet to be installed there. Its origins as a church tell a story of Victorian philanthropy. The Worcester Journal says that there was huge concern over the lack of divine service within walking distance for the residents of Hollybush. This concern was exacerbated when the Mormons swooped in and carried thirty families off to new lives in Salt Lake City and so stimulated the great and the good of the area to take radical action. Miss Mary Selwyn lived in a house called Glenberrow, in the middle of Hollybush, and was a woman with excellent connections – her aunt was local gentry, Catherine, Countess Beauchamp over at Madresfield Court – and you get the impression she was a lady to whom it was difficult to say no once she'd got a plan in mind. The Church Commissioners donated a chunk of common land, the Eastnor Estate donated the stone with which the church was built, and a famous architect of the time, Frederick Preedy, was commissioned to design the new church building and three stained glass windows to go above the altar, which still occupy pride of place in the church. This means that the church only exists because of the strength and determination of one woman – Mary Selwyn, which is inspiring in itself.

It's also the place where I was baptised, so where my own journey of faith began, and where my maternal ancestors are laid to rest in the graveyard. The church also played a part in my vocation journey. The first inkling that God might be calling me to something other than being a member of the congregation happened here in Hollybush, when another strong and determined woman – Reverend Joy Birkin – preached a sermon on the parable of the talents. Her message was 'don't bury your gifts, use them'. I never felt I had many gifts, but a good strong reading voice was one of them – one of my earliest memories is standing on a chair in a school assembly in Sandford in Devon to read the parable of the lost sheep. That sermon of Joy's started something, a nagging little voice inside pushing me forward, but I would never have guessed in a million years where that very tentative beginning would lead me. All in all, Hollybush was a place of beginnings and endings for me, so a very appropriate place to begin and end this walk.

Fig 1. Sparky, Vanessa, Me, Simon and Cathy, ready for the off.

Fortunately, I knew exactly where we were heading for today – up to the majestic Malvern Hills to walk the ridge from Midsummer Hill to the end, and then a short walk across country to the village of Storridge. We milled around for a bit as you do and took various start of walk photos (see fig 1).

I had thought I might go into the church and be a bit holy, but it somehow didn't feel right – too many people, too much noise. Revd Julie blessed us and we set off uphill, the first hill of many that day. A car whizzed past and tooted its horn – it was Liz and Derek, on their way to Ledbury, wishing us good luck. I remembered how I'd walked up this same stretch of road with Reverend Mike Rogers, another vital step on the path to ordination, with me giving him all the very valid reasons why I'd make a lousy priest, and him dismissing them one by one – it was a long walk!

After that initial response to Revd Joy's sermon, I'd become more involved in church life, reading and leading prayers, and playing my part during the interregnum – another fancy church word, which means the gap of twelve to eighteen months between one priest leaving a parish or benefice and the new vicar arriving. That Easter a group of us had done a dramatized reading of the Passion of Christ, the events leading up to Jesus' death on the Cross. We had sat in the choir stalls at St Faith's, Berrow, and I had suddenly got an overwhelming feeling, a knowing if you like, of a voice that was not a voice, internal yet not of me, saying 'This is where you should be' – as in at the front of the church, leading services, not in the congregation. I would have dismissed this, rationalised it away. Then, after the service, my friend Angela, fellow member of the prayer group and a woman of a deep and active spirituality came up to me and told me she felt strongly that God was calling me to be a Reader – that is a lay rather than ordained minister. To have that happen at the same time, in the same place, was a 'coincidence' which even I couldn't ignore. And so began the lengthy Church of England discernment process, of which my walk up this very bit of road with Revd Mike was a part, culminating in me being ordained deacon in 2010 and priest in 2011. How a shy and retiring, lacking in self-confidence loner gets to be discerned to be priestly material is a story for another day – back to the walk!

Part way up the road we passed Hollybush Quarry, now gated and shut off, but one of the main reasons for All Saints Church being built in the first place, to cater for the quarry workers. My maternal great grandfather, George Prosser, had worked there well into his seventies, going down on a rope to place the explosives into the hill face and then setting light to them to bring the Malvern stone tumbling down. He was killed in that quarry on the 14 November 1951 at the age of seventy-three, ironically by being run over rather than blown up. The coroner recorded a verdict of death by misadventure, which even now seems odd, and my mum has always reckoned that was to prevent the Eastnor Estate having to pay my great grandmother any sort of compensation for his death, in what would now be termed an industrial accident.

It's thanks to my great grandparents that Mike and I are lucky enough to live where we do, in a house in a dip called Eight Oaks, surrounded by orchard, looking up the Malvern Hills. George and Susannah Prosser bought the house when it was still being run as a pub in the 1920s – hence the name The Plough, which still confuses delivery drivers to this day. How much of who we are comes from the family we grew up in? I think that's one of the questions I was trying to answer on this walk, to remind myself of where I'm from, not just physically but genealogically as well. 'Who do you think you are?' is the question the celebrities try to answer in the TV series of the same name, so what do I know about my maternal family, and how have they influenced the person I am today?

My great grandmother, from the photos I have of her, was a handsome woman with great poise and presence.

She attended the Birmingham Conservatoire to study violin and piano, winning a violin scholarship to what was then known as the Birmingham and Midland Institute in Paradise Street, Birmingham for the 1895–96 session when she would have been just fifteen years old. Given that her father's occupation on her marriage certificate is given as castrator and the family lived in Wyre Piddle, near Pershore, I am curious as to how she managed

Fig 2. Susannah Elizabeth Prosser nee Lock

to tap into her musical talent and get herself to Birmingham Conservatoire – the sign of a strong-minded, talented and determined young woman. I suspect she really didn't see herself as the landlady of a front room pub, but the family apparently moved to Castlemorton for the benefit of my great grandfather's health, and I guess moving to a pub would initially have involved continuing to run an establishment which, from the clay pipes and bottles we've found in the garden and the mark on the outside wall where the urinals stood, would have been a bit rough and ready. We couldn't work out why there would even have been a pub here, with the Plume of Feathers and the Robin Hood both within walking distance up on the main Malvern to Gloucester road. But then we thought about all those quarrymen up at the Gullet, walking home after a hot and dusty day's work. The Plough would have been a good fifteen to twenty minutes closer than the other two pubs – and that's a long time to wait when you've built up a really good thirst! She kept the pub going for a little while once she and my great grandfather George and their children, Dorothy, Monnoa and Clarence had moved in. We still have the cellar and you can see where the steps would have led up from it to the front room bar so that bar staff could nip down to tap off a pint straight from the barrel. I also wonder whether they made a lot of their own alcohol from the many perry pear trees which still dominate the skyline in the orchard. Unlike cider apple trees, perry pear trees can live for up to three hundred years, and like all pear trees tend to reach for the sky. We love them, and Mike has recently started replanting some of the old varieties to replace those we've lost over the past few years.

Within a short time of arriving at The Plough, my great grandmother shut down the pub. She became a sheep farmer of some note – at its height she and her son, my great uncle Clarence, had over one thousand sheep which they kept on the common land which surrounds us and down on Longdon Marsh, where they rented land from Francis Bradley-Birt, owner of Birtsmorton Court. The same Birtsmorton Court which is now used as a wedding venue, and which keeps the church next door in business because of couples who still want to have a church wedding, especially one so handily placed right next door to their venue of choice. Of course, the sheep being sheep would stray from time to time and Clarence was never very swift about bringing them back. Maybe as someone who liked to stray himself he had sympathy for the sheep and their desire to roam over pastures new.

The other family legend relating to my great grandmother is about the fire, which seems more than just myth, as Mike has revealed burnt timbers while he's been renovating the house. The building caught fire when a wooden beam that went into the fireplace caught alight and half of the house burned down – with only my great grandmother's precious piano saved from the blaze. That same piano is the one I attempted to learn to play on, although I definitely lack her talent. It's currently in my parents' dining room, but I'd love to return it to The Plough one day.

My great grandfather is a much more shadowy figure than his wife or his three children, Dorothy, Clarence and Monnoa. He doesn't appear in any of the old photos we still possess. I know he was a blacksmith in Wyre Piddle and a quarry worker up at Hollybush, but other than that I know far more about the manner of his death than I do about his life, which seems wrong somehow.

You don't think of the dangers involved in quarrying now when you see the beautiful Malvern stone walls and cottages dotted around the hills, but I'm sure George was far from the only person to lose his life during the quarrying process. And very sadly people are still dying in quarries on the hills today, as hot weather tempts them to cool off in the icy waters of the Gullet Quarry, not realising that it is likely to cause their hearts to stop. A few years ago, there were two deaths in two successive days, both young people. Now the water in the quarry is fenced off with many warning notices – but I still see people down there occasionally when I walk through. Of course, we all think we're immortal when we're young.

Climbing up Midsummer Hill as ever proved to me that I am far from young and definitely not immortal, as the pounding of my own heart filled my ears. Sparky the dog kept us entertained, running back and forth between Simon and Vanessa, and checking in on Cathy and myself as we walked along behind them. I will confess I had been nervous about this whole walking together business, as I'd not really walked with people other than Mike – and he would stride ahead finding the way while I lagged behind, so making conversation really wasn't a problem. And I worried about

Cathy because she was still recovering from cancer herself, and it didn't seem to me all that long ago that the cycle of chemotherapy, operation and radiotherapy had come to an end. I knew she really wanted to walk part of the way with me – and I knew that with her easy, open-hearted character and wide range of interests she would be good company on any walk, but I was concerned that the climbing of many hills on this first day meant that it might not be the best one for her. As it turned out, it was a good job she did accompany us that day, and she coped brilliantly, never complaining, never slowing, always glad of a rest and a break – but then I certainly always was too. I also sensed that it was important to her that she did this. That in a way it would prove something to herself about her recovery, that she wasn't going to be defined by her illness, that she could still push herself physically and her body would cope, and that she was part of raising money for a cancer charity like Macmillan. And I worried about Simon because he was someone I didn't know at all, and I definitely worried that my pace would be too slow for him. In fact, when he first offered to come, my immediate response was to warn him that I was slow. But he couldn't have been kinder, and just fitted in right away. It helped that I quickly discovered that he was a cricket enthusiast – of which more later – and was in demand as an umpire as well as a player. Thanks to being brought up in a cricketing home, and living with a sports mad husband, I could talk the cricketing talk as we walked. And then I discovered that he was a baker by trade which was even more exciting, as I'm a novice bread baker and could get top tips from a real life professional.

Eventually we reached the top of Midsummer, enjoying the view of the Eastnor Obelisk on our way, and paused by the construction which always reminds me of a bus shelter – an impression reinforced by my memory of climbing up to it from the Roughs through a hailstorm one day, only to find a gang of teenagers taking shelter in it! In fact, it's a memorial to a member of the Somers-Cocks family who own Eastnor Castle. Simon and I tried to locate our homes down in the valley while Cathy checked out the bus shelter – sorry, memorial. On we went, down Midsummer and then along a nice wide track to a crossing of pathways – right to the Gullet Quarry, left up to the Eastnor Obelisk, straight on to the rest of the hills. Here we said a fond farewell to Vanessa and Sparky and headed on through the woods of the Eastnor Estate along a track where you sometimes need to step aside to allow the Range Rovers of the Landrover Experience to pass. After a gateway waymarked for the Three Choirs Way, we then headed up the relatively gentle incline to Swinyard Hill, past one of the big round stone direction givers you find dotted throughout the Malverns. We walked on along the ridge, admiring the views on either side, descended a little to the track which leads down to the Swinyard Hill car park – not used as much as the local residents would like now that the conservators charge for it – and then headed back uphill to Hangman's Hill and the wide open spaces of Broad Down, with the imposing hill fort of the Herefordshire Beacon ahead and to our left. I voted to avoid the climb to the Beacon and to take the lower route, which still had elderflowers growing in proliferation along it and gave us a view down over the reservoir and out towards Worcester and Bredon Hill. Finally, we made it to British Camp car park, with its handy coffee shop and public toilets. Simon took the opportunity of a pit stop and I realised that we were almost due our first two-hourly stop so needed to be on the lookout for a handy bench. Walking on, past the Malvern Hills Hotel and up through another car park we soon came upon a bench with a view, where we stopped to take on much-needed food and water. As we looked out at the view, we tried to work out what the big house in the distance could be – maybe

Evendine Court? Possibly even Brockbury Hall? Speculation made the break time fly by and, in a nod to modern technology, Simon was able to do some organising of cricket matches from his phone while we sat, and soon we were on our way again.

This leg of the walk was more up and down, with stiffer climbs than the first leg, so sometimes I was too out of breath to talk, and Simon did have a naturally quicker pace up the big hills but would always wait for us at the top. We walked along Black Hill, Pinnacle Hill and Jubilee Hill, looking down over Colwall, the village where I was born. It's where my maternal grandparents lived for a large part of their lives, so let's spend a few minutes getting to know Ronald and Monnoa Lewis – or Ron and Mona as they were better known, Nan and Grandad to me. I have very vivid and predominantly happy memories of them both, despite the fact that life had not always been kind to them. Grandad's first wife, Gladys, after whom my mum is named, died very young from peritonitis. Hard to imagine people dying from appendicitis today, but only a couple of generations ago, that's what happened. Happily, Grandad then married my nan, the wedding taking place at St Gregory's, Castlemorton, with the reception held in Castlemorton Village Hall. They lived in a bungalow he built, Roisel in Colwall, and had a daughter, my mum, Gladys Elizabeth Ann, named for Grandad's first wife, but always known as Ann. All was going well until Ron had an industrial accident while working as a carpenter on a roof. The scaffolding he was working from hadn't been erected properly and it collapsed under him, so that he fell from a great height and was lucky to survive. It left him with brain damage, unable to work and prone to very painful and debilitating headaches, which I remember as a small child. This was very hard on the whole family – my nan, who was now the only breadwinner, and my grandad himself. To be dependent on your wife was not a common thing at all in the

1950s and '60s. Nan had to fight for compensation, and it was a long hard battle, lasting four years, which she only won because she had the support of the trade union. My mum remembers them stepping in when pressure was brought on my nan to make her daughter, my mum, leave school at an early age so that she could go out to work. Nan resisted strongly, the union backed her up, my mum stayed at school and went on to have a long and successful teaching career, and was always a member of a union because of all that they had done to get that compensation for my nan. Very different from the case of my great grandfather, my nan's father, killed in the quarry and with no compensation – maybe Nan learned from her mother's experience to hang on in there and keep fighting for what was owed to her. I can remember her working on the Christmas post in the days when they took on extra staff to cope with the extra volume of work. And of course, she still kept sheep over at The Plough and sold the lambs. Grandad found his salvation in gardening, in particular the growing and showing of chrysanthemums, and dahlias to a lesser extent. He had a fabulous greenhouse – huge and L-shaped – a child's paradise – smelling of tomatoes and old tobacco tins. In one half of it grew the biggest vine which produced a ton of grapes – a little sharp and pippy for my taste. So, I am the granddaughter of a shepherd and a gardener, and I have become a priest, kind of a shepherd but with a human flock, and a gardener. If I was trying to find roots and influences, here were a couple of large clues!

I was born in their little bungalow in Colwall in the days when first babies were still born at home. Given that I took three days to make my entrance into the world and half killed my mother in the process it's not a great surprise that I'm an only child. I remember staying with them there as a child – the green glass sugar bowl always on the table, Fred the postman always calling in for a cuppa and smelling of cigarettes, the big old-fashioned radio up on its own high shelf when we all had to be quiet so that Grandad could listen to the weather forecast, and the *Farmers Weekly* always around, provider of recipes for Christmas cakes. The design was unusual in that the kitchen sink was in a corner of the main living/eating room and the rest of the kitchen was down a step, across the corridor that led to outside and in a separate room. There my nan cooked lunch for her mother-in-law every day and carried it across the garden under a plate to the massive house where Dandy lived alone until her death at the grand age of 101. I remember the cake my mum made for her hundredth birthday with icing portraits of all the monarchs whose reigns she'd lived through. She got a telegram from the Queen *and* received Maundy money, but where that went nobody knows. I remember her as a tiny figure in a massive armchair, doing tapestry work, a lady from a bygone age. Down the side of her chair was always a bible, illustrated, with tiny print and a magnifying glass, and I used to enjoy looking at the pictures.

And in all these years, it's never occurred to me to wonder how a working class family, made up of carpenters and plumbers, was able to afford to build or buy that magnificent house and the land surrounding it, where Dandy's sons built houses for themselves and their families – until now. And amazingly, the answer turns out to be, yet another industrial accident. My great great grandfather, John King, known as the Red King on account of his bright red hair and beard, lost the sight of his right eye whilst working up at Barton Court, then owned by Miss Cabrera. By way of compensation, he was given outright an absolute title free from incumbrances of three parcels of land – a meadow, an orchard and a cottage, totalling some 1.5 acres in the middle of the village, and this was how our family was able to own and build their own houses. How amazing that in each generation – great great grandfather, John

King, great grandfather, George Prosser and grandfather, Ronald Lewis – all three men had their lives taken or radically changed by accidents at work.

Once Dandy had died and her estate was up for sale, Nan and Grandad moved over to The Plough full time. More happy memories of Saturday high teas, counting the sheep in and out with Nan, orphan lambs being kept warm in the bottom oven of the Rayburn and seeing their little tails going nineteen to the dozen when I fed them from the bottle. Nan and Grandad came on family holidays with us down to Cornwall and loved driving up to Scotland themselves on holiday, often with their great friend Gerald, an honorary uncle of mine. As they grew older, so their health deteriorated, with my grandad having to have a hip replacement at a time when the operation was still in its infancy. My nan always seemed the fit and well one, but then she went down with a pituitary problem, and she had to go and drink a radioactive drink to treat it, which seemed like science fiction to the young me, but which did the trick. However, one evening as we were leaving, she stepped onto the step from the dining room to the kitchen and her leg went – I was close by and able to give her an arm but it turned out her leg was broken. This was the beginning of the end for my nan, and through a long stay in hospital, bravely borne, she never fully recovered and died in 1983 just before I was due to go away to college. I don't quite know what would have happened to my grandad if my paternal grandmother, long since widowed, hadn't suggested that she could move in and look after him. It was an arrangement which worked brilliantly for both of them and they thrived – but more of my paternal family later. Suffice to say that I come from three generations of strong, hardworking and determined women – there's a thought to stiffen the sinews!

And they probably needed a bit of stiffening by the time we

reached the aptly named Perseverance Hill. However, by now the Worcestershire Beacon was well in sight, which was a great incentive to keep going. We descended to the Wyche Cutting, and then it was onward and upward to the Beacon via Summer Hill. By this stage, I opted for the gentler tarmac track rather than the more direct and steeper route across the hills, and so we arrived at the highly popular Worcestershire Beacon. We reminisced about the café which used to be at the top, and which every now and then folk talk about reinstating. And about the plan to set up a cable car system to enable people to access the Beacon, which seems a strange proposed use of public money when the Hills are after all, only hills, and not mountains. The Worcestershire Beacon is even accessible via Landrover and a friend of ours has been instrumental in getting Landrover Jaguar involved in a scheme to allow folk who are unable to walk up to be taken to the top so that they too can enjoy the stupendous views. It was a wee bit windy up there – Cathy and I both had to hang onto our hats a few times – and, as Simon pointed out, the strange thing about the Worcestershire Beacon is that there's a very walkable and clearly defined path up one side of it, but not down the other side of it. We picked our way down gingerly and worked out where our route onwards lay, with the confirmatory help of another of those handy stone roundels. It was time for our next break, and by now it was just a case of finding a handy bench and never mind about the view! We squatted down on a bench by the side of the path, facing back into the hills, and took our ease. Four hours down and we were nearly at the end of the Hills. However, the feeling that we were nearly at the end of the day's walking gave us a false sense of security, as there was still quite a way to go and I was now entering unknown territory, never having walked further than this along the hills, and so felt somewhat out of my depth – a feeling I was to become very familiar with over the next three weeks.

We set out again and Simon kindly took the lead in attempting to find our best way down and on into West Malvern. After a couple of false starts, he led us past Sugarloaf Hill and round the back of Table Hill until we descended via the aptly named End Hill into the outskirts of Malvern. It felt strange to be walking on pavement and past houses, but then we walked past a house which had been featured on the Channel 4 show, *Grand Designs*. It had been built on a very unpromising plot straight into the hill, and was looking magnificent now it had had time to weather in. I'd always wondered exactly where it was. Simon headed on up front, keeping a look out for our next turning, which turned out to be the only overgrown bit of the entire day's walk – a short downhill cut through from Old Hollow to Cowleigh Road. It was a bit uneven underfoot, not helped by the fact that you couldn't easily see where you were treading owing to the verdant greenery. However, the three of us reached the Cowleigh Road safe and sound, coming out close to one of the many wells and/or sources of Malvern Water which are dotted around the hills. Soon we were back in the relative safety of a farm track and following the blissfully well waymarked Worcestershire Way. It was lovely to get a little shade from a spot of woodland and then to walk through several well-kept orchards, heavy with fruit, which I guessed might be going to make Knights Cider. I was tiring now and looking forward to the day's end, so kept anticipating the end being in sight too soon – the disadvantage of not following your route on a map and relying totally on someone else to navigate for you. I was soon to be taught the error of my ways! But Simon did a brilliant job and soon we were crossing a minor road and I was able to hear the whizz of traffic that signified a major road was close by and then to see the untiled roof of the pub undergoing conversion – hoorah – we were nearly there. One more field to cross, and then we were out onto the main Worcester to Hereford road, and could see Mike and the Skoda waiting to take us home. Simon had been taking photos all the way through the walk, and at one point said it was to show we really had done the walk. This made me think we needed to make sure we did beginning-of-day and end-of-day photos so that my sponsors would be reassured that every step of the way had indeed been walked. So, the three of us posed in the layby, the eviscerated pub behind us, and then Mike drove us home, via a mildly circuitous route, so as to remind Cathy how to get to us for Friday when she was planning on walking with me again. Up New Road, across the Common and the Roughs and then Mike dropped Cathy back at All Saints Hollybush where she'd left her car and we carried on and dropped Simon back at his home in Coombe Green. He can't have had too terrible a time, as he said he'd be in touch once he'd checked his diary to hopefully walk another day or so with me, maybe over towards Hay. Then it was just the two of us, and we headed for home. I really wasn't feeling too bad, not as bad as I was expecting to feel at the end of day one, but I was way too cautious to feel triumphant about this as I knew I had days two to five still to come in the week. Once we arrived home I got into my end of walk routine, which I will only detail once for you. I put the kettle on for a much-needed cup of tea, filled an old washing up bowl with cold water and added ice, and treated myself to a bagel and peanut butter, together with the cup of tea, while plunging my feet into the ice bath. This sounds weird I know, but trust me, once I got over that first icy shock, it was bliss. Then, once the tea was finished and the ice had melted, I'd pour the water onto the garden and head upstairs for a good soak in a bath filled with Arnica and Seaweed foaming bubble bath in its little blue glass Neal's Yard bottle. I attribute my lack of excruciating aches and pains to this regime – but it might just have been the massage I had before I started the walks, or the slowness of my pace! Then I'd devour whatever lovely tea Mike had got planned, download photos and write my blog. That first week I managed to put updates on my JustGiving pages as well as the blog, but by weeks two and three with the increased travel and walking time it was just too much so I focussed only on the blog. I really had to keep it updated that first week, as my mum and dad were holidaying on the Isle of Wight and Mum in particular was nervous about me doing the walk solo – although for most of the first week I had company. So, I had to get the blog up so they could read it and be reassured that I'd survived the day's walk. Having to do it that first week got me into a routine, so that I automatically continued it in the weeks that followed – and then I started getting positive feedback about it, which was lovely. Finally, I'd keep on top of work emails, watch a bit of telly and head to bed, knowing that I had it all to do again the following day.

Stats for Day One

   Start time – 9.00 am.
   Finish time – 3.05 pm.
   Duration – 6 hours, 5 minutes.
   Distance walked – 13 miles
   Total ascent – 4,047 feet.
   Total descent – 4,070 feet.
   Max elevation – 1,371 feet.
   Average speed – 2.4 mph.

Day Two: Into the Jungle with Julian
Storridge to Bromyard

2 July 2019

I'd managed to complete day one, but how would I fare on the next day and the day after that? Luckily, I had people booked to walk with me for the rest of the week, which I knew would help, but day two was set to be a challenge because on day one, most of the walk had been familiar to me, and Simon had kindly taken on the navigation for the unknown bits. Day two and pretty much all the other days were into the unknown completely, I'd never walked any of it before and would be relying on my phone primarily – or so I thought – with the map as backup. Like many people, I have a great fear of the unknown. I'm an inveterate planner, like to have all the detail nailed down well in advance and worry very much about all the things that could go wrong. One of the many lessons which the Amble was to teach me was that learning to deal with the unknown, to step out of my comfort zone, that's where the magic is, that's where you really learn who you are – when you push yourself. Staying forever in your comfort zone is a great way to stagnate, growth comes from pushing yourself to go for it, embark upon that adventure! Fortunately though, to ease myself into the scary rest of the walk, I had a secret weapon on day two, which was that I was walking with Julian.

Who is Julian, what is he? I hear you ask. Julian is our nearest neighbour, living just down the road with Diana, his partner, and their two big black fluffy German shepherd dogs, Inky and Echo, together with assorted pet sheep. He and Mike are fellow perfectionists and bonded almost instantly, each seeing a fellow sufferer and helpmate in the other. They are locked in mortal combat to see who can be the first (or last) to finish renovating their respective houses. Yet each of them willingly helps out the other, using some arcane system of days of help given and owed. We have our lovely winding slate path because Julian helped Mike to lay it. He and Diana make a great and sparky couple, disagreeing about almost everything yet in a comradely and caring way, each wanting the best of all worlds for the other. Julian has been a hang glider, a balloonist and currently a kayaker. He is definitely a man of action as well as a man of thought and word, and he is someone who walks many miles daily both to exercise Inky and Echo and to carry out his many renovation projects. So, I was a bit trepidatious about him walking with me, again because I feared my pace would be too slow and boring for him. Also, while I knew him to be an immensely kind man, and a great conversationalist – Mike would disappear down the road for a cup of tea and be gone for hours – I would be spending more hours alone with him than I ever had before and was worried in case we ran out of conversation – I needn't have worried.

Julian is also someone who prepares carefully and well for everything he does, and he'd been up and mentioned about making sure we had paper maps of the route to take with us, as he mistrusts technology and thought it probable that either the GPS on my phone wouldn't work or it would run out of battery. We were confident in the phone as I'd done all that work testing it on practice runs over many hours and there had never been any issues with either the battery or the GPS. However – and it was to prove to be a pretty big however – the day Julian walked with me was the day Mike decided to try out the Beacon Buddy he had recently installed and got working on my phone. It should have been working the day before, automatically sending him a signal every hour so that he could gauge where I was, how quickly I was going and so have a better idea of when he'd need to stop what he was doing to come out and pick me up. But it didn't work, so what we agreed to do was that I would manually send him a beacon signal through every two hours when we stopped for our patented Dave breaks. At this stage we still thought I would navigate using the phone, with the map as a failsafe backup in case something went wrong with it. I'd had a few issues on one of the practice walks, when the scale of the map on my phone went out of whack so I just got a blank screen. I'd worked out how to fix it eventually, but it gave me a nasty few moments. When it happened on that practice walk, I was in countryside which I knew well so it was irritating but not fatal. However, for it to happen in the middle of nowhere on a day when I was walking alone would not be good, so we'd got all the maps ready to go as well. And, just in case for some random reason the phone battery did start to go, Mike gave me his portable charger and full and frank instructions on how to use it – you must make sure all four lights come on he told me that way you know it's working. Fateful words as it turned out!

All began very well indeed. Julian arrived bang on time at 8.30 am as we knew he would and we headed out, back to Storridge and the start of day two. We set off at 9.05 am prompt. Already my mind was boggling with the thought that I was about to walk to Bromyard – Bromyard was somewhere you drove to and it seemed to take a long while to get there in the car – a good hour – how was it possible that I was going to walk there? One very big lesson the walk taught me and will hopefully go on teaching me is the pointlessness of looking too far ahead. When faced with a massive task, break it down into its constituent parts, and focus on the first one, and only the first one. Be in the moment, don't miss out on the good parts of the experience by worrying about things that may well never happen, just keep putting one foot in front of another.

We set off, back on the clearly waymarked, well maintained Worcestershire Way. And the weather was once more absolutely lovely, couldn't ask for better weather for walking, fine, dry and sunny. The first part of the walk took us through more well-kept orchards, then along a track to what looked like a very newly renovated house with gorgeous views out across the plain and back to the Malvern Hills. It looked like it had some sort of blue plaque on it but we couldn't read it from the path and hadn't brought binoculars – though as Julian suggested, to point binoculars right at someone's house seemed somewhat intrusive . . . Turns out though that binoculars are potentially a useful addition to the solo walker's equipment list, not for spying on people's houses, but for scanning field boundaries, attempting to spot stiles or waymarks – maybe next time . . .

As we walked uphill to enter some woodland, we suddenly realised that we were on the wrong side of an electric fence, but, looking back we could see that a gate had been deliberately left in the fence so that we could let ourselves in without letting the sheep out. We continued up through the woodland, and I sent us the wrong way a couple of times. In my defence, Mike the master route finder had been worried about today's route. In particular he'd been worried about the network of paths he'd had to knit together to get us from the Worcestershire Way to the Three Choirs Way. Most of all he'd been worried that I'd miss the moment when we needed to turn off the Worcestershire Way and just carry on walking along it, ending up way off track. This made me totally paranoid and, as a result, I started looking for the turn off miles before we came to it. As Dave later pointed out, quite forcibly, this is the disadvantage of following the route on the small screen of a phone – you can't see very far ahead at all. However, now that I look back on the map, the first mistake wasn't mine but the map's – the path had been re-routed round a house, where Julian stopped for a quick chat with the lady of the house who was lovely but not especially helpful. However, we were soon back on track, heading down a minor road and across fields to another road which led us into the village of Longley Green. From there, still following the Worcestershire Way, we headed up into woodland on the Suckley Hills and I'd managed to work out that we'd turn off the Worcestershire Way in order to leave these woods – but where would the turn off come?

Turned out that I didn't need to worry about that for a little while because we'd been going for two hours so our mandatory stop time was fast approaching. Where would we find a suitable spot on which to sit down and take our ease? As if by magic, a stone bench appeared at the side of the path. On closer inspection, it wasn't a bench as such but a large chunk of rock, positioned over the grave of a local farmer who had asked to be buried right there in the middle of the woods. We figured that George wouldn't mind us purloining his protective stone to use for a bit of a sit down, and we found ourselves speculating on how on earth the massive chunk of rock had been manoeuvred into the middle of these woods. But it did the job brilliantly and, rested and refreshed, we carried on. In the end it was easy to see where the turn off was because we came to a T Junction in the woods and my phone told me that the Worcestershire Way went right, and we needed to go left. Julian was at first unconvinced but I stuck to my guns and so we headed off piste, away from the woods across fields and a bit of road walking into the village of Suckley Green where we were to pick up the Three Choirs Way. Something of note happened as we picked our way across fields. We arrived at rather a fine field of potatoes; the sign pointed the way over the stile directly across this magnificent crop – our conundrum was how were we to get across the field without causing any damage to the potatoes? Then we realised that the farmer in the field was mowing off an entire row of this prolific and very healthy-looking crop in order to allow walkers to cross his land. He'd made it a dog leg to avoid some electric pylons, but it was an excellent walkway. Julian stopped to chat to him as we passed and we both thanked him very much for making a path for us. It wasn't to be the last time that the timing of the walk was uncannily almost to the minute precise, coinciding with paths being cleared for us just as we arrived at them. However, sadly our luck was about to run out as we headed for the Three Choirs Way. This should have been a doddle. It's a major long-distance path, and so Mike had assumed it would be clearly waymarked and well maintained. From the start that was not the case, and things were to get a lot worse before they eventually got better!

We should have known all was not well when it took us ages to even find the path. We found the pub it was next to – sadly not yet open. We found the fingerpost sign for the footpath, pointing straight into someone's garden, but after that we couldn't find hide nor hair of the path, not a waymark in plain sight. I came across this problem a few times, usually in close proximity to someone's house or farm buildings, and while I sympathise with their wish to limit intrusion by the public into their private space, the reality is that you actually prolong people's visit to your property by removing signage, and positively encourage them to explore areas which aren't on the right of way, simply because they can't find the correct path owing to lack of decent signage. If you really want people to go away – show them where the right of way goes and 99.9 per cent of all walkers will follow it!! Rant over. Eventually we worked out which way to go and headed off across fields.

Our first misstep came at Upper House Farm, where a whole load of paths converged. We found the right path taking us into a field, but where to go from there? As was often to be the case in the days to come, it was really easy to be misled by an obvious path leading across the field to a gateway – and that's the way we headed. It was the sort of mistake which was rewarded as Julian spotted a muntjac deer in full flight and pointed it out to me. It looked like no deer I'd ever seen before and I read a recent description of a muntjac as looking like an overgrown hare, which seemed right to me. Too big to be a hare, it seemed to move in a hare like manner, but I trusted Julian's identification skills totally and was glad to have added muntjac to my list of wildlife spotted.

We realised we'd headed in the wrong direction, but it took us a while to spot our onward route, which turned out to be a green lane running between fields. I was double checking the phone map yet again to reassure myself we were in fact on the right track when Julian spotted another piece of wildlife, but it moved so fast that by the time he'd alerted me and I'd looked up it was long gone. Julian described it as like a cat, but bigger, yet not as big as a fox. A few days later, having done some research he reckoned it was a pole cat, which apparently had been sighted in the area. These are the things you see when you walk. You make so much less noise than any machine that you can get up close to a wild animal before it runs. Sitting here typing this, I get to see a squirrel close up and be fascinated by its movements, so quick and lithe. Nature is all around us if only we take a moment to stop and stare and be aware that we share this planet with others – it's not all about us.

I love a green lane – you're not in fields so you don't feel like an intruder, but you're not on roads so don't have to worry about traffic. You're surrounded by green, hedges and trees, which gives you a fabulous feeling of being protected somehow, wrapped in nature, and in history as some green lanes date back hundreds if not thousands of years. This one delivered us out to cross over a track leading up to a farm but we kept going straight on, along a field margin then through an opening and into another field which turned out to be orchard, with well-kept lines of apple trees. As we came through the gap in the hedge, the way ahead seemed clear, a track leading to a gate, thoughtfully propped open so we continued on through it and into the fields beyond. By this time, we were deep in conversation about people's inability to take the initiative and organize stuff for themselves, rather than leaving it to mugs like us, when I thought to check where we were on the phone route as something about the way we were heading suddenly didn't look very pathy. Sure enough we'd been misled by the temptation of a wide open gate and needed to backtrack and re-join the path which actually led up through the orchard we'd just left.

Thinking about this later, it struck me that most of us, definitely including me, follow the obvious path. Not always because me becoming a priest was definitely not the obvious path. But we can be so distracted with the busyness of life that we keep heading through each open gateway without really thinking: is this actually the way I really want to be heading? We go with the flow, go with parental or societal expectations – school onto university into a job, marriage, kids, etc – often without stopping at each stage to ask ourselves whether that's really the way we want to go. As children, it can be easier to know what we want and just go for it. Once we arrive at adulthood, the oughts and the shoulds come into the picture, and muddy the waters. As a mature adult, it can be surprisingly hard to work out what you want to do, and then just go for it. It's important to realise that not making a choice is still making a choice – you're choosing to stay on the obvious and conventional path, stay well within your comfort zone, limiting yourself to the safe and known, when life might be richer away from the obvious path. It can be so easy to let busyness give us tunnel vision, but sometimes this is an excuse for not pushing yourself, testing your limits. This was a large part of why I was doing this walk, I wanted to push myself physically, mentally and spiritually and see what I was really capable of doing. It had taken a lot of organization and hard work but the key first step was daring to dream that this was something I wanted to do and then having the courage to voice that decision and work to make it happen. If I hadn't had the courage to say this is what I want to do, how can we make it happen, then I would have stayed stuck in my tram tracks and never have done it.

Back on track, we kept going for a few hundred metres, heading into woodland and then crossing over a stile bridge – so definitely on some sort of footpath, but then the phone showed us we'd deviated off our set route once more and left the Three Choirs Way. We walked back up the slope we'd just walked down and, coming from this direction, were able to see the Three Choirs Waymark on the back of the post we'd just walked past. Coming from this direction, the way was obvious, which was lucky as the 'path' was so overgrown we'd never have believed that that was the way to go without that waymark. We hacked our way through the nettles, down to the bottom of the field where a stile and another waymark confirmed we were still heading the right way. By now it was time for our second break, so we sat down on a handy pile of logs, and I attempted to manually send Mike a Beacon Buddy signal to let him know where we were. It seemed to work. However, the battery on my phone was now down to 35 per cent – it had gone down much faster than usual – was this the effect of the Beacon Buddy app running in the background? Who knew? Certainly not me! I got out the mobile charger, plugged everything in and switched on but

I couldn't see any lights on at all, let alone four. I swapped cables around, turned it off and turned it back on again – still nothing. I texted Mike to let him know there was a problem and then break time was over and we carried on. The next few fields were lovely short cut grass, a blissful change from the jungly conditions just encountered. We also came across waymarks for the Beata Way, which I'd never heard of and made a mental note to look up once we got home. What I found out was that The Via Beata is an amazing project to establish a pilgrimage route spanning the UK from east to west at its widest point, with Christian artworks at key points. The route runs from St David's in the west to Lowestoft in the east, over four hundred miles in length, and it's still a work in progress but a very fascinating one. To find out more, go to https://www. viabeata.co.uk.

Then it was a nice bit of road walking – I'd never been a fan of road walking in the past, moaning like a drain at having to cope with passing cars and lorries, but these were tiny country lanes with very little traffic, so all was well. And you really do know where you are on a road!

However, it was when we followed another fingerpost pointing us away from the road and up a short track leading to a house that we hit our most challenging obstacle of the day. The track up to the house was fine, clear and easily walkable, but the route continued on past the house, over a stile and into a field. The way to the stile was blocked by undergrowth – mainly nettles – that were taller than I was. Did I mention Julian was wearing shorts? Perfectly fine gear for the hot weather but not for walking through nettles. It was so absurdly bad that Julian took some photos (see fig 3).

I went first with my stick trying to beat down some sort of path for us both. We made it to the stile, but once over the stile our problems were not at an end. We found ourselves in a field

Fig 3. Anthea and nettles

of corn where the field margin was just as congested with nettles, docks and thistles as the bit of path we'd just navigated. We had no choice but to walk through the crop, keeping to the edge and doing as little damage as we could, but the farmer had left us no option. This happened a few times – most notably and potentially disastrously on the Monday of week two. And I understand it, I really do. As Julian said, doing the walk in July wasn't the best idea from this point of view in that it was just before harvest time and at a time of the year when nature in all her glory was going into overdrive and the margins were likely to be overgrown.

It strikes me now that this also describes part of my faith journey. Having been brought up as a Christian, and been part of a Christian community at university, it was when I started work up in London that the rest of life kind of took over and obscured the faith pathway. There was so much else going on, work and play, that I never quite got round to finding a new Christian community to belong to and so I definitely wandered from the pathway for quite a few years. To quote from the parable always used at harvest time, the seed had landed, had germinated but then it got overgrown by the weeds and thistles of life. That's how easily it can happen. Fortunately, God never gives up on us and is always there like the father in the story of the prodigal son to welcome us back with open arms. But I wanted to be clear that just because I'm a vicar now, doesn't mean I've always been a faithful and observant Christian, and our life in London marked the beginning of a time when faith hardly featured in my life at all for almost twenty years.

Back at the walk and facing a battle up a very congested field margin, or through the crop, I reminded myself that we had also walked through fields where the margins were kept mown for walkers. I knew it could be done. Some landowners choose not to do this, just as some landowners choose not to maintain their stiles or keep their waymarks updated. I can see that this is never going to be your top priority when you're trying to make a living. But the consequences are that walkers will trash your crop because, like us, they don't have an alternative. I hated doing it, and I particularly hated doing it whilst walking up the field towards two cottages, but it was the only way we could keep going. We emerged onto the road and then had a considerable stretch of road walking to do which again was a blessed relief. And the deeper we got into the countryside the more beautiful it became. The view over the countryside as we walked down the road, the hedgerows, the fields, the birds flitting in and out of the hedges – it was wonderful.

Sadly, we arrived at the point where we needed to turn off, head up a farm drive and circumnavigate some farm buildings – yet again, it took us ages to find a waymark, but when we did it pointed us toward a field where a clear track had been left through the crop to enable walkers to cross the field. By now we'd reached Lower House Farm, and still had quite a way to go to reach Bromyard but it was 3 pm and the phone battery was fading fast. I sent another Beacon Buddy off into the ether and texted Mike to warn him that there was a problem with keeping in contact. He phoned me – it felt surreal to take a phone call in the middle of a field. He was already in Bromyard and offered to come out and pick us up when we next hit a road. Julian was some way ahead because he'd kept going while I stopped to take Mike's call, so I couldn't check with him, but I said 'No' for both of us. When we'd ended the call, I tried plugging the phone into the charger again, but got a message saying you shouldn't charge the phone while it was switched on. By now I was thoroughly fed up with mobile technology, so turned the phone off and put it away in the rucksack, still attached to the charger to see if that did any good. I then caught up with Julian who was happy to continue using good old-fashioned map reading skills, which luckily, he possessed in abundance. I suspect a little part of him was actually quite smug about the fact that all his misgivings about relying on technology were proving to be correct – though he gave no indication of this at all and carried on being a kind and stimulating companion. We headed for Upper Venn Farm the next major landmark on our route, reaching it after quite a long trek along a farm road. It was a sad landmark, a once great and sizeable farm now fallen into disuse. Whole chunks of the brickwork of the farmhouse were literally held on with baler twine, windows were broken or just missing altogether, and the huge barns stood empty.

However, the good news was we were finally off the Three Choirs Way – hoorah – and onto the Herefordshire Trail which was so much better maintained and waymarked. The only bad news was we still had quite a way to go before we reached Bromyard, but there was only one way to solve that – keep going, keep putting one foot in front of another. We headed up a lovely accessible field, along a track which led us through hopyards, the first time I'd walked through one though I'd seen them often enough as I'd whizzed by in the car. Hop fields had played a part in my family history as I remembered Dad telling me that his mum, my gran, had worked as a hop picker, so it was really interesting to be able to walk through one and I was so impressed that I took a photo, using Julian to give a sense of scale!

Fig 4. Julian in hop field

We came to a set of farm buildings which couldn't have been more different to Upper Venn Farm. This was Brook House Farm, well maintained and a very impressive operation comprising a modern farmhouse, some self-catering lets and buildings, with free range chickens thrown in. However, we were unsure of which way to go until one of the farmers came to our aid and pointed us in the right direction, and soon we were heading across fields again, only to emerge onto the lane at Avenbury to find a familiar looking Skoda waiting for us and Mike chatting to someone. For a moment I thought it was Dave who was due to arrive by train from Shrewsbury that afternoon. In fact it was someone mowing his lawn, who thought Mike was a potential burglar or shady character, but was soon convinced of his mistake and very happy to chat. I was a bit thrown to see Mike there and didn't quite understand what was going on. By now it was 4.00 pm so we'd been going for seven hours, less the two breaks we'd had. Mike had very kindly driven over to give us the option of cutting the walk short, finishing there and then before we reached Bromyard with the logic that it didn't really matter as Dave and I could just start from there the next day and add the distance on to day three.

Now this is where I really surprised myself. Had you asked me at the start of the day I would have said I'd have jumped at the chance of the early finish. We'd been going for seven hours, it was going to take us at least another hour to make it to Bromyard, I'd never walked for eight hours in my life and wouldn't have thought it possible . . . but the music of my heart was 'No. Thank you for thinking of us, and suggesting it, but No'. I could see Bromyard from where we were standing. True it would take us another hour to get there, but it was within sight. And how would it seem to my supporters, those people who had pledged all that money, if I gave up and went home early on day two? And what sort of sign would it be for the rest of the walk? If I fell short this early in the proceedings and started adding bits onto the next day, would I ever finish? I did give Julian the option, but he felt the same way as I did. We'd made it this far, we'd keep going until the end. So we did.

However, it was useful for Mike to be able to check out the phone/charger situation, if somewhat irritating that when he checked it the charger had obviously been working all along as the phone was now back up to 75 per cent battery. This meant I could reactivate the tracking system for the last bit, which was comparatively easy walking, well-marked, eventually leading us uphill and into Bromyard. Eight hours after setting out we sat on a bench under a Bromyard sign for the end of day photo. We were tired, battered and bruised and with nettle stings, but we'd made it. On the way home we stopped off at Great Malvern station to pick up Dave who had signed on to walk the next two days with me. And thank goodness he did!

When I reflected on this day afterwards, many things about it surprised and astonished me – the fact that I'd walked to Bromyard, the fact that I'd walked for eight hours, the fact that I turned down the chance of a lift and kept going even when it meant hacking through head high nettles. But in some ways what surprised me most of all was that I managed not to whine, whinge or lose my temper – all things I have done repeatedly when out walking over much shorter, easier distances with Mike. This makes me feel a sense of shame – and so it should – but also confirms something I say on every marriage prep day to our brides and grooms – that we often treat the people most dear to us far worse than we do complete strangers or acquaintances. We are polite and restrained with them whereas with our nearest and dearest we feel free to vent our anxieties, frustrations and general bad humour with impunity. I don't have an answer for this, I just hold my hand up to admit my guilt in the hope that it will improve my behaviour on future walks. And a huge thank you to Julian for maintaining his sunny and even temperament and being willing to stick it out with me – heroic behaviour above and beyond the call of duty and for which I remain hugely grateful. Definitely wouldn't have made it to Bromyard without you!

Stats for Day Two
  Start time – 9.05 am.
  Finish time – 4.56 pm.
  Duration –7 hours, 51 minutes.
  Distance walked – 11.8 miles.
  Total ascent – 1,613 ft.
  Total descent – 1,567 ft.
  Max elevation – 622 ft.
  Avg. speed – 1.9 mph.

The mathematicians among you will have noted that the mph makes no sense. This is because my phone record tells me we walked for six hours and fifteen minutes – presumably because it was turned off for a chunk of time. I've not recalculated it as that would be way too depressing, even now!

Day Three: An Education in Map Reading
Bromyard to Pudleston

3 July 2019

Day three dawned bright and sunny again, and Dave was up and about early to make sure he had time for the seven or so cups of tea he would inhale before we set off. I exaggerate, it was only three. Footnote on kit – I had by now added a buff to my kit list. A buff is basically a tube of wicking type material you have round your neck, and in my case it served the quite disgusting purpose of being there so that I could push it up to my hairline to prevent the oceans of sweat I was generating from dripping down into my eyes and obscuring my vision. You don't fully realise how salty your own sweat is until it's running into your eyes and making them sting. But my trusty buff prevented this and had become part of the nightly quick wash ritual when that day's kit was flung into the washing machine, hung on the drying rack to dry, and was then good to go the day after next. Rinse and repeat, rinse and repeat and so on. Just reassuring the reader of delicate sensibility that I was clean and sweetish smelling when I set off each morning.

Now, I knew that Dave had a cunning plan, which he had confided in Mike, which was to make me lead the walk, get lost and then he would teach me how to do it properly. This is a classic Dave teaching method – and one that is pretty universal I would imagine. The pupil needs to realise that they need the knowledge before they are going to be willing to take it onboard. However, having had a blow-by-blow account of our many disasters the day before, he had slightly revised this plan. He still planned to teach me the Zen art of map reading and navigation, but he realised he could skip the getting lost bit as I'd already done plenty of that and so had already prepared my mind to be receptive to a bit of help and guidance. I suppose at this point I should tell you something about Dave and our sort of unlikely friendship.

Dave and I first met when we were both working at a company called Wrox Press based in the Birmingham suburb of Acocks Green. In fact, when I joined it was based in a terraced house in Acocks Green and employed about twenty people. Dave joined once it had grown a little, and when I left it employed about two hundred people and had offices in Paris and Mumbai as well as the Chicago sales office which it had always had. It was all the brainchild of Dave Maclean, a serial entrepreneur, and a genius with a very low boredom threshold. He was mercurial and magical, hugely charismatic, could charm the birds off the trees, but could also turn on people for no apparent reason – I'd sat in meetings where he had reduced people to tears. He was totally open to new ideas wherever they came from. If a reader phoned up to complain, that was like catnip to him. He'd want to have a proper conversation about the complaint, understand where it came from and then do something about it. He'd originally set the company up using Russian programmers to write books in red covers explaining how to code C++ largely for the American market – hence the Chicago sales office, run by his younger brother, Adam. But when I joined the company, he'd moved on to focus on Microsoft technology, hired British physics and maths graduates as editors and used American coders to write the books which our highly talented editors would turn into readable, useful prose. I didn't need to know anything about coding – which was handy – I just needed to manage the people, liaise with the printers and hit the book delivery deadlines (sound of hollow laughter). Dave Galloway came onboard as a project manager and in a sense he's been project managing me ever since! How to describe him? He's one of the most real, grounded, authentic people I've ever met. He's calm, relaxed, pragmatic and practical to a fault. Nothing fazes him. He'll accept the reality of any situation and then work out what the best way is to deal with it, without wasting valuable time and energy getting stressed or emoting. That's why, although I greatly mourned the sudden and tragic death of Ann, I knew that he would treat being widowed as a project to be faced up to and got on with. That doesn't mean I thought he wasn't devastated by her loss, didn't mourn her or miss her – just that I knew he wouldn't allow himself to mope – particularly as that would be the last thing Ann would want – but would get out there and get on with life. My impression had always been that he doesn't give a fig what anybody else thinks of him, he is who he most gloriously is, take it or leave it. So in many ways he's the polar opposite of a people pleasing emotional wreck like myself – hence we work well together! He loves his family, his friends and Birmingham City, not necessarily in that order. The measure of the man I guess is in the fact that his closest friends like Clive are people he has been friends with since school. He is loyal and true, will always give you a totally honest opinion – how scary is that – and has a wicked sense of humour and a great love of walking, cider and real ale. I am very lucky to have him in my life.

Dave left Wrox before I did, head hunted to a job in the health service. We stayed in touch and when I too left Wrox and re-trained as a garden designer, he asked if he could be part of the business too. Said he'd enjoyed working with me and would like to be involved not because it would make both our fortunes, but for the experience and enjoyment of it. Mike was particularly keen that I take Dave up on this kind offer, fearing that otherwise I'd never do anything with my shiny new garden design qualification. With Dave's help, we came up with a name for the company, Midfeather Garden Design. This was based on a term taken from his old mining dictionary – his degree was in geology. A midfeather is a pipe which, when joined to another two pipes, makes the whole thing work better. We thought that this was a good metaphor for what a good designer should do – be the conduit between client and landscaper, making the implementation of the design run smoothly – and it gave us a nice feathery name so that Dave's mate, Mike Ashton, could create us a nice feathery logo. We met monthly while Dave and Ann were still based in Bournville, then, when they moved to Shrewsbury, we tended to do things by phone, and we still have our monthly phone meets to this day. It's a handy way of checking in on each other's lives as well as ensuring I'm keeping up to date with the business admin. The business never has been a roaring success, rarely turning a profit, but if all it's done is kept me out of mischief and kept Dave as a part of my life, then I'd say it's been worth doing. These days I'm far more of a gardener than a garden designer, and that suits me fine. I work a couple of days a week as an under gardener at a local big house with the most beautiful grounds and gardens – a real privilege to work there – and still have a few private clients of my own. I still love gardening. There is something about spending time outside, head down, hands in the soil, which is calming, quite literally grounding, and keeps your ego firmly under control – all good!

So, where were we? Back at Bromyard taking the day three start of day photo outside Bromyard Public Hall. Dave nipped off to the loo before we began which left me to talk about my day-three nerves with Mike. I had good reason to be nervous. I'd never led a walk before, and I knew that both my husband and my father were deeply sceptical about my ability to read a map. However, my mother is a brilliant navigator, so maybe some of that would have rubbed off, genetically speaking? I've always been more comfortable as follower rather than leader. Or is that true? As a child, I was much more comfortable taking the lead, making the running, coming up with ideas and getting others to join me in putting them into practice. Then puberty and an all-girls secondary school happened, and suddenly I was a little fish in a truly massive pond and my confidence took a real beating. Ever since then I preferred to stay safely in the background. There was something about being out front, exposed and vulnerable, that sent me running for cover. Even as a manager I worried, didn't see myself as leadership material, lacked the confidence to speak up and speak out. But now I was thinking that maybe this was just a form of laziness. Instead of shy and retiring, lacking in confidence was I instead just happy to coast along on other people's coat tails, happy to let Mike always lead the way on our walks and then complain if his short cuts led us through mud or brambles – or both – as they usually did?

This would also explain why I was ambivalent at best about my call to the priesthood – no hiding away there, you are definitely up front with bells on, singled out by the funny clothes and the dog collar, an authority figure and no mistake, however much I'd like to pretend otherwise. My discomfort levels at putting on the dog collar for the first time were off the scale, truly I did feel on the leash. And yet, and yet, it's only through being in that position, having that mark of Cain, that I have been able to be of service to people, to come alongside them in times of great joy or great pain and do something to help. Maybe it's not about authority after all. Maybe the being up at the front bit is the least important thing about being a priest for me. The most important thing? It's the people, which is what I'm also discovering as I look back over this walk. It's all about the people, people who've made me the person I am today, people who continue to influence and to form me – we're all a work in progress, or, as Michelle Obama put it, 'Becoming is never giving up on the idea that there's more growing to be done.' Maybe today was the day I would grow into a map reader . . . And maybe this whole trip was partly to show me that there was more growing to be done. That in my mid-fifties I wasn't done yet, not ready for the pipe and slippers. I could still challenge myself, push myself out into the unknown, in spite of – or maybe because of – my self-limiting fear.

Anyhow, time to confront my fear of maps – big style. Dave and I headed off out of Bromyard and within minutes I'd led us off track and straight into a graveyard. Great idea, let's take the man whose wife died four months ago on a detour into a cemetery – classic. I'm sure Dave wasn't fazed by this at all, focussed as he was on project 'Teach Anthea some basic map reading skills'. Instead, he guided me gently but firmly through the arcane mysteries of the map.

The first lesson was to look around you not just at the map. I gave him all the reasons why I thought we shouldn't be going into what looked like somebodies front garden only for him to point out the footpath sign which confirmed that that was exactly where we should be heading . . . He explained that one of the great things about walking with Ann had been that he would always be head down scanning the map, while she would be looking out and ahead, scanning the landscape for signposts, waymarks or stiles. Yet another reason why the two of them had made such a great team. Looking back on it now I realise the day must have been soooo boring for Dave, but it was totally fascinating for me. How often do we learn a new skill at an advanced age? Maybe you do, but I know that fear of failure and fear of looking a fool are both things that have held me back in the past – not anymore!

So, in case you too fear the map, I will pass on some of Dave's amazing wisdom.

Tip One

Always look ahead of where you are actually walking. When you do this you know what to look out for, what you're expecting to see before you see it. That's why he favoured the paper map over the phone map. On the phone's tiny screen, following its tracking of our track, you can't see very far ahead. As Julian and I had found out the day before, the time the phone comes into its own is to confirm that you've gone wrong and to help you get back on track. Dave's point was that by using the paper map and anticipating where you're going and what landmarks you're looking out for, you should be able to avoid going wrong in the first place. And we did – thanks to Dave.

Tip Two

Field boundaries. How did I live without an awareness of the value of the field boundary?? And I'm not even joking. Field boundaries are fab, field boundaries enable you to orientate yourself, and trust me, knowing where you are is pretty key to getting to where you need to be. The human capacity for self-deception is pretty remarkable and the number of times I've made the landscape fit where I think I am rather than looking at it properly and working out where I really am are innumerable. And if that isn't a metaphor for life, I don't know what is. Accurate self-assessment is a skill, but one which Dave possesses in abundance – maybe that's what makes him such a good map reader and teacher of map reading.

Anyhow back to field boundaries. By assessing which boundaries the path takes you across, which side of the boundary the path lies, how many boundaries you should be crossing before you hit the road, whereabouts along the boundary the path crosses over – is it in the corner of the field or half way down the field? – all these things enable you to be far more confident in knowing where you're going. Even if you can't see the stile or the waymark, you do at least know roughly where they ought to be and it's amazing how many times the stile or waymark suddenly emerges out of the hedgerow, if you head in the direction the map tells you to go. This is a particularly valuable skill to cultivate in high summer when the vegetation is at its lushest, often concealing vital clues to where the footpath goes.

Tip Three

Contour lines and other landmarks. Now, to be fair to me, I had already experienced the joy of contour lines. It was during one of my practice walks, where part of what I was practising was walking in places I'd never walked before but still being able to find my way. This meant walking off the end of the Hills, beyond Chase End, and down into Bromsberrow, which was great. On this occasion I'd decided to try out a new route back to Whiteleaved Oak via Howler's Heath and the High Wood. What I hadn't been observant enough to notice was the contour lines suddenly got really very close together in the middle of the wood. Until that is I was standing at the top of what looked like a vertical bank, trying to find a way down. With the help of my trusty stick I made it, but it did alert me to the importance of observing and correctly interpreting the contour lines ...

But Dave taught me something much more valuable than that. He showed me that you can use contour lines and other landmarks like church spires or woodland or houses as confirmation that you are where you think you are. Kind of a double or treble check that the data you are taking in with your eyes and processing through your brain really does match with where you think you are on the map. For example, if you think you should be going downhill but find yourself going uphill or if you think the church spire should be away to your left but find that it actually appears to your right – then you're probably not where you think you are and you need to go back to the map and recalibrate.

There's plenty more where that came from but for now, let's head back to the actual doing of the walk. We headed out of Bromyard on the Herefordshire Trail and we were to stay on that trail for the next couple of days, at least until we reached Leominster, which was the first really major milestone of the walk. The walking itself was becoming increasingly beautiful. This morning we started out with water meadow walking, following the River Frome until we turned away from it and headed up past some houses and then down towards a sports field near to the main road. Then we were back into fields, walking up field margins, and then down through some gorgeous meadowland and on through a field where a bull was threatened but thankfully didn't materialise. I think it was at this point that Dave made me aware that field boundaries can change – just when they'd become my best friends – and that often the hedges or boundaries shown on the map have been removed to create larger fields. Stunned by this revelation, I managed to carry on navigating us towards Edwyn Ralph and its church, using the spire as a reassuring landmark. The field before the field before the church was one where we should have been able to cross diagonally but there seemed no way through the crop – that old chestnut. We were able, just about, to navigate our way round the margin, although the change in level from margin to cultivated land was a trap to break the ankle of the unwary, particularly when both were in full growth. Dave showed me another trick of the trade when we arrived at the stile/bridge – overgrown with nettles and bindweed. If you stood at the stile and looked back, *then* you could see the route we should have come, as the stile on the opposite side was clear. Sometimes, it's all about having the good fortune to approach from the right direction, but it also made the point that looking back can be educational and filed away for future use.

Similarly, it can be a good idea to take some time out on a regular basis to look back on life and to see how far you've come. These days we're all about the future, all about the next item on the to do list, onward and upward is the mantra, no looking back. But sometimes, it's only when we stop to reflect, to look back at where we've come from and what we've left behind that we might see that we're missing something. That in our rush and hurry to move onto the next thing and the next and the next, to justify our existence by being busy happy shiny productive people, we lose some of the things that really do make us who we are. I think that's how I was feeling, and a large part of why I was doing this walk. To reach back to my roots, to where I'd come from, the people and places which had formed me, to find my way back to my authentic self. Either that or it was a straightforward midlife crisis disguised as a charity walk – you decide!

We crossed the final field and arrived at the church. It was slightly early to take our break, but my inside knowledge of all things ecclesiastical led me to believe that we should be able to find a bench or two in the churchyard, so it was worth taking a break early in order to get a comfy seat. Sadly, this was a rule I didn't always follow when walking on my own but it's a good rule of life to stick to – always go for the comfy seat when it's on offer, you never know when the next one will come along. Edwyn Ralph had always intrigued me – it's an unusual name for a village and every time I drove to Bromyard I'd be fascinated by the signpost pointing off to Edwyn Ralph.

Now, here I was, sitting outside its beautiful twelfth century Church taking in the view and enjoying a rest. I also remembered to put the phone on charge, now I knew to shade the lights with my hand and to listen for the little beebop sound that told me it was working – see, not a Luddite at all . . . Before we moved on I nipped into St Michael's as I find it fascinating that buildings used for the same purpose, possibly even built about the same time, are all totally different. But also, I love the peace, calm and tranquillity of a church building. It calms and centres me and puts me back in

Fig 5. Effigies at Edwyn Ralph

my proper lowly place in the overall scheme of things. And beauty is always a balm for the soul. Edwyn Ralph's church has the most amazing effigies.

In fact, the most important collection of medieval effigies in the whole of Herefordshire. All are members of the Edefen family – or Zeddifen (spellings vary) and it is this family, here since Domesday, who gave the village its name. There are seven effigies in all, the

earliest dates back to 1290, a knight in full armour, his shield
bearing the Zeddifen arms, feet resting on a lion, slumbering next
to his wife. Then a slightly later knight with his two wives beside
him, and a fourteenth century effigy, described as either a very
small woman or a child. Finally, there is the grave slab of Maud
de Edefen, dated 1325, a fine example of a pardon monument. This
means it has an inscription asking those who pass by to say a Pater
and an Ave (Lord's Prayer and Ave Maria) for the soul of Maud
de Edefen and in return the Bishop of Worcester will allow them
thirty days of pardon and the Bishop of Hereford will allow them
sixty days of pardon. Good old Bishop of Hereford says I, and boo
to the stingy Bishop of Worcester! But it does give you a real insight
into the power the Church once wielded over people's lives, and
the very potent fear of lingering in purgatory or even worse, which
could be alleviated by the prayers of those still living. Even though
the loss of that power has seen the Church drift into a much more
peripheral position in most people's lives, I still feel it's healthier to
live life following the teachings of Jesus because you want to and
believe they make the world a better place, rather than out of fear
of the hereafter or societal pressure. But the effigies and especially
the pardon tomb give a very real insight into the medieval world and
are also phenomenal works of art, both moving and very impressive.

Break over, we continued back on our field walk towards
Pudleston. At one point someone had put huge bales of black plastic
covered silage blocking the way and they were so close together that
I couldn't fit between them while wearing a rucksack. This proved
to be a problem with narrow kissing gates as well. But Dave looked
at the issue logically as ever and found a way round for me which
didn't involve removing my rucksack only to have to put it straight
back on again. Another lesson really – don't assume there's only one
way through. Take a moment to look around you and see if there's

an alternative. This was a lesson which was repeated later in the walk and one which I put into practise a couple of days later. And it applies to life too. The most obvious way through is not always the best, or most efficient, sometimes you need to do a little lateral thinking around the problem to find the best way through.

The path from this point on had been rerouted around a farmhouse and you could see the stile we were climbing over and the fence it was set into were both brand new. Another example of keeping your wits about you and looking at the reality on the ground as well as the directions on the map. I was growing in confidence by now and a little confidence can be a dangerous thing... We crossed the road leading up to the farm and navigated our way round pony paddocks, climbing over a stile and coming down onto the driveway to another house. I looked at the map which seemed to show that we could either carry on along the path and the fields and then follow the road back to the path, or just leg it up this drive to the road, which would be trespassing, and would bring us out virtually opposite where we need to be. Dave shrugged. 'Up to you', he said in his Zen master role. We legged it up the drive. Apologies to the homeowner, and obviously you should never do this yourselves...

On we went, following the waymarks, the path taking us between houses, showing us some massive and well-kept gardens, always a matter of interest for me. We paused to chat to a lady doing a little light weeding, who warned us against taking one of the paths ahead of us as it was impassable, but luckily we were heading the other way. Again, typical of the kindness of strangers I was to encounter time and time again on this walk. The path took us through a lovely bit of woodland, providing very welcome shade, then we turned uphill along a field margin, followed by a nice bit of downhill to the road, startling a BT engineer who'd parked his van in the gateway – happily it opened inward rather than outward! Then a good bit of road walking, admiring the big houses we passed and finding a fledgling who'd obviously flown the nest a bit too soon. We found where we thought we should be walking. Another top tip – if you think you're in the right place but want another cross check, walk a little further than you think you need to, just to be sure. This links in with something Dave tried to explain to me a few times, but at that stage it was a bit too advanced for where I was – try to cultivate a good understanding of time and distance, in other words, know your own pace as another cross check on knowing how far you've walked and so where you are on the map. Time and again when walking on my own, I'd overestimate how far I'd come, and need to recalibrate based on the reality of the landscape in front of me. Dave's words of wisdom came back to haunt me but also to reassure me. So, we knew we were in the right place, but the way through the hedge was very overgrown.

Further top tip, look around you to see if there's an alternative route via which you can pick up the path again slightly further on. Luckily in this case there was. We could walk down a track and find the stile in the hedge which we would have come over if we'd been able to get to the stile on the roadside. Then it was on past some farm buildings, up a field margin and out into a green lane up to a road. Crossing the road we carried on across the fields which were mainly pastureland and so blissfully walkable. We encountered some cows, and I learned Dave's patented method for crossing a field containing cows – ignore them, just keep walking and they'll move, and whatever you do, don't run. This worked and then we found ourselves in a field full of crop and Dave had another lesson to teach – take a look at the crop and see if there are tracks running through it, tracks made by machinery but which can then be used by a walker looking to find an easier way through if the field margin is impassable. Luckily for us, there were tracks like this going up this large field so we follow them right to the top, crossed a road and we were at Velvet Stone – I'd love to know how some of the places round here got their names! Again, the path took us close by houses and gardens, which always feels quite awkward to me. A new build was going up so I was worried the right of way might have been at risk, but when we emerged onto the road, the waymark had been replaced and was there pointing the way still. We availed ourselves of the newly built kerbing to sit down and have our second break.

Dave and I talked a little about the challenge and scariness of suddenly finding yourself on your own at our age. Thinking about this many days later, I found myself relating it back to field boundaries. It struck me that many of the folk who walked with me or met me on the way had lost their spouses way too young and unexpectedly. It was like having the future all mapped out and then someone comes in and grubs up all the field boundaries and moves all the landmarks. Suddenly you are in unknown territory, having to start again from scratch. You are forced to rebuild the life you thought you were going to have and take a very different route, not through choice but through necessity. Looking at it from the outside in, it must be very disorientating – and would also apply to anyone coping with any life-changing situation – the death of a child, divorce, serious illness. The landscape has changed forever, there's no going back, you can only keep moving forward, in hope and expectation that someday you will start to notice the landmarks once more, to reinstate some hedges, make new paths, build new connections and bridges. It's a tough ask, and it takes time, a lot more time than others may expect or allow you, but it can be done. I see it in Cathy and Ruth, works in progress as we all are, and I know I will see it – am seeing it – in Dave.

Break time over we crossed the road and headed across more

fields, culminating in walking right through someone's back garden – which was the right of way, we weren't trespassing this time, honest! Finally, we'd made it onto the road, which was a relief to me as navigator as, for a short while at least, I could put the map down. Turns out that the challenge of the walk wasn't so much physical – which is what I had been most worried about – but mental. Could I find my way along the route without getting lost? The following week I was due to be walking alone every day, so Dave's day of tuition was invaluable, and made me aware of how cavalier and naive I'd been to embark upon this whole crazy enterprise. I think I'd assumed that all footpaths would be well maintained and well waymarked and I'd just need to follow the signs. I was already learning that was far from true. Thing is though, if I had known, I wouldn't have dared do it. And there are times when you've just got to shut your eyes and take a leap in the dark – and I'm the last person in the world I'd expect to do that – but here I was, in the middle of rural Herefordshire, walking to Pudleston. And enjoying it – did I say that yet? Enjoying the open air and the wide-open spaces, enjoying the beauty of the English countryside, enjoying challenging myself physically and mentally and just about winning through. And enjoying the simplicity – get up, get ready, walk, eat, blog, rest and repeat. Life boiled down to these essentials was restful on the psyche. Yes, it was good. I mean after day two, anything not involving nettles and getting lost was going to be good, wasn't it?

We walked past chocolate-box cottages with verdant, blousy front gardens til we came to another church, which I identified from its noticeboard as Hatfield St Leonard. As time was moving on and we were nearing our destination I didn't go in – which was a shame as when I got home and looked Hatfield St Leonard up for the blog I discovered it's something like the third oldest church in

Herefordshire – always take the time to go in is the lesson there. Dave prevented me from leading us off in completely the wrong direction – self-preservation was beginning to override education for him I suspect – it had been a long day!! We followed the road leading us over a cattle grid and up toward a lovely big house set on the side of the hill. As I passed the edge of their garden, puffing my way uphill, I was glad of the excuse to pause and wait for Dave to catch up. I pointed to the Easter Island head taking pride of place in the garden, a reminder for us both of a garden we'd done for Jane, a great friend of Ann's, the only person ever to ask me to design a planting scheme round an Easter Island head! Hopefully we did a good job.

We turned off across fields, one of them a hayfield, cut but not yet baled. As we walked a tiny mouse scuttled across our path into the safety of the hedgerow. We were approaching the end of our day together, and as we were crossing the final few fields, Dave talked about Ann's illness and the days leading up to her death. I just listened, because that's all you can do. But I do believe it's important to listen, to allow someone to talk through the detail of these traumatic events if they want to. I've noticed when visiting bereaved families that it can be helpful for them to tell you the detail of the last few days of a life, and I wonder whether talking about it helps to make it more real for them, helps finally in the long process of starting to accept what has happened, particularly when a death has happened suddenly and unexpectedly, as Ann's did. The problem is, often these days we see death and bereavement as problems to be fixed, or problems that can't be fixed, which makes us even more uncomfortable around bereaved people. But in my experience, those who have lost someone very near and dear to them just want the opportunity to talk about that person. They know this isn't something that can be fixed, but they need to be able to talk openly and honestly about the person they love who isn't around anymore and the pain and grief that this is causing them. Just listen. It's best to not interrupt with 'helpful' suggestions, listen, ask questions about the person, don't deflect, don't try to change the subject, just listen. It's not easy, and there have been

Fig 6. Pudleston stained glass

times when I've literally bitten the inside of my lip to stop myself jumping in to try to suggest things, but I do firmly believe that giving folk the time and space to talk about their loss is one of the best, most helpful and most healing things you can do for them. I was glad to be a listening ear for Dave, knowing he would always do the same for me. We had a bet that whoever saw the church spire first would get the first round in at the pub that evening – which I unsurprisingly lost as we were nearly on top of the church before I spotted it!

Our driver wasn't in sight, so we went in search of somewhere to rest our weary limbs, but before bums could connect with seat, the Skoda hove into view. I took a quick look inside the church before we headed for home. There was a fabulous ha-ha on the other side of the graveyard, keeping the sheep from the churchyard, and clear evidence of the swifts finding a roost in the porch. Inside there was some sensor-activated nifty lighting, which I must mention to the ecclesiastical electrician, him indoors, a very ornate font and some fab psychedelic stained glass above an ornate carved reredos.

Another fascinating church made more fascinating by the notice on its board that told us that they were planning a Winnie the Pooh-themed flower festival. End of walk photos safely taken we headed for home along the somewhat potholed Herefordshire road, but past Landrover heaven, a point of interest for our driver at least.

Footnote to the day – once home, washed and refreshed with tea and toast, the plan was to walk down to the pub at the end of the road, the Robin Hood, as they do a really good range of gluten-free dishes and Dave is coeliac. Sitting round our lovely outside table in the sunshine, Dave suddenly asked – 'How many bikes have you got?'

'Two and a half,' Mike replied and so it came about that, having walked eleven miles that day, I then cycled down to the pub – and back. I hadn't cycled anywhere for approximately 10 years, so getting onto the bike was . . . interesting, but sadly not as interesting as getting off. This I decided to do at a discrete distance from the Robin Hood car park, both for the avoidance of embarrassment and for the avoidance of having to cycle across the main road. I employed my own patented method of dismount – laying the bicycle on the ground and stepping over it. All would have been fine, had a peloton of cyclists not picked the precise moment of dismount to cycle past. Hopefully the amusement they clearly felt will have been a temporary distraction from the lactic acid coursing through their legs . . . .

However, it wasn't all bad. The food was great as ever, and I bumped into Matt and Nicola, a couple I married a few years back, with their two gorgeous daughters who I'd baptised. This is an example of the great privilege of priesthood – you get to be a part of people's lives at the happiest and most joyous of moments, as well as the challenging and tragic ones. And once you've made that connection, you sometimes become the family priest who they come back to on other occasions, which is such a joy and a blessing. I can't tell you how humbled and honoured it makes you feel. As we were chatting with Matt, a hot air balloon went overhead, and he told us he'd never ever want to go up in one as it looked scary. Given that I knew he rode to hounds on a regular basis this seemed suitably bonkers but shows that everyone has different fears and phobias. I went over to chat to Nicola before we left and she offered to sponsor me, so all was well with my world – once I'd made it home and been able to once more dismount from the damn bike!

Day Three Stats
    Start time – 9.07 am.
    Finish time – 3.12 pm.
    Duration – 6 hours, 5 minutes
    Distance walked – 11.1 miles
    Total ascent 1,095 ft.
    Total descent 919 ft.
    Avg. speed – 2.3 mph

Day Four: In my Father's Footsteps
Pudleston to Monkland

4 July 2019

Today was the day when I was due to reach the first major staging post of the walk – Monkland Church, where my paternal grandparents are buried. Grandad was a great grower of sweet peas so suddenly it seemed right to pick some that were growing in our garden and ask Mike to bring them with him when he came to pick us up so I could put them on his grave. Dave was going to walk with me again today and then get the train back to Shrewsbury, so he was going to be carrying a full pack just in case we didn't make it to Leominster in time for all of us to go onto Monkland and return in time for Dave to catch his train home. I say all of us because Ruth was going to be walking with us today as well.

I worried about this – is there anything on this walk I haven't worried about? Anyhow, I was worried about how Dave and Ruth would get on, but, as ever, I needn't have been because they are both the sort of people who are able to get on with everyone and anyone. Ruth is another friend made through church, so friend and parishioner. She's one of those amazing people who always has a smile and a cheery can-do approach to life, so a godsend on a walk like this one! She's someone who just gets on with the job and is willing to be there helping out a lot, which is totally invaluable in church terms, particularly as she's quite a lot younger than many of our other volunteers, with boundless energy. With her energy and enthusiasm she sometimes reminds me of an eager young puppy, with a real zest for life, though much more focussed and productive. However, despite her incredibly positive, always look on the bright side outlook on life, Ruth was widowed at a very young age, when her beloved John fell ill with the cancer, which would eventually be the cause of his very sad and untimely death. Reverend Mike, our previous incumbent, remembers sitting in his study with John, who said to him 'other than dying, what do I have to do to get into Berrow Churchyard . . .' to which the answer was no need to do anything. He and Ruth lived in the parish, within sight of St Faith's and Ruth lives there still, next door to her great friend Mel, in a pair of houses with the most fabulous views up to the Malvern Hills. She is a great lover of all things equine in fact of wildlife in general and the beautiful countryside which surrounds us. She and John also had a shared passion for VW campervans and Ruth is the proud owner of two of them, one up and running and still heading out on adventures and one about to be fifty-year-old campervan, called Lucy, which doesn't stray far from home these days. She also has a very powerful and tuneful soprano voice, which is great for our benefice choir, and is chair of the local Parish Council. Someone very sociable, very community minded, but also someone who knows very much what it is to grieve the loss of a loved one. Her beloved mum, Patricia, had died just about a year before we did the walk. I'd had the great good fortune to take home communion to her in Tewkesbury a few times, to attend her funeral in Tewkesbury Abbey, where she was a regular worshipper, and to lead the service to inter her ashes at All Saints Hollybush, with the most amazing singing from Ruth's cousin Susannah, and the joy of a horse passing by, which would have totally delighted her mum, who loved horses almost as much as Ruth does.

True to her keen character, Ruth showed up bang on time, so we got the show on the road on the hottest day of the walk so far. Mike drove us all the way back to Pudleston – that would be pretty much four hours on the road for him that day, so he was fast reconsidering his driving commitment as we got further and further from home. However, for the moment he was there at the start to take the start of day photo for us, after which we set off – but not until Ruth had had a chance to have a quick look round the church. Dave suggested I take the lead again. I've decided I'm not good at beginnings and was all set to lead us off in totally the wrong direction, but thankfully he intervened. I'd investigated a little way down one of the alternatives, but not quite far enough. So, we headed off down the right road, turned right up another road and came to our first field next to a small group of new houses. The route took us up and over a stile but, learning all the time, I volunteered to go over and scope out the lie of the land – et voila, Dave and Ruth could just walk up the driveway to where we needed to hop over the next stile. It was then that Ruth unveiled her superpower – she could spot a stile or footpath sign a mile off, way before I'd even started looking. This was to come in very handy! Dave did caution that just because you spot a stile or sign doesn't mean it's the one you're looking for. But in this case it was, so we headed up the field, over the stile and through a little bit of cooling woodland, from where we made our way along a field margin for a short way then across grassland and fields to a road. Left and then immediately right brought us to another field of pasture with grazing sheep. Making our way across through one open gateway was fine, but the field lying ahead of us didn't make it easy to work out which way we should head next. I led us off in what I thought was the right general direction, and Dave described a technique whereby you scope all the way round the edge of the field, which means that you can be certain sure you've not missed the way forward and are far more likely to find it.

We worked our way along the field margin and soon found the waymark we were looking for, partially concealed under an overhanging tree. We had to disturb a few sheep to get through the gate, but then we were on our way and soon reached Bache Camp, an iron age hill fort. The fort is now quite overgrown so it's harder to make out the distinctive ditches and ramparts, but in its day, it must have been quite something, covering an area of over six acres and with three separate entrances. Strange to think that this now remote and overgrown place would once have been a hive of noise and activity, smoke from cooking fires, wooden shelters, people getting on with their day to day lives living so differently from the way we do now and yet still being very much the same people in terms of finding love, bringing up children and feeling the same emotions – fear, joy, anger, hope, grief, excitement. However, something else had caught Dave's eye, which interrupted my historical musings and brought me back down to earth with a bump, or rather a tump. Ant tumps to be precise. These are quite rare earth formations created by ants, and Dave took a photo of them to pass onto the Shropshire Wildlife Trust for whom he volunteers, using Ruth and myself to provide scale. A great way of putting us firmly in our place in the overall scheme of things!

As we climbed up and then left towards Upper Bache Farmhouse, with its listed dovecote, Dave and Ruth began to discuss the nature of friendship, how there were some people you just clicked with and knew were going to be friends for life and others who just weren't on your wavelength. I think I've been very lucky with my friends over the years, and it's interesting how this walk became partly a tribute to the lasting value of friendship. The idea started in grief at the loss of one of my best friends – Marianna – and then was really pushed into action by deaths of three other close friends – Matthew, Benny and Ann. But I also don't think I could have done it without

the help of the friends who walked with me, and the friends who
supported and encouraged me with donations, but above all with
moral support and the belief that I could do what seemed like a
crazy idea to me. It strikes me that often the best friends we have
aren't people who are like us or who agree with us all the time, but
people who are very different from us, who challenge us and who
enable and inspire us to push our own boundaries. A few years
before, Dave and Ann had come to stay, with the idea that we'd
head out on a day's walking the next day. When we all awoke, it had
snowed in the night, which as far as I was concerned meant game
over. I'd been worried enough about being able to keep up with
Mike, Dave and Ann anyway, but to go walking on the hills in snow,
surely that was just too dangerous? Of course, to Dave and Ann, it
was nothing, something they'd done loads of times and in fact just
added to the experience. Not wanting to be the wet blanket of the
party or be seen to make a fuss, I went with it and we had a really
amazing walk because once up on the tops of the hills it became
clear that while there was loads of snow on the Worcestershire
side of the hills there was none at all on the Herefordshire side.
A beautiful and stunning sight, and one I would never have seen
had it not been for Dave and Ann. And that's what I mean about
good friends being those who push us, firmly but gently, out of
our comfort zones to find that we can do a lot more than we ever
thought we could. Dave was definitely doing that again for me on
this walk. And it strikes me now that that's what Jesus did when
he plucked fishermen and tax collectors from their day to day lives
and turned them into disciples, apostles and evangelists. Or God
did when he appeared to Moses in the burning bush, choosing him
to lead the people of Israel from slavery in Egypt to freedom in
the Promised Land. Moses' response? Please Lord, send someone
else. Which, coincidentally, was very similar to my own response

to being called to the priesthood! It's not easy to step out of your comfort zone, but it is usually very rewarding, and I say a huge thanks to all those family members and friends who supported me while pushing me gently but firmly forward.

Dave and Ann had walked the Herefordshire Trail in its entirety some years before and we were about to come up to a bit he remembered – which was good because I was all set to lead us the wrong way again, until he suggested we maybe try another way. You can go off people you know! However, I knew enough to know I was looking out for a sign taking us off this track to the left and sure enough there it was. A prime example of putting yesterday's learning into practice – if you know roughly what you're looking for it's a lot easier to find it! We climbed a stile and made our way around the field margin, which was fine at first, but when we crossed another stile into the next field it became slightly more reminiscent of the Three Choirs Way, and not in a good way. However, we made it through and soon afterwards found a spot in the shade by the lane where we could squat down and take our first break of the day. Dave pulled out a cut down square of old camping mat to sit on which I instantly coveted – so handy and so light. Yet another thing to learn from the Master.

Soon we were all set to go again, beginning with a nice bit of road walking to get us in the mood and give me a slight break from the map reading. On the way we passed a huge crop of orange wildflowers growing on the verge, the same variety I'd seen walking with Julian a couple of days earlier – hawkweeds – very handsome but very invasive. Then it was back to a mixture of fields and orchards until, suddenly, the sound of traffic meant we were descending towards what sounded like a major main road. This could only mean one thing – we were closing in on Leominster, which was seriously good news, except that the trail took us alongside a very busy main road and you never quite know whether there will be pavement or not. We were in luck, not only was there pavement but after quite a short walk the path took us over the other side of the hedge from the main road along a path which had clearly been recently strimmed – huzzah! We walked alongside the River Lugg, where Ruth attempted to make friends with a horse in a field, and through Easters Wood, a Woodland Trust nature reserve, nearly all the way into town, which was very pleasant. Going under the

Fig 7. Marvellous mosaics

main road we saw a beautiful mosaic of some dragonflies, which it seemed a shame to hide away in such a non-promising place, but it did really brighten it up and lift the spirits.

Then it was over the river, and over the railway, and amazingly, there we were in the middle of Leominster, and, even better, Dave knew of a handily placed pub. And so it was that we took our next break in the luxury of the beer garden of the White Lion – having purchased ourselves some refreshing soft drinks first, of course! I texted Mike to give him an update on where we were, and he wasn't happy we'd found our way to the pub – apparently that wasn't on our itinerary! However, given what was to follow, maybe we should have been on the hard stuff rather than sticking to soft drinks.

The day had got even hotter by the time we set off again at 2.00 pm, heading away from the railway station and up into the town. This time we were relying on the Black and White Trail footpaths to get us from Leominster to Monkland, so we were veering off the main waymarked paths. All went well initially, though it was a long, sweaty pavement walk all the way out of the town. All a bit counterintuitive as I knew this as the way to go back home, and yet here we were starting by walking away from, rather than towards, Monkland. Eventually we arrived at our turnoff, down Passa Lane, which it turned out was a rat run for cars which zipped along the narrow lane rather fast. With some relief we found where we were supposed to turn off down a green lane – only to discover that it was totally overgrown and impassable. Luckily, Dave found us a way round and from here on in, he definitely took over leading the walk, with Ruth and myself trailing in his wake. I suspect he knew that if he relied on me to get us to Monkland, he might well end up missing his train! We walked across the water meadows of the River Arrow, along the road through Newtown and then turned right to do our last little bit of fieldwalking before we reached Monkland Church, which we saw in the distance a while before we reached it – a real hoorah moment. Dave was still a fair way ahead of us, and as he exited one field, a herd of what looked like young bullocks came galloping en masse past Ruth and myself. A couple of them reared up and kind of body popped each other – maybe some kind of rival head of herd face off going on? It was dramatic and slightly scary, even though they clearly couldn't have cared less that we were there, caught up as they were in their own testosterone filled games. We

Fig 8. Dave with Monkland Church in the background

Fig 9. Jones family

swiftly made our excuses and exited that particular field, attempting to keep at least Dave's hat within sight.

The final stages of that day's walk involved crossing over quite a springy single plank bridge, walking across a very dead looking field and navigating our way in and around the buildings of Manor Farm, and then there it was – Monkland Church, which I remembered very well from funerals and baptisms.

Mike was waiting for us and I quickly grabbed the sweet peas and jam jar from him and went to find the grave, wanting to take a few moments on my own to go and see my paternal gran and grandad.

Molly and Cyril Jones lived on Monkland Common, in a tied cottage situated next to the Moor Brook. Dad was brought up there, the eldest of three boys. In fig 9 you can see my grandad Cyril and gran Molly and their three sons – my uncle Mike on the left, my father Derek on the right and my uncle Dave, the baby of the family, seated.

Both my grandparents worked for the Bengough family, Captain and Mrs Bengough, at The Cottage, Upper Wall End, a short walk up a lane from their house, grandad as gardener and gran as an ace cleaner. I remember a lovely walled garden and Captain Bengough as a very old man – to me – in a motorised wheelchair. Grandad was a hard taskmaster in gardening terms, and Dad can remember being recruited to work in the garden as a child, particularly on the sweet peas, where there was a very specific way of digging the trench, planting and tying up the plants and woe betide anyone who got it wrong. Grandad was also a type 1 diabetic and I remember Gran buying special diabetic chocolate for him at the chemists, back in the days where that was where you bought your olive oil too. They supplemented their income by selling flowers and poultry at Leominster market, and Gran used to often walk from Monkland to Leominster and back. She walked everywhere at an incredibly swift pace – faster than most people could run. At Christmas time they prepared the turkeys and geese for selling and I can remember the whole family getting involved in the plucking, drawing and dressing – the smell of meths seemed to fill the house because you would sprinkle it over the turkey and set light to it to singe all the fluffy down off the plucked bird. The kitchen was tiny – a galley kitchen with pantry – but the living/dining room was huge and the Rayburn was in this room so most of the cooking was done on that. I remember Gran making me Rayburn toast spread with Lurpak butter. And she did the most fantastic stews with fresh peas, and a really great roast dinner – roast duck or goose is what I remember, all of us sat around the big old wooden table with the green cloth on it, and the blue china with the Chinese garden pattern on it. The sitting room was kept for best, but in the end had a TV in it on which Gran watched the soaps.

I was still quite young when Grandad got ill. I can remember him picking away at a spot on his toe with a pin, and eventually he got blood poisoning and as a diabetic this was really serious. He had one leg and then the other amputated, and then he died. In a way, the loss of his independence, ability to work and to be outside would have ended his days anyway. He was a very proud man. I remember him lying on the sofa in the living room when he came home from hospital, and pressing a coin into my hand, as apparently he loved having grandchildren and had a particularly soft spot for me as the only girl at that point – my cousin Lesley was born not long after his death. Gran stayed on at Monkland and continued to work for the Bengough family. She went to clean for them at Great House in Canon Pyon, the home of Colonel and Mrs Bengough, the old man's son and daughter-in-law. Mrs Bengough in particular was very kind to her. I would go and stay with Gran in the school holidays, and share her deep feather bed, with its flannel sheets – very different to home – as the only other bedroom was occupied by my uncle Dave, her youngest son, who had turned the only other room in the house into a dark room for his photography. I played with the children who lived next door – Sally Ann and Sue, whose dad was a lorry driver and used to park his big rig on the Common. We played in the big pond just round the corner from the house. We'd walk up to the village shop and buy sweets. Gran always had bottles of pop in the house, and we'd take the bottles back to get the deposit back. Sometimes a mobile shop would come round, with big steps you climbed up to get into the back to do your shopping.

It was a hard life, with not a lot of money to go round. A reminder that on both sides of my family I come from a very rural working-class background. Dad can remember Gran taking him hop picking with her when he was little. It was a case of turn your hand to whatever you could to bring an income in and supplement that by growing a lot of your own vegetables, keeping poultry to sell and to eat, etc. But I don't remember any of this as a child, all I remember is that it was a great place to go and stay because there was so much freedom to roam. Back in those days, children would be sent out to play all day, no worries about stranger danger, or us managing to drown ourselves in the pond, we could just head out and do our own thing, use our imaginations, go off and have adventures. I don't remember

worrying about this at all at the
time, just enjoying it and making
the most of it. Time to rekindle
that childhood freedom of spirit
and love of adventurous play.

Once Grandad had died and
Uncle Dave left home, Gran didn't
really take very good care of herself.
She always hated cooking, even
though she was a really good cook.
It just didn't interest her; cleaning
was her passion. So she lost a lot
of weight, and as she'd always
been lithe and slender to begin

Fig 10. Gran and Grandad

with, this caused a lot of worry and concern to my dad and his
brothers. It seemed an insurmountable problem, until an innovative
solution appeared, good springing out of a very sad situation. As I
mentioned earlier, my mum's mum, Monnoa Lewis, who I called
Nan, died suddenly after a short stay in hospital, just before I went
up to university. My grandad Ron was still very sharp mentally, but
physically unable to look after himself – what to do? Gran stepped
in and offered to become his live-in housekeeper, and this worked
brilliantly. Two people who would otherwise have been living all
alone found company and companionship, and, because she had
someone else to cook for, my gran ate well again and soon returned
to a much healthier weight.

They lived very happily together until my grandad's death in
2001. When Gran also passed away in January of 2004, her funeral
was held at Monkland Church, and she was interred in the same
grave as her late husband Cyril, the grave I was now standing in
front of, about to place my jam jar of sweet peas.

I don't remember that much about my grandad Cyril, but I remember my gran very well. I admired so much about her – her apparently endless capacity for hard work, her ability to keep three growing boys and a husband fed and cared for on very little money, her speed walking in the days before that was even a thing, her love of clothes and her colourful wardrobe, and her love of the sun – she rarely sat down for any length of time, but a nice sunny spot would tempt her to linger. Above all, I remember her laughing at some outrageous remark my grandad Ron had made, or the way he cheated in the most obvious way possible at cards. I'm not sure there was much by way of laughter in her early life, so to see tears of laughter rolling down her cheeks was always an absolute joy. I now realise what a strong woman she must have been to simply keep going, keep managing, keep the family fed and clothed. She also suffered serious illness in middle age, which was what brought Mum, Dad and myself back from a brief spell of living in Devon to return to Herefordshire to be nearer to the grandparents in general and Gran in particular. She overcame so many obstacles, and in a life which didn't contain many, if any, luxuries until quite late on, she found joy in her dedication to cleaning – often rubbing the silver plate off items through excessive polishing! – in her three boys, of whom she was inordinately and rightly very proud, and in her grandchildren, whom she loved. I'm thankful that for the last twenty years of her life she had the time and means to treat herself, to go on holidays, to be part of village life and to enjoy a happy and funny relationship with my grandad Ron.

It's a good reminder to me, at this stage of the walk, maybe even at this stage of my life, that perseverance pays off and that I come from a line of strong women on both sides of my family. They had endured much greater hardships, both physical and emotional, than I'd ever known, but that meant that I'd got some of those endurance genes in me and their example to inspire me on my way.

I miss all my grandparents, appreciating them more as the years go by, so it was good to take a few moments to give thanks and to remember Molly and Cyril. But of course, we couldn't linger too long, as we needed to get Dave back to Leominster station to get his train to Shrewsbury, and to get Ruth home so she could put her feet up after a long day of walking.

So, we took the end of day photo and then it was back to Mike and the car as we headed for home, with a grateful hug of thanks to Dave as we dropped him off in Leominster. The knowledge and wisdom he'd managed to get into me in two days of walking were to prove truly invaluable in the days to come!

Day Four Stats

Start time – 9.10 am.

Finish time – 4.14 pm.

Duration – 7 hours, 4 minutes

Distance walked – 10.5 miles.

Total ascent – 252 ft.

Total descent 636 ft.

Avg. speed – 2.2 mph

Day Five: Going Solo
Monkland to Woonton

5 July 2019

Friday dawned fair again. The weather so far had been magnificent, for which I am exceedingly thankful. However, the start of the fifth day of the walk was beset by confusion and miscommunication. Like many clergypersons, we have two phonelines, one for church business and one for family and friends. The church one can be silenced so that when we're away on holiday and my mum and dad are here cat-sitting, they aren't bothered by it. Reasonably enough, given that I was pretty much out of the loop for three weeks, Mike had turned it to silent so that he wouldn't be disturbed by it as he worked. The problem was that this meant we didn't hear the phone when Cathy rang to tell us that she wouldn't, after all, be able to walk with me that day. So I sat at home, ready to go, increasingly puzzled, and a little worried about Cathy's non-appearance. True, there was always the explanation of Powell-Chandler time, and the family's reputation for lateness – but Cathy had assured me that she would be on time, she'd been very on time for the start of the walk on Monday, so I was surprised as 8.00 am came and went and still no Cathy. Normally it wouldn't have mattered – whatever time we started, we'd just keep going until we finished. But the night before, my aunty Pat had phoned. She lives in Leominster and knew that part of my reason for doing the walk was because her late husband, my uncle Mike, had died from cancer in 2013, so was keen to meet up with us at some point, preferably at Monkland. Meeting up at the end of the day was tricky because I never quite knew how long each leg would take, but meeting up at the start of the day should be straightforward, so I told her we'd be at Monkland Church, ready to resume at around 9.00 am the following morning.

Time ticked on, and Mike sensibly suggested I give Cathy a call to see what the problem was. Of course, her first words to me were – 'you've picked up my messages then' – which was when I found out she's been leaving me messages since about 7.00 am that morning! The problem was that her gorgeous black Labrador, Rex, had been poorly all night, and, as she was heading off on holiday the next day, she needed to stay with him, possibly take him to the vets, to ensure that he was well enough to travel. So having wished her and Rex well, I got into the car and headed for Monkland. Mike had been finding the driving took up far more of his day than he'd bargained for when he kindly offered to chauffeur me around, so today was going to be the first day I'd driven myself to the start point – thus cutting his time spent driving in half. Now it had turned into the first day I was going it totally alone with the walking as well, so it was with some trepidation – as well as a little excitement – that I followed the very familiar roads to Monkland. I remembered them very well from the times Mum and Dad would take me to visit Gran and Grandad even down to yelling out when I saw the milk factory, aka the Cadbury's factory, on the outskirts of Leominster.

I finally made it to Monkland to find Aunty Pat still waiting faithfully for my arrival. I'm so glad I did, partly because it's always lovely to see her, and she gave me a very generous donation for Macmillan, but also because she had brought with her a photo of Uncle Mike, so that when she took the start of day photo, he could be included in it too. This was incredibly important, as it was another representation of all those lives cut way too short by cancer,

Fig 11. Uncle Mike

which was a huge motivation for me to do the walk and raise money for Macmillan, who do such a great job of supporting families like Aunty Pat and my cousins Paul and Lesley when they were going through the trauma of Uncle Mike's illness and death.

Uncle Mike was the middle of the three Jones boys, very bright as they all are, and someone who loved and excelled at all sports, particularly rugby, which was a lifelong passion. He was originally intending to study at Loughborough and become a PE and craft teacher but, thanks to the interference of his headmaster, he became a police cadet at Hendon instead. He served two years in uniform before joining the CID, where he remained for the rest of his police career. He was a man of great integrity and high standards and expected the same of others. He had a very dry wit and a great sense of humour, a love of the outdoors, of gardening, of cooking and of family, but the police and rugby took up most of his early and mid-life. He worked long hours, but in a job he thoroughly enjoyed. On retirement, he continued to do more of the same, travelling the world investigating ticket fraud for Pan Am and then various insurance-type frauds. I think Aunty Pat thought she would see more of him when he retired, but I'm not at all sure that was the case until eventually they moved back to Leominster, reuniting with old friends and particularly with the Old Luctonians rugby club. Mike was now refereeing rather than playing, but his interest in and passion for the game remained undimmed. It seems so unfair that just as he was able to relax a little and enjoy life, particularly loving spending time with his grandchildren, that illness should have arrived to limit the life of this hugely active, charismatic and vital man. He was a big man in every sense of the word, and his death has left a huge hole in the lives of my aunty Pat, my cousins and all of our family.

I think what meeting Aunty Pat that morning showed me is that remembering is really important too. Much as we miss Uncle Mike, our lives have continued pretty much as before, whereas for Pat, Paul and Lesley, life changed forever when Mike died. And while they may no longer be aware of that loss every minute of every day, yet still in many ways the wound is as raw as it was at the time of his death. It may have scabbed over a little, but the hurt is always, will always, be there. And I think we the family, and we the wider world, and we the Church, don't always realise the enormity and longevity of grief and hurt, aren't always sensitive enough to the seismic shift that the death of a beloved family member or friend causes. That's why continuing to hold All Souls services where people can come and mourn the loss of a loved one, hear their name read out and remembered, is so important no matter how recent or how long ago the death of that person occurred. Loss is loss, every human being is unique, there is no replacing or filling the gap left behind, particularly when the person no longer there is such a force of nature as my uncle Mike was.

Batteries recharged and determination reinforced by my encounter with Aunty Pat and having agreed that we'd call in and see her on Monday evening so that we could have a longer catch up, I headed off on my first solo walk of the entire trip. Of course, it wasn't my first solo walk – all of my training walks had been done alone, and in many ways, I enjoyed this, finding it a time to clear my head and almost reset myself, reboot my soul and outlook, if you like. If I felt in need of company or the sound of the human voice, I'd just plug into my iPod and either listen to a podcast or my music. It was strange to find that other people thought that walking alone was either a brave or foolish thing to do, whereas to me it seemed like the most natural thing in the world. The only thing that made me even vaguely apprehensive was the thought of getting lost and not being able to find my way to Woonton. However, I had Dave's tuition and all his wise words in my head, I had my map in the map holder round my neck, and the route on my phone which was tracking me provided I remembered to turn it on. I was all set and ready to hit the trail.

I made my way out of the Church and along the main road until I spotted a footpath sign guiding me through a cattery and on out into open fields. Mike later said this wasn't quite right, but hey, it got me heading off in the right direction, a first for me on this walk so far! Initially I did feel the need to keep stopping and double checking that I was still going the right way, and this did prove invaluable early on in preventing me walking off in completely the wrong direction. My main problem was that, despite Dave's fantastic tuition, I still tended to overestimate the distance I'd walked and so be looking for turns and waymarks way too early. It was lovely easy field walking in beautiful countryside to begin with, and at one point I was able to look back at the way I'd come and to see Monkland Church in the background, which was reassuring. Having crossed several fields, I came to a point where I could see I had options – I could continue through a field to the road and walk along there, or I could put off the road walking a little by following the path through three more fields before hitting the self-same road. As Mike the master route planner had said fields, then fields it was.

These field margins were much more accessible than the ones earlier in the week but still needed full attention as I walked and

I was, as ever, glad of my trusty walking pole to aid my balance. Crossing over stiles as I went, I eventually arrived at the final field, knowing there was a short walk between houses to get me to the road. As I got closer to the stile to enter this short walkway between houses, I could see equipment of some sort lying just beyond it. Sure enough, as I climbed over, there was an abandoned hedge trimmer and as I walked along it was clear that someone had been cutting back the undergrowth very recently. As I got towards the end of the walkway, I came upon a chainsaw, protective visor and ear defenders and abandoned shirt. This meant that when I saw a topless man approaching me, I wasn't alarmed but glad that I could thank him for doing such a great job of clearing a pathway for me and other walkers. His reply kind of took my breath away as he told me that if I'd attempted to get through even the day before I'd have stood no chance as it had been very overgrown for many years and never used – what were the chances? It felt as if angels had been at work, clearing the way for me at just the right time. You may well scoff, and put this down to coincidence, and also point out that if it had been blocked, I could easily have retraced my steps and accessed the road via the earlier path. This is true, but as it was my first day of walking on my own, I think that would have hit my morale quite hard, whereas this had the opposite effect of boosting me up and making me give thanks to God for the selfless act of this gentleman in clearing the right of way for all walkers just in the nick of time.

I reached the road, turned right and could now relax a little as it was road walking for quite a long stretch and that was easier to navigate than field walking. I felt I'd completed the first challenge of the day. And it also enabled me to appreciate one of the joys of solo walking – you get more time and space to appreciate the beauty of the countryside all around you. I don't know whether it was successfully completing the first couple of hours of solo walking, or that Herefordshire was looking particularly beautiful on this glorious summer's day, but I found myself stunned by the beauty which surrounded me, so much so that I stopped to take a photo, although no photo can really do it justice.

I walked onward, ever onward but along blessedly quiet roads, only the odd car to disturb me and every now and again a village or hamlet to give me other points of interest in examining the

Fig 12. Glorious Herefordshire

variety of houses, and especially gardens, as I passed. It was by now approaching the two hour mark, and as I had taken Dave's injunction to stop and take on water and nutrition seriously, I was on the look out for an appropriate place. Churches became a favourite resting place as they generally had benches in the churchyard which welcomed the weary walker, but alas no church or roadside bench came into view. Consulting the map, I decided I would get myself across the main road which I was about to reach, and then focus on finding a stopping place. I made it across the staggered crossroads, reassured by the roadsign pointing to Dilwyn, which was my first major staging post, and walked only a short distance further when I saw a promising looking bridge. Its stone walls came up to seating height for a weary walker, so without further ado I took off my rucksack and plonked myself on it. The sight of a middle aged woman sat on a wall caused surprise and some consternation to the 4x4 drivers who whizzed by. However, I really didn't care, as I sat there feeling not only my body, but also my soul being restored by the sheer beauty and majesty of the landscape, which even included a few poppies on the edge of the harvest field. According to my map, the bridge was Ventnor Bridge over the Stretford Brook, which made me smile, as Stretford is where my lovely husband was born and brought up for the first few years of his life, but his Stretford is the one from which you can see the floodlights of Old Trafford!

There's something about being by water that is particularly soothing and refreshing. Watching the water flow by, hearing the babbling of the brook, made me feel very serene and relaxed. In my priestly role, I associate water with baptisms – not the most relaxing part of the job, given that the baby is generally screaming their head off at the sight of some strange woman in weird clothes tipping water over their head, followed by oil on their forehead. But there is something deeply elemental to that start of the journey of faith, the use of water for cleansing but also creation – nothing survives for long without the water of life, and oil for anointing you as you start out – as Julie had anointed me the day before I began this enterprise – and the light of Christ, the little flame of the Holy Spirit on the candle which we generally hand to a godparent rather than a babe in arms. Water, oil and light, Father, Son and Holy Spirit, all that symbolism of faith is rooted and grounded in real items that you can touch and feel and see. When Jesus meets the much-married Samaritan woman at the well, he describes himself as living water and tells the woman that those who drink this living water will never thirst again. She rushes off to tell all her friends, becoming the first ever Christian evangelist. And of course, back in the day before there were even church buildings, baptisms would have taken place in rivers and brooks just like this one and are still done there today – a much nicer method of total immersion baptism than hopping into a birthing pool! This walk made me think about the way Christianity used to be a faith of the outdoors, a walking faith – the Gospels are full of Jesus walking from place to place, teaching, preaching and healing – a faith very much in touch with nature and the great outdoors. Yet now we seem to have almost shut it away in our buildings, made it very formal and stiff, lost touch with how wonderful God's creation is and how spiritually refreshing it is to be out in that creation, giving thanks for all the beauty which surrounds us.

Refreshed in body, mind and spirit, I stood up and prepared to move on, deploying my trusty iPod to get me through what promised to be a lot of road walking to get me to Dilwyn and then onto Weobley. I always carried my iPod with me, but I didn't use it when walking with others as that would have been downright rude. I had often used it on my solo walks, and even when walking with Mike, as he tends to walk much faster than me and is generally beyond conversation distance when we walk together. I've found that podcasts or music can be good distractions when the going gets tough – particularly on big hills – but I did a deal with myself that the first part of any walk would be iPodless as the downside for me was that by taking away the sounds of a walk you slightly detached yourself from the world about you. This could be a good thing when that world involved aching muscles but losing the birdsong and other natural accompaniments wasn't something I did lightly.

Once I'd got back into the rhythm of the walk, I seemed to arrive at Dilwyn quite quickly – in fact I seemed to be making relatively good progress overall, probably because of the high proportion of road on the route. I didn't really get to see much of Dilwyn as I took the road signposted to Weobley on the outskirts of the village and kept on along the road. I knew it was a fair way until I picked up the next footpath marker to take me across country to Weobley which was the next big staging post and where I planned to have my next stop. I found the footpath sign without any problem, close to magnificent farm buildings set part way up a hill – Fields Place. The route continued along past a forestry plantation, then across fields which were clearly waymarked – wonderful. I even encountered a very cheery farmer who waved from his tractor. I'm always slightly apprehensive about farmers' reactions to walkers as – even though I'm always ultra-conscious of closing gates, sticking to marked paths and avoiding going through crops – I feel bad about going across their land. However, every farmer or farm worker I encountered on this walk was without fail helpful and friendly – so huge thanks to the farming community who enable us to enjoy the land they care for so well. The other fab thing about this part of the walk was that the spire of Weobley Church was a major landmark from quite a way out, reassuring me that I was heading in the right direction and there wasn't that far to go.

Our church buildings, especially the massive medieval ones, are a huge presence in the rural landscape. Those who built them will have done so with that intention in mind, to build to the glory of God, a magnificent building bigger and grander than anything else around with spires reaching up to the heavens and containing bells which would ring out across the countryside, calling the faithful to prayer and worship. As a sign of God with us they are fantastic, and as historic and sacred spaces they have a wonderful atmosphere and feel all of their own – those centuries of prayer and worship really do soak into the stonework. But they are also hugely costly to maintain. They lack most of the facilities like effective central heating and toilets which most people have come to expect as standard wherever they go. And most of them are now very much too large for the average weekly congregations who love and use them. Smaller congregations and a dwindling band of ageing volunteers do their best to care for these magnificent places, but it becomes ever more apparent as the years go by that some tough decisions will have to be taken in the quite near future. The nub of the problem is that the vast majority of people want the church to be there for them when they need it – and generally these days that's for weddings, baptisms and funerals – but don't feel the need or inclination to give regular support in terms of time and/or money which is so desperately needed to keep the show on the road. I don't have any magic solution for this problem, but it struck me as I went from place to place, enjoying the time, space and hospitality provided by these wonderful buildings, to wonder whether someone doing this same walk in ten, twenty or fifty years would find them still functioning and welcoming, or converted into housing or some other use. I very much hope not, but fear that the days of these wonderful, historical and sacred buildings may be numbered.

Nearing Weobley, I came across a family having a picnic in the back of a pickup in a field, so despite there being a lovely bench nearby I didn't really feel I could stop without intruding on their privacy. However, I knew that my route was about to take me round and past Weobley Church so hoped for a friendly bench and wasn't disappointed. Weobley Church is MASSIVE! I quickly found a shady bench which allowed me to sit and appreciate this beautiful building on this amazingly fine day. The church looked magnificent against the backdrop of a cloudless blue sky. I didn't go in as I'd noticed what looked like a grave-digger's car – complete with coffin shaped template – waiting outside the church so assumed that there was to be a funeral that afternoon. A brief word on funerals here, as I know some people dislike them and find them gloomy and sad occasions, hence the proliferation of private cremation firms advertising on daytime TV at the moment. But to me a funeral is such an important milestone in grieving the loss of a loved one that I would urge everyone to make sure they have something appropriate. Not necessarily a church funeral, but some sort of event where you are brought face to face with the reality of death. We are very good at ducking this one certain fact about life – that it will end. I know that coming face to face with a coffin at the church or crematorium is incredibly hard – I've been to the funerals of friends and family, and even conducted some like my uncle Mike's funeral at Kingsland Church, and it's never easy. But it's also the chance to celebrate and to give thanks for lives well lived. To remember all the good times you shared with them. To come together with friends and family to talk about them and exchange memories. To laugh and to cry together. Grief is such a lonely and isolating experience. Coming together to comfort and help each other to bear that loss is, I believe, a vital stage on the grieving journey, and one that we shouldn't omit without very careful thought or consideration. So, if you are thinking, I don't want a fuss when my time comes, I'll just go the private cremation route, bear in mind that by making that choice you may well be depriving friends and family of their last opportunity to show how much they love you and how thankful they are to have shared your life.

As I sat in blissful shade, looking back at the church, I was kept very well entertained by watching the swallows – or possibly swifts – duck and dive around the church porch. It's not just our church buildings which can be havens and sanctuaries, our churchyards can also be great places for wildlife to flourish. At St Faith's, Berrow we have a very acrobatic swift population who return year on year, and insect and lichen populations which are astonishingly varied and rich. And if you ever get the chance to go on a bat walk in a churchyard, or around a church tower, I would definitely recommend it as these amazing creatures are losing their habitat of old barns and so find a new home in our church buildings, where they are very welcome – except when we need to carry out repair work! Even then, rest assured, we always work round them and with them, as we love and cherish them as part of our church community.

I texted Mike to let him know I'd made it this far, so that he would know when to set off to pick me up, then picked up my rucksack, plugged myself into my iPod and headed into Weobley for the last leg of the day. This looked dangerously straightforward, and to begin with it was. I headed into the middle of Weobley and turned right along the road to head out of town, once more passing some very fascinating looking houses and gardens. Then I needed to nip across and along a very main piece of road, the main road running from Leominster to Hay, the A4112. Mike had talked me through this bit, explaining that he'd deliberately designed it so that I spent as short a time as possible walking along this very fast and busy road. So it was with some relief that I found my way to the footpath sign taking me offroad and into a field which should have led me out onto a quiet lane. I say should have because for all my attempts at putting Dave's words of wisdom into effect I could not for the life of me find my way out of that field! I spent what felt like hours wandering to and fro consulting my map. I did try to consult the phone tracking map to see exactly where I was relative to the exit from the field but was greeted only by a blank screen. This was another bit of the learning curve we were both on – Mike hadn't downloaded the maps to my phone, thinking that I'd always be in phone signal range, but this field was obviously a black spot for data loading so the phone was no help.

In the end, I did use Dave's words of wisdom – if you can't find the way you're meant to be going, can you see a good alternative? I could. If I went a little further up the scary main road, I could turn onto the lane which the lane I couldn't find would have led me onto. Leaving the field defeated, I made it along the main road and set off up the lane via Little Sarnesfield. I was starting to tire now in the heat of the day after a long week, but the iPod and the prospect of being nearly there kept me going. I found my turn off the lane up a farm track towards The Birches. The stile to let me onto the path to skirt round the farm buildings was not obvious at first, being in the middle of a slightly overgrown hedge, but I managed to both spot it and get over it. The waymarks at this point were reasonable, but there were quite a few obstacles to get over – nettles growing in front of gates which I had to clamber over in lieu of stiles, then a final very overgrown field margin to walk along to a virtually impassable stile – how I wished I had my secateurs with me, but sheer bloody-mindedness and tiredness enabled me to force my way through, emerging bloodied but unbowed onto a nice easy bit of road. Never did I think I'd be thankful for a bit of road walking, but this became a fairly constant theme of the walk. Now I just had to walk up to the crossroads, turn left and it was all downhill to Woonton. Even better, as I turned onto the main road, I saw Mike walking towards me with some chilled water in his hand – wonderful! We took the end of walk photo by the parish council noticeboard, and then headed back to Monkland, which, rather annoyingly, we reached in no time at all by car. Mike dropped me off, and as I got into my car, I noticed that the thermometer was showing 30 degrees – no wonder I was a bit tired and hot! I drove myself home singing along to an Abba CD, tired but very happy and also proud of myself for not just enduring but also enjoying a whole day of solo walking. And for solving the problems myself when they came up, not giving up but keeping going. It had been a good day of walking to bring Week One to a close.

Day Five Stats

    Start time – 9.39 am.

    Finish time – 3.36 pm.

    Duration – 5 hours, 56 minutes.

    Distance walked – 11 miles.

    Total ascent 276 ft.

    Total descent 105 ft.

    Avg. speed – 2.3 mph.

Day Six: Pride Comes Before a Fall
Woonton to Kington

6 July 2019

Having had a lovely restful weekend – apart from taking two services, where I talked about the walk – Monday dawned once more bright, sunny, blue sky and warm. The weather was still being very, very good to me. Actually, rewind slightly as I've kind of passed over those services. Ideally, I wouldn't have taken them, but it turned out Revd Julie needed to be elsewhere that weekend for very important reasons, so I was happy to cover for her. And you know what? Those services were really restorative for me. Particularly the 8.00 am service at Pendock Cross. I know a lot of priests don't have much time for the Book of Common Prayer communion, and I totally understand why – the language is very much of its time, and that time is 1558, so it's not exactly accessible for youngsters or those who are unfamiliar with its wording or the sudden jump of pages that happens mid-service. But for me, the language has a beauty and a rhythm all of its own, and you don't necessarily have to understand each and every word to gain a sense of what is happening – like opera sung in a foreign language, you just drink in the overall sound and are upheld by that. And when I thought about it a bit more it is the eucharist in its purest form – no hymns, no intercessions, just priest and people united in the memorial of Christ's body and blood.

Eucharist, communion, whatever you call it, the sharing of the

bread and wine is central to a priestly vocation, certainly central to
mine. There are very few things in the church which only a priest
can do – consecrating the bread and wine for communion is one
of them, marrying people and blessing people are the other two.
During the time in a communion service where the priest is behind
the altar, reading the eucharistic prayer, he or she is basically being
a channel for the Holy Spirit to come and inhabit the bread and
wine, and to pour out over the congregation. A very wise man once
described it to me as being like a garden hose or watering can – it
sprays liberally out over the congregation, but focuses narrowly
down to consecrate the bread and the wine. Roman Catholics
believe in transubstantiation whereby the bread and wine are
somehow changed into the body and blood of Christ. Anglicans
believe a whole range of things, from transubstantiation through
consubstantiation – the doctrine that the body and blood of
Christ co-exist with the bread and wine – right the way through to
eucharist being a re-enactment or remembering of the Last Supper,
in accordance with Jesus' instructions to us. All I can tell you is
there is something indescribably mystical about being the hands,
the feet, the body which gets to be in that situation, to be that
channel, to be in that liminal, numinous space, standing between
God and his people.

And the people who attend this particular flavour of the eucharist
are folk who have been coming to this service all their lives, many
of them not needing the prayer book because they know the words
off by heart. There was something about the service that morning
at Pendock where the response of those few in the congregation
came through loud and strong and lifted me, supported me, gave
me the strength I needed to carry on – and I was very much to
need that kind of strength and determination today! Also, 8.00 am
communion has another dimension for me since Benny's death, as

he blogged that during his illness, he found he preferred the BCP Communion over other services – whether it was the quiet, the calm, the purity of it, or whether it was the comfort of the words he'd known all his life, I'll never know, but I do know that every time I lead this service, he is in my mind and heart and I give thanks for him.

Monday was another driving myself day, so I headed back to Woonton, parked the car and then had to work out how to take a selfie on my phone for the start of day photo. Not particularly beautiful, but functional! Having established I was back in the right starting place, I headed off away from the main road, along a path past an old Friends Meeting House and into a field, newly harvested, with a keen rabbit population! This was the eponymously named Woonton Farm, and I progressed across its fields, using my newly acquired field boundary skills to successfully navigate my way to a moderately overgrown track past houses and down to the road. It became a rule of thumb that footpaths on the edge of human habitation, be it town, village or hamlet, were likely to be in better condition because the dog walkers of the locality, God bless them, kept them well walked.

A tiny bit of road walking towards Logaston took me past the house of a fellow pilgrim – or at least someone with an interest in pilgrimage – as on the side of their house nearest the road they'd written the mileage from Logaston to Santiago di Compostella and from Logaston to Rome. This made me smile and think of a fellow pilgrim currently on the road to Santiago di Compostela – my friend Tina's husband Nick. He was doing the full walk as a way of marking a big birthday, retirement, the recent death of his father – all the usual mix of things that goes into the decision to do something as different as a pilgrimage. It's a bold move, to step out and walk any distance at all, to claim that time for yourself in our busy, productivity obsessed world. My latest favourite quote, from the theologian Richard Rohr, is 'We do not think ourselves into new ways of living; we have to live ourselves into new ways of thinking.' Maybe Nick and I were both walking ourselves into new ways of thinking and living. And this pilgrimage was also a reminder of the days when we were a nomadic people, always on the move, walking was our natural state. And more recently than that, walking or cycling or riding were pretty much the primary modes of transport before the invention of trains and cars, which isn't that long ago in the overall human scheme of things.

Philosophising over, I saluted Nick in my mind, hoped all was well with him and the friend he was walking with and carried on with my own pilgrimage, aiming to arrive at Kington in one piece. I was gaining in confidence about my walking and navigational skills, and, as we all know, a little confidence can be a very dangerous thing. The route Mike had planned for me saw me continuing to walk down the lane and onward via some farm buildings. As I'd rather avoid farm buildings if at all possible, and the footpath in front of me looked wide and walkable and I could see it joined back up with my route soon, I took the wide and walkable path, encountering another cheery farmer who had come to check his crop along the way. However, wide and walkable soon turned into overgrown field margin and no way out of the field where there should have been a way out of the field according to the map – serves me right for not staying on the approved route!

I didn't panic, which was progress in itself. Instead, I kept on keeping on along the field boundary and eventually came to a footbridge across the stream, waymarked the Vaughan way, and suddenly found myself back on track. The onward way was clear and obvious, with waymarks and visible stiles, and although the final bit through a verdant field of potatoes was hard going, I finally made it to the road and to Almeley village, where the sound of play time at the nearby school confirmed that I was where I thought I was. I could now relax a little as it was road walking all the way from here to Eardisley and I could enjoy the sights and sounds of another lovely Herefordshire village. Ameley had another massive church, a running bus service, a very striking war memorial, and a very tempting bench. I was sorely tempted to stop and have my break there and then but I hadn't quite achieved the requisite two hours of walking so I carried on, a decision I would come to regret. And one which made me aware that a bench in the hand is worth any number of potential benches further on down the road.

I carried on along said road, leaving Almeley and its very attractive manor house behind, crossed the bridge over the river and then hung a left along the road to Eardisley which ran alongside the disused railway line so it was very long and very straight but ran alongside some magnificent woodland which contained some huge old oak trees – a feature of the Herefordshire countryside. Then on the other side of the road, Upcott farm had some wonderful orchards, row upon row of laden apple trees, a reminder of Herefordshire's past and present cider heritage. I continued on past Gypsy Hall and went over Gypsy Hall Bridge, sadly not a bridge you could sit on, and the outskirts of Eardisley were in sight. Then I had another dilemma. There was a pub in Eardisley but it was right over the other side of the village. Did I take a chance on it being open and willing to provide me with coffee and a seat, or did I stick with the route and turn off the road and carry on across the fields? The footpath sign beckoned me on, so I turned off into the field, but could go no further, and having now well exceeded my two hours and with no bench or friendly bridge in sight I just sat down in the field and had my break. It wasn't exactly comfortable, but it was much better than nothing!

I didn't linger, and was soon underway again, walking the field margin and then crossing into a field of oil seed rape, where the farmer had very considerately left a gap from one side of the field to the stile on the other side. This always lifted my spirits and made me very grateful. Up the length of a field of pasture I went and then through a waymarked gate in the fence and down into Holywell Dingle, a lovely shady piece of woodland with waymarks all of its own, and several fallen trees to get under or over. The variety of criss-crossing paths could be a bit confusing, but I managed to emerge in approximately the right place, although confusingly the manor house whose grounds I was walking alongside had changed its name – shouldn't be allowed!

Having spent all of my time so far on day six walking through fields or on quiet country roads, I was now approaching an A road, the A4111 to be precise and could hear the traffic noise from a way off. Thankfully I only had a short distance to go along it, which was more than enough as the traffic was moving very fast, to my walker's eye, and there were lots of heavy lorries as it was the main road into Kington. I was relieved to be able to turn off down a quiet lane, and to pick up the footpath into a field very soon afterwards. Using a combination of map and the route description of the Black and White Village Trail, thoughtfully provided by my dear husband, I made it across Queest Moor – a couple of fields – and into Queestmoor Wood. The dilapidated condition of the stiles made me feel that possibly this landowner wasn't that keen on welcoming walkers and that maybe the Black and White Village Trail wasn't that regularly used. This suspicion was confirmed all too soon. Once into the wood, the instructions told me to look out for a gateway and a bridge across a stream. The path I was following seemed to disappear quite quickly but I saw no sign of either gateway or bridge, so I convinced myself that it had reappeared and kept on going through the woodland, which also entailed walking through a pretty huge badger sett. I kept going right to the far end of the wood to find only a fence, no gate or stile and no waymark. I climbed out into the field to see if I could orientate myself using either my map or my phone and pretty soon realised I'd gone quite a way off course. I spent a little time looking around the field to see if there was any way I could get myself back on track without going back into the woods – but there wasn't. With a heavy heart, I climbed back over the fence, fought my way back through the woods to the stile I'd climbed in over and set off again looking out for the gate and bridge, which really shouldn't have been that far into the woods. This time round I spotted what looked like an old gate post next to a massive fallen tree which I assume had taken out the bridge. By stopping to look around more carefully, I could just about make out a very overgrown waymarked stile on the other edge of the stream. As the water level was very low, I was able to step over the stream, haul myself up and over the stile and, beating away at the nettles and brambles, land up in the field on the other side. Now, this was the point at which I should have looked at what lay ahead of me and decided to make alternative arrangements, because there was no sane way through this field. The field margin contained nettles, docks and thistles that were as tall as me, which meant walking through the crop, something which I'm never comfortable with doing, partly because it just seems plain wrong and partly because you can't see where you're putting your foot, the ploughed furrows are uneven and it makes you prone to falling, and/or breaking an ankle, neither of which particularly appealed. However, several things mitigated against this sane and sensible decision, the main one being my own bloody mindedness. It had taken me ages to find my way back on track, this was the way the footpath lay, and I was ruddy well going to walk it, come hell or high water. Plus, on a more prosaic level, my alternative route would mean walking for quite a long way along the scary A4111 with those lorries thundering past in close proximity. At the time, this seemed like the worst of my two options. Had I only known, dicing with death under the wheels of a heavy goods vehicle would have been a picnic compared to what I was about to experience! Of course, I told myself that this was only one field, and the next field would probably be better (it wasn't) or pasture (it wasn't).

Grimly determined, walking pole in one sweaty hand and written directions clenched in the other, I set off along the edge of the cropped field. Within minutes it was clear that this was far, far worse than I had imagined. Walking through waist high crop is hard going at the best of times. Walking through waist high crop, which is also infested with goose grass, that sticky long weed, is nigh on impossible as it grabs at your legs and entangles you in its all too persistent embrace. I can't remember whether I fell over two or three times getting across that field, but I do remember I got steadily more and more angry and upset. Whether it was physical tiredness, frustration or fear, or a bit of all of the above, I was not in a good place either physically or mentally. Finally, after what seemed like hours but was clearly only minutes, I reached the hedge on the other side of the field. The good news was that I could see the stile, the bad news was that I couldn't get to it because of all the nettles, bracken and brambles in front of it. Putting my anger and frustration to good use, I beat the obstructive foliage back a little with my stick to clear a path and stepped forward into nothingness. My foot went down and down and I ended up on my back in the bottom of a ditch – a ditch which still had a little muddy water in it just to make my day complete!!! Now I was really cross – but also still sane enough to realise that I had been very lucky. I hadn't hurt myself falling into the ditch and from my vantage point lying down there I could see a plank bridge had been put in to enable walkers to cross but had been so overgrown as to be completely invisible. I hauled myself out, and discovered, thankfully, that my phone had stayed dry in my pocket, although the written instructions in my hand had got a bit wet and muddy.

In one way I think the fall was a wakeup call for me. I'd been guilty of letting anger and frustration – and sheer pig-headedness – blind me to the danger of where I was and the terrain I was walking through. Yes, it was a field in the middle of rural Herefordshire, but if I had fallen awkwardly and broken an ankle or a leg, I would potentially have been in real trouble. Nobody would have been able to see me in the bottom of the ditch, there were no houses close by to hear me shout, yes I had my mobile phone on me but sod's law would probably have meant I didn't have any signal – and how would Mike have been able to find me? And it also showed that there was a bit of a downside to walking alone. I suspect that if I'd been walking with any of my previous companions, we'd either have decided that trying to force our way through the fields wasn't worth it and gone back to the road, or if anyone else had been mad enough to try it with me, they would have been able to go and raise the alarm if I had seriously hurt myself. As it was, my pride was the only thing in pain. I had been incredibly lucky or incredibly blessed, depending on your point of view. All of which went to show that often it's good to have someone else around to talk through options and possibilities because it can prevent you from charging on with your plan when there might well be more sensible alternatives available.

However, none of that changed the fact that I was where I was. And it could have been much worse. I could have injured myself falling, or I could have been walking after a spell of wet weather, in which case I'd have been soaked to the skin from walking through the vegetation. Although, my contemporaneous notes remind me that my forearms were badly stung by the four-foot-high nettles I was having to beat back to get to and over stiles. The fall had calmed me down a little and got rid of much of that dangerous adrenalin. I also really didn't fancy retracing my steps again, now that I'd made it across one field. The only alternative was to keep going, but hopefully in a calmer and less dangerously hot-headed manner. I did this and, after another couple of crop walks through fields, arrived at some pasture which provided blessed relief – never thought I'd appreciate a field of grazing land so much! I navigated round some farm buildings, up a farm lane and then was out onto a country lane which I knew I needed to cross to continue along my route. I'd agreed to text Mike when I reached this point so that he would know when to pick me up. I managed to do this, but then struggled to find my onward route. I was definitely due another two-hour pitstop but was so tired and fed up that I decided I just wanted to press on and get to Kington, get the day's walk done and put it behind me. Mistake number three of this day of learning . . . although in my defence, I hadn't really come across anywhere suitable to sit down and take a break, no welcoming churches or conveniently placed benches. Tuning into the rhythm of life, the rhythm of the seasons, the rhythm of work, rest and play which our brains and bodies need is not an easy thing to do – or certainly I don't find it easy. This example of being tired and grumpy but not taking a rest is classic me, just push on through, just get to the end, get it done. What I've learned from the walk, but also from what's happened since in terms of brain and body, is that rest is vital to our health and general well-being. Rest is not a luxury, it's a necessity. Rest is when we rebuild mind and body and spirit, ready to go again. Clergy are terrible at modelling this for their parishioners, which is ironic when the concept of Sabbath, of resting for one day out of seven, is there right at the start of the Bible, throughout the Old Testament, and then very well modelled by Jesus, who would always take himself away to a quiet place after an exhausting day of giving out in terms of teaching, preaching and healing. Whereas for clergy, I sometimes think it's a badge of honour to have a packed diary, something I struggle with as much as anyone. That's why Quiet Days and retreats are so vital, taking time out on pilgrimage too, but actually find the time day to day to rest, relax, be still and be present – that's the hard part but the key learning from this incident. Make it part of your everyday – don't neglect your rest.

Eventually I gave up on finding the right way and just decided to go for it. I made my way up what looked like a green lane running alongside a house. I arrived at a field gate with no comforting waymarks, but I knew from the phone route tracking that I was headed in the right direction, so carried on – getting daring now – or desperate! I walked on up the field, scaring a herd of cows, and eventually found a waymarked stile up in the corner, which I clambered over, only to find a farmer in a tractor working on the other side. Seeing me, he drove over and turned off the engine so we could talk. I was bracing myself for a telling off, but on the contrary, he was interested in what I was doing and took a look at my map to make sure I was headed in the right direction. In fact he told me he'd walked down one of the paths I was headed toward but it was a bit overgrown ... Heartened by his help, I made for the corner of the field, and across one more cropped field – not so bad this time and then onto pasture walking, looking out for a right turn through the boundary line. Knowing what I was looking for – thank you Dave – I found it nicely marked and leading onto a clear trail across and down some meadowland. Walking through a clear path in the middle of long meadow grass is probably my favourite type of walking. Something about being surrounded by waist high grasses and flowers, beautiful sights, sounds and textures. And the movement of a meadow as the wind passes over it, like a green grassy sea. It really lifts the spirits to discover a meadow on your walk. I continued on and passed through some sort of donkey sanctuary until I made it to a main road. The fact that arriving at a main road was a cause for major celebration tells you everything you need to know about how tough the previous bit of field walking had been.

Now I knew that I only had to cross this road to reach the back road into Kington and from then on it was good old road all the way – no worries about navigation, no concerns about overgrown field margins, just lots of lovely tarmac, and the odd oncoming car. It was in all honesty a long hot slog at the end of a frustrating and exhausting day – both mentally and physically – but this was where the iPod was an absolute godsend and plugging into my music made the journey go with a swing. And on the meandering backroad there were houses to be eyed up, gardens to delight in, dogs to see me off their property and the almost meditative state of knowing that I just needed to keep putting one foot in front of the other and I'd be in Kington in the end. Walking as meditation, as a way of being in the moment, being in the rhythm of your footsteps, being in your body, on the road, in the middle of the countryside. It stills the racing mind and calms the soul.

But fate had one last curve ball to throw at me that day. I knew Kington pretty well as we love to holiday in this beautiful part of the world, a quintessential time out of mind borderlands market town. When I came over the river and into Kington itself and saw, where my mapped route said I should turn left, a sign saying access to a business only, I thought blow it – or words to that effect – I'm not even going to risk not being able to get through, I'll go the long way round to get to the car park where I'm due to meet Mike.

What I didn't know was that he had arrived early and decided to walk along the mapped route to meet me and walk back with me, knowing I'd had a rough day. This meant that I ended up in what I thought was the designated meeting point only to find no Skoda. I phoned Mike, who was by now heading out of town on foot and becoming increasingly concerned that he'd not come across me. He set me straight, I needed to walk just a little further to a short stay car park and there I would find the Skoda, my trusty chariot, awaiting. And sure enough, there it was with a very welcome bench nearby so I sat and rested my weary legs until Mike arrived a few minutes later. Thankful that this particularly tough leg of the walk was at an end, we loaded the rucksack into Skoda, and headed back to Woonton, a dishearteningly short drive away, so that I could pick up my car for the drive home.

We debated whether to stop off at Aunty Pat's on the way home, as I was tired, hot and pretty fed up by this time. However, we'd said we would so we did – and I was so glad we did. For a start, Aunty Pat had laid on a wonderful selection of baked goods, including a custard tart – and you can't beat a custard tart for immediately making you feel better about life. And it was just really lovely to spend time with her, to hear a bit about her life, to have a walk round the garden, admiring all the hard work she'd put in, and just to enjoy each other's company. When I finally drove home, I was feeling very much restored by tea, custard tarts, but mainly by a reminder of how good it was to spend time with those you love, and of the reason I was doing the walk in the first place – to raise funds to help those like Aunty Pat who continue to grieve the loss of someone totally irreplaceable in their life.

What had I learned from this somewhat manic Monday? That we can all get tangled up, overwhelmed, lose our way, end up down in the bottom of a ditch – either physically or metaphorically. And that what gets us back on track, for me anyway, is a combination of family, friends and faith. And the kindness of strangers – that farmer stopping to make sure I was headed in the right direction changed the tone of the day and really lifted my spirits. He also confounded my expectations that farmers would be hostile or irritated by walkers crossing their land, and it's always good to have your expectations confounded. We often need someone from outside our situation to put us back on track with a few well-chosen words or kind actions or an innocent question. In faith terms, after a long spell of not going to church, my young niece, Bex, asked one Sunday when she and her family were visiting 'Why don't you go to Church?' Church and faith were such a part of her family's life that she genuinely couldn't understand why they weren't part of mine. And as I couldn't come up with a good explanation for her, I did start going back to church, was made to feel very welcome, particularly by my good friend Susan, and eventually ended up getting ordained as a priest in the Church of England – and all because of an innocent question.

Similarly, that lovely encounter with Aunty Pat sorted me out and got me back on track because it reminded me of one of the major reasons why I was doing the walk – to raise money and awareness for Macmillan. What was a bit of hurt pride and a few fields of tricky walking for me, compared to the difficulties encountered by cancer patients and their families? She helped me get things back in perspective.

And the final bit of learning was that nature is red in tooth and claw. In full growth she can be rampant and destructive and for every gorgeous wildflower filled meadow there is likely to be a stile surrounded by nettles. Which is just life, isn't it? We all experience times of great joy, but also times of pain, frustration, grief, sorrow. We can't avoid it, but we can try to deal with it well, which I definitely didn't do to begin with on this day of the walk! There's a thin line between perseverance and courage tipping over into stubbornness and stupidity and I was definitely on the wrong side of that line when I ended up in the ditch. Maybe today's lesson was never be too proud to ask for and receive help when you really need it, no matter where it comes from.

The worst day of the walk was over – though of course I didn't know that at the time – and the best really was just about to come.

Day Six Stats

Start time – 9.32 am.
Finish time – 4.26 pm.
Duration – 6 hours, 53 minutes
Distance walked – 12.7 miles.
Total ascent 584 ft.
Total descent 476 ft.
Avg. speed – 2.2 mph

Day Seven: Kington to Hay
From the Ditch of Despair to the
Heights of Hergest and Hay

7 July 2019

My contemporaneous notes on this part of the walk begin with – 'After miserable Monday comes tip top Tuesday – so far at least!' My caution stemmed from a lingering concern about getting lost again – although this pretty much disappeared once I'd started on Offa's Dyke proper. And then there was the potential length of today's walk – a stonking sixteen miles. I'd been managing twelve miles okay which I still found astounding, but an extra couple of hours on top of that – I wasn't sure I'd be up to it. Mike reassured me that I could stop earlier if I wanted to – and the official schedule did stop in a layby on the road into Hay – but that it would make much more sense if I could manage to keep going and make it into the car park in the middle of the town. This illustrates what an amazing job Mike had done in getting the route together. One of the limiting factors for him was that each day had to end at a point where he could easily stop the car to pick me up and a point with an obvious landmark which I couldn't miss, like a church or a pub. This meant that he couldn't simply chop the 150 miles up into fifteen legs of ten miles each – it just didn't work that way – with the inevitable result that some legs, like today's, were longer than others – but today was set to be the longest of the lot.

I promised him that I'd give it my best shot, so he dropped me back at Kington Museum and took the by now traditional start of day photo. I headed off up the hill and out of town to where I knew I would pick up the Offa's Dyke Path. There was a lot of comfort in beginning the day somewhere I knew well, even though that meant that I also knew it was going to be uphill all the way for quite a while. I huffed and puffed my way through the fascinating and vibrant market town, with its array of independent shops, a craft gallery, a cookshop and a very tempting looking coffee shop. All sadly would have to wait for another day, as I continued on up the hill, taking a short cut across the churchyard of St Mary the Virgin, Kington. I would have liked to stop and take a look inside the church, but it was way too early to take a break, so I continued on along the road until I came to the sign for Offa's Dyke, pointing up to the left. I knew this bit of the path well as it leads past Hergest Croft Gardens, a fabulous place, owned by successive generations of the Banks family. It has wonderful planting and a particularly good selection of trees to admire – also a good café. At the other end of the same estate, also owned by the Banks family, is Hergest Court, reputed to be haunted by the Black Dog, the inspiration for the Hound of the Baskervilles. Happily, all the dogs I met on my walk were very friendly and well behaved and not at all terrifying!

Once more I resisted the temptation to divert from my path and carried on up, up and up. A few cars drove slowly past me and then drew up to park near the gate which lets out onto the hill up to Hergest Ridge – pronounced Hargest. I'd always pronounced it Hergest until we stayed the weekend of Mike's birthday at the fabulous Harp at Old Radnor – great pub, great food and drink, absolutely stunning views, highly recommended. Over an equally amazing breakfast, we told the landlord that we were going to take a walk up Hergest Ridge only to have our pronunciation very gently but firmly corrected, so it's been Hargest for me ever since.

On our walk that day we'd climbed the ridge from a different starting point, but we'd descended via the route I was about to take, so again, I was walking along a familiar path which was helpful, particularly with the experiences of the day before very fresh in my mind. I got through the gate just ahead of a group of ladies who obviously walked together frequently and headed on upward, ever upward. What a gorgeous walk – lovely wide well-marked path, clearly leading you in the right direction – such a contrast to the day before! Off to my right I could see the highest golf course in England, and thought of Mike, who I believe has played golf there. I also seemed to remember that we'd walked across bits of it during one of our stays in Presteigne. This whole area, and even this path, was well loved and familiar to me, which made such a difference. It meant that I was able to relax and enjoy the amazing views, the wonderful scenery and not have to worry or keep checking my map and/or phone all the time, I could just 'be' which was marvellous. Before embarking upon this life changing adventure, I naively thought it would be a time of meditation and contemplation, being one with nature and reviving and renewing my spiritual side. Any experienced walkers will be laughing their Bridgedale socks off by now, because what I discovered along the way is that you have to be really focussed and concentrate hard on where you are and where the next landmark or turn should be otherwise you are likely to get very lost very quickly. However, this bit of the walk I could just enjoy for its own sake, and very lovely it was too – did I mention the weather was really good again???

I was overtaken near the top of the hill by a man wearing very professional looking kit and walking sandals, and something about the way he was walking – swiftly and without any maps or guides – made me think this was a path he walked frequently. When I reached the group of trees and bench which mark the top and let you know that you are now very much on the ridge, he had stopped and sat down. This was good because it meant I wasn't tempted to do the same. But instead of just passing by with a nod and a smile, something made me ask him if he did this walk regularly. He replied that he did it every day and that it was 'his church and his gym' which gave me pause for thought as I wished him good day and walked on. His church and his gym. The gym bit was the easy part to understand – to walk from Kington town up to the top of the ridge and back every day, rain or shine, would keep anyone fit and be much more pleasant and interesting than working out with loads of other sweaty people on machines in a gym. Nothing against gyms – well, okay, loads against gyms in the sense that they aren't really for people like me, and there's something about the concept of exercising on machines while being indoors watching screens or listening to music that just seems very sterile and monotonous. However, it clearly works for many people, and on the basis that taking exercise in any form is much better than not taking exercise – and that my second eldest niece, Hannah, is now a very successful personal trainer, spending much of her time in the gym – then I'd better just say they aren't for me and leave it at that! Walking in nature, enjoying the sights and sounds of the changing seasons, feeling the sun on your back, the wind blowing your cobwebs away, even the rain pouring down on you somehow makes you feel alive and connected to creation in all its glory, so I totally got what the gentleman meant by this walk being his gym.

But being his church – now that took much more thought and I think I'm still working through it. In the early days of Christianity, a lot of worship would have been outdoors – at preaching crosses like the one in Berrow Churchyard – and in sacred spaces – by streams, or yew trees, or wells or the sea. Sites which had been used for pagan worship were then colonised by the new religion of Christianity, at least the Celtic version of it which came over with St Columba from

Ireland. Since the walk I've read a fascinating book on this subject called The Naked Hermit by Nick Mayhew-Smith which gives a really interesting insight into this whole area. When the Roman version of Christianity won out over the Irish Celtic version at the synod of Whitby in 664 AD, the faith almost became imprisoned in buildings of wood and then stone, and even our buildings today – beautiful though they all are – are very inward looking. We have magnificent stained glass, but it obscures the view to the outside world and what windows there are tend to be set high up so that while you are able to gauge what the weather is doing and rejoice in blue sky and sunlight you can't actually see much of the outside world. This is clearly deliberate so that congregations would not be distracted from their worship and could instead concentrate on the word of God. However, it does seem a shame that in doing so they cut themselves off from his creation, from feeling the sun on your back, the rain on your face, the springiness of the grass under your feet – the beauty of holiness. As George Fox, founder of the Quaker movement, put it 'God is not only found in steeple houses.'

There is now a Forest Church Movement and the Quiet Gardens Movement and I benefit greatly from spending a day a month in silent retreat at a Quiet Garden in rural Herefordshire. And there is also the very wonderful Caring for God's Acre Movement which encourages churches to maximise the potential for wildlife in their churchyards – although that is always a balancing act between a churchyard being tended and cared for so that bereaved families can get to their graves, and leaving areas to grow long for wildlife so that cowslips and primroses can self-seed. We are also blessed in some of our medieval churches by the company of bats – and while some parishioners find them a pain as they dictate when repair and restoration work can and more importantly can't be done and leave us small offerings of bat poo to mark their presence which needs clearing up before each service, I am very honoured that we are able to provide a much needed home for these fascinating creatures who can struggle to find roosts as agricultural buildings become converted into homes.

Right, back to the concept of Hergest Ridge as church. If by church we mean somewhere where we feel the presence of God and where we can find peace and tranquillity to sit, to meditate, to pray or just to contemplate the glory of God's creation, then Hergest Ridge is one of the finest churches I know. Also gloriously maintenance free . . . However, church is more than that – church is a landmark reminding us of the presence of a worshipping community down the centuries, church is a building with history and a place of great beauty, church is important for the milestone moments in people's lives, somewhere they come to celebrate happy times like a marriage or a birth, and to mourn in sad times when they come to celebrate the life of a loved one who has died. And church is somewhere for the community to gather, a sacred space but also a communal one and sometimes the only communal space left in a village as rural pubs and shops close and village halls struggle to sustain themselves as the older population dies out and commuting couples with families move in. During the first lockdown of 2020, the fact that no one was able to enter a church building, even to sit alone and pray, was a very real deprivation, showing that there is great love for and valuing of these sacred spaces – but they definitely don't have a monopoly on God. Finally, and in many ways most importantly, church is the people, not the buildings. Church is the coming together of a worshipping community to share prayer, to break bread together, to support each other, and their wider communities. The body of Christ in any place, where two or three are gathered together – that's church or Church.

So, yes, I agree with him that for an individual to experience the transcendent, the liminal and numinous, a beautiful place in nature is ideal, and I have definitely had some of my most moving spiritual experiences, overwhelmed by the generosity and creativity of a loving creator God while being outside in the middle of beautiful common land or on the tops of mountains or by a lake or the sea. There's something about the top of a hill that is particularly good for this – and it features in the Bible on many occasions – Moses

Fig 13. Hergest ridge view

meets with God at the top of Mount Sinai, Jesus goes to the top of the same mountain with his disciples and there meets with Moses and Elijah and is transfigured into all his glory – there is definitely something about being up high and looking at the land all around you, the views, the tiny settlements down in the valley below, to put things into perspective and remind you that you are but a tiny insignificant part of a much bigger world, and that the troubles or worries which may seem so important today are just ripples in a pond or seeds blown on the wind – all things will pass, good and bad. A salutary reminder to me that even this walk would fairly soon come to an end and that I would miss it.

I continued walking along the ridge, and you can see that compared to all my travails yesterday, this was luxury walking along the pedestrian equivalent of a motorway – lovely broad well-kept paths. This time I even saw some of the wild ponies which live up on the Ridge, and walked along past the old Victorian racetrack where horses used to compete from 1825 until around 1880. Soon I had passed the point where Mike and I had walked up to the Ridge and was into unknown – but very well waymarked – territory. The key thing was to spot the way down off the ridge and into the village of Gladestry, and I'm happy to report I did manage this, pausing on my way down only to marvel at the sight of a beautiful vintage car unexpectedly encountered parked quite a way up a very bumpy track.

It was clearly very well looked after, and positively sparkled, which made me wonder whether it was used as a wedding car, this being around peak wedding season. I pressed on down the track and soon joined the road into Gladestry. As I walked past some nice bungalows on the way into the village, I was hailed by a couple in their front garden who informed me that the pub hadn't yet reopened – which was a bit of a blow. Apparently, it would be reopening on Friday of that week to be run by a lady who is a really good cook – well worth a revisit then. But the good news was that they told me if I went on up to the church, there was a kitchen where walkers could make themselves a cup of coffee, and, as I was to discover for myself, most exciting of all – a toilet!

With a spring in my step, I headed up through the village and found St Mary's Church, Gladestry. And it was just as the nice couple had told me – mugs, tea, coffee and squash all laid out for

walkers to refresh themselves and clear signage to a toilet which
was left open during the summer for walkers to use. This was yet
another benefit of walking the Offa's Dyke Path which was clearly
a superhighway in long distance walking terms, very well used and
therefore well maintained and with good facilities and signage –
certainly along all the bits of it that I walked. As I didn't really have
the spare change on me to take advantage of the tea and coffee on
offer, I headed for a handy bench in the churchyard with a lovely
view back up the way I'd just come.

It was very satisfying to be able to sit in comfort and look back
at the hill that I'd already conquered! Nice to have a bench to rest
upon and be able to consume my two-hour snack and drink some
more water, even make some notes on the walk so far. I was also
able to have a chat with a lovely lady who had come to tend her
husband's grave. He'd been dead three years, hardly any time at
all, and coming to the churchyard was clearly and understandably
a big part of her life. My conversation with her made me reflect
upon all those connected to the walk like Dave, Cathy, Ruth and
Aunty Pat who were all trying to find their own ways of dealing
with the grief of the loss. Not just how to deal with grief but also
how to even begin to think about starting over, trying to make a
new and very different life, a life which wouldn't include the person
they loved dearly and with whom they'd shared their lives for many
years. And trying to reconstruct or reimagine their lives in ways
which didn't in any way diminish either the pain of the loss or the
joy of the life lived before their bereavement. In turn, this made
me ponder what else we as a church can do to help with this huge
adjustment and reminded me of the important role which graves
and churchyards can play in providing people with somewhere to
go, a place to come to express their grief and ongoing sense of both
loss and gratitude in the way they tend their graves.

After these profound thoughts, I did the much more prosaic and practical thing of testing out the Gladestry toilet – highly appropriate as part of the reason for this walk is to fund the installation of one in Hollybush Church. She's a waterless bioloo, very sensitively and successfully installed in a Grade 1 listed church building. St Mary's is a much larger church than Hollybush so they've obviously managed to adapt a part of the existing building to create the toilet – memo to self to get in touch with them to find out details like costs, architect, supplier of toilet etc. However, more to the point at that moment, time to get back on the road and head for Hay.

I left the churchyard, and followed the Offa's Dyke footpath sign along a lane, then crossed over a couple of fields and a couple of minor roads before emerging out onto more common land where the path turned right in the middle of a wide open space but with a large sign post to make sure the unwary walker turned the correct way. It was good to be back out in the open and up on the tops and to see a few other walkers with big packs, obviously doing Offa's Dyke the proper way, but generally going in the opposite direction to me. The descent down into Newchurch was pretty steep so quite hard on the knees, and also brought me out walking through someone's front garden, right in front of their house. I was definitely following the correct right of way but I always feel quite self-conscious about walking through someone else's private space, and scurry past, eyes fixed ahead of me or on the ground to give the message that I'm really not being nosy. I walked on along the road, passing the Methodist chapel and continuing on to the Anglican Church, another St Mary's, which advertised itself as being open with refreshments for walkers on its noticeboard. I poked my head around the door and once more saw the tea, coffee and squash all available for a donation – no loo visible this time though, but that was okay. Again, I took myself off out into the churchyard where they had a very rustic cartwheel bench, upon which I sat and took my ease, enjoying my second break of the day. As agreed I texted Mike to let him know I'd arrived in Newchurch so he could estimate when to set off from home to meet me. The graves in front of the bench were quite recent, judging by the gravestones and one was particularly sad as it was for a young lad, in his early twenties, from one of the local farms. In fact, most of the stones mentioned which farm the person was from, a lovely tradition for rural farming areas, which really gives a feel for the deep connection with the land and sense of place found within the farming community.

After an all too brief respite, I settled the rucksack back on my back, picked up my pole and plugged into my iPod for the first time that day – hoping that a dose of Simon Mayo and Mark Kermode discussing films and so much else – the aptly named Wittertainment – would see me through the miles still to go. I turned left out of the churchyard, headed down a brief bit of road, then a farm track and then up the rather steep field – not for nothing known as Little Mountain on the map. Then the route took me into a very nice bit of green lane – confusingly marked as Red Lane on the map, across a road and onto another part of the path which couldn't quite make up its mind whether to be field or green lane, and finally out onto the road and a slightly too close for comfort encounter with an Asda van. Then I heaved myself up and over a stile to cross a couple of fields and cut off a little bit of road walking, before dropping back to the road for another spot of road walking – which I've come not to mind half as much as I did. With the security my phone app gave me of knowing I was on the right road and headed in the right direction, road walking on these little used lanes could be quite relaxing, provided you kept an eye out for where you should be turning off. God bless King Offa, his path was so well way-marked that this wasn't a problem, even for a novice long distance walker like me. Particularly as this turnoff had a set of very new looking wooden steps to commend it to the walker. I knew this final section of the day – in theory – would bring me out onto the main Hay road at Cabalva – somewhere we'd had another holiday a few years before. As is so often the way, when you think you're on the home stretch it takes much longer to walk than you think – and the first part down to the waterfall was quite steep and had some quite keen brambles to either side, keen to get their hooks into the unwary walker. But with the aid of my trusty stick, I made it down the steep slope and it was lovely walking, through woodland and beside fields until I hit first of all a minor road and then, finally, arrived at the A438 main road into Hay at a layby just by Cabalva Farm.

I turned immediately to the right to try to see how far along this busy main road I needed to venture before picking up the onward path on the other side and was about to set off when there was the perp of a car horn from my left and I turned to see the familiar Skoda parked up with Mike at the helm. He'd come to see how I was feeling and whether I'd rather have a lift from there to our accommodation the other side of Hay or felt up to walking the additional couple of miles to get me to the centre of town. I'd been walking for around seven hours by then and done fourteenish miles, so was feeling pretty tired, *but* I could really see the sense in pushing on to Hay. It was only another couple of miles, and it would be a much nicer start to the following day to leave from the safety of a car park in the middle of town, rather than leaving from a layby to walk along a busy main road. The decision was made easier by the fact that I knew I was heading up into the Black Mountains the next day so needed all the help I could get! Decision made, Mike zoomed off and I yomped on. The bit along the main road was unpleasant and went on for longer than I'd assumed it would judging by the distance on the map – but again, I think that was more psychological than anything. I managed to make it across the busy main road and picked up the Offa's Dyke Path once more. I'd been assuming it would just follow the River Wye all the way into Hay, so was surprised to discover that there was a fair bit of field walking first – but along lovely clear well marked margins, nothing like the trauma of the day before. I switched to music on my iPod and kept it there for pretty much the rest of the walk that day – although shuffle on my iPod also brings up things like episodes of Cabin Pressure, which it did on this occasion. If you don't know of it, Cabin Pressure is one of the best comedies ever written or performed, about the crew of a hapless air charter business called MJN Air. It has the most fantastic cast – Stephanie Cole, Roger Allam and Benedict Cumberbatch together with its writer and Arthur, John Finnemore. There are also the most amazing guest stars – Timothy West, Prunella Scales and Anthony Head to name but three of them. Seek it out if you don't know it – it's well worth the search. So, iPod shuffling to the Rotterdam episode as I approached another field of cows was just what the doctor ordered – although happily these cows were far more interested in munching away at the pasture than in a stray walker. I'm guessing they are well used to stray walkers – so I passed through the field without incident. I then started encountering dog walkers, which is always a cheering sign that you are not far from a town or village, and the route took me alongside the river, so I knew I was approaching the end of the walk. Then suddenly there was Mike, sitting on a bench waiting for me – what a wonderful sight. We still had a little way to go to walk up through town to the car park to take the end of day photo underneath a sign proclaiming that Hay was twinned with Timbuktu in Mali – another hilarious Cabin Pressure episode, coincidentally! This had been my longest walk ever – I felt like I had walked to

Timbuktu and back – but the main thing was – I'd done it! Mike loaded me into the car, and we headed for Dorstone. We love this village and Hodson's House, another holiday cottage we've stayed in around here – you might be getting the impression by now that we like this area! Luckily, we got to know its owners, Jo and Tom, and they also do bed and breakfast, so I'd booked us in for the night. We got a wonderful welcome from Jo – with apologies for the overwhelming scent of aftershave – her two other young male guests had just headed for the pub in a pungent cloud of Lynx! We climbed the spiral staircase to a wonderful spacious, welcoming room and while I did my usual end of day ice bath for my feet, Jo booked us in at that same pub, The Pandy Inn. After a restorative bath, I even managed the mile or so walk to the pub and back and a really wonderful meal. And so to bed, having done the longest leg of the walk and lived to fight another day!

Day Seven Stats

Start time, 9.41 am.

Finish time – 6.11 pm.

Duration – 8 hours, 30 minutes

Distance walked – 16.4 miles.

Total ascent 1,697 ft.

Total descent 1,906 ft.

Avg. speed – 2.3 mph

Day Eight: Hay to Capel-y-Ffin
Into Clarence Land

8 July 2019

The good news about today's walk was that at just over eight miles I only had to walk half the distance I'd walked the day before. The bad news was it would be mainly in a vertical direction as I had to walk up to Hay Bluff, along Gospel Pass and down into Capel-y-Ffinn where my great uncle Clarence is buried.

However, the day started very well indeed, when Jo delivered a fabulous tray of breakfast to our room. And what a breakfast! Fresh fruit salad, Greek yoghurt, croissants, butter and jam – very much my kind of thing and a great start to a new walking day. We said our goodbyes, thanked Jo profusely and headed back to the car park in Hay for that start of walk photo in which I look so much fresher and happier than I did in the end of day photo from yesterday. With a spring in my step, I set off out of the car park, down a side alley between houses and picked up the Offa's Dyke Path again heading out of town across fields. The weather was dry and fine again – so lucky with the weather. The first part of the walk was quite flat, along very well-marked paths, including crossing a stream via a kissing bridge – not something I'd ever encountered before . . .

The route then skirted round the village of Cusop a pleasant walk alongside the Dulas Brook, followed by a right turn along a field edge and then a climb out onto a lane. After a very short bit of road walking, I was back into fields and the climb began, gently at first but also taking me past a remarkable but vertiginous garden seemingly in the middle of nowhere, providing a welcome distraction from my aching limbs and pounding heart! However, soon after passing it, I came out onto a track leading to a house, where, I suspect, the garden owner lived. I crossed over the track and then the going began to get really steep! Another much fitter female walker zoomed past me, but I found this heartening rather than depressing, as I hadn't seen many other lone female walkers. It was either men on their own or a man and woman together, so I didn't mind being overtaken as I would have hated to hold her up. I would love it if this book were to encourage more women to go it alone and get out there and walk or run or cycle – or anything really. Yes, absolutely, we all need to take sensible precautions – Mike knew exactly where I was going, I had my phone on me at all times, and if I hadn't turned up where I was meant to be at about the right time, he would have come looking for me. In the same way that the negative voices in our heads can prevent us from doing things, the negative perceptions and fears of others or portrayed in the media can circumscribe us as well and make us live smaller, bounded lives. There is something about getting out there and just going it alone which is incredibly empowering – it's challenging, undoubtedly, and as you've already read, I had a lot of help, but this walk has given me confidence and self-belief in spade loads because I dared to do it on my own, as well as with company.

The good thing to be said for the steepness of the way up was that you did get really panoramic views back down to Hay. And it was wonderful to be walking this path mown through meadowland, which just confirmed to me that orchards and meadowland are my two favourite types of terrain to walk through – both beautiful in their own ways. The meadows are relaxed and informal, the orchards very controlled and formal, all straight rows, so you couldn't get a much bigger contrast, but both of them are havens for wildlife, seas of green and have an atmosphere of calm and reflection all of their own. After managing to make it to the top of the meadow without having to send out for more oxygen, I came out onto a lane and turned left which brought me up to the farmhouse and buildings of Cadwgan Farm, home to a very vociferous dog who wasn't that keen on stray walkers. Thankfully he was all bark and no bite and the kind owner did appear to call him off. Still following the waymarked path I headed out onto moorland and for the first time since joining Offa's Dyke started to worry about losing my way. But then I saw a lone (male) walker heading straight towards me and shortly after that was overtaken by three young male walkers, so I followed them and started seeing waymarks painted onto boulders, all of which reassured me that I was on the right path.

During the course of the walk, the hymn 'O Jesus I have promised' kept dropping into my mind, particularly at times like this when I was worrying that I might be going off track and losing my way. The last verse, with the lines 'O let me see thy footmarks and in them plant mine own, my hope to follow duly lies in thy strength alone', was the one which kept recurring. I can't tell you how reassuring it was at times of doubt to see either boot marks on the ground headed in the same direction, or other real live walkers, and it amazes me how often this happened at exactly the right time to keep me going. Another example of guardian angels popping up at just the right moment. And a reminder that humans are made for community, we need each other – for help, support, reassurance – fun! One of the many reasons why Covid was such an incredibly hard time for so many, that lack of contact with other human beings continues to take its toll. Also a good reminder for me that while I love my alone time, I also love spending time with friends and family, and would miss them dreadfully if I couldn't do so.

I was certainly up in the mountains rather than hills this time! I carried on walking across the open moorland and eventually arrived at the road, turned right and followed it on along, waving goodbye to the Offa's Dyke Path for the moment and to the three young men who continued on it and up toward Hay Bluff. I took my first – and hopefully only – stop of the day, squatting on a boulder marking the edge of a really packed parking area. According to the map there had been a stone circle there and I could understand why. You had the mountain of Hay Bluff behind you and the most amazing panoramic view in front of you. The day wasn't by any means clear but even with the cloud cover the view was something else again. And it was more than that, there was a feeling to this place, a sense of majesty and awe, you felt as if you could see the whole world spread out before you, that the view went on for ever. It felt like a sacred space, a space very fitting for worship. Reminded me of the top of Hergest Ridge with its monkey puzzle tree cathedral. You got a real feeling of eternity, of the unchanging nature of these mountains and this vista, a real mountain top moment of reflection and restoration.

I was now at about the halfway stage of the walk in both time and distance. It was day eight of what we'd planned as being a fifteen-day walk and I was nearing my ultimate destination of Capel-y-Ffin. After which it felt like I'd be turning for home. So why had I wanted to walk all this way, who had drawn me to this wild and beautiful place up in the Black Mountains? Great Uncle Clarence, that's who!

My great uncle Clarence was what is known as a 'character' – every family has one. I don't know a lot about him, but everything I do know is fascinating and unusual. He was a bright child, winning a scholarship to Evesham Grammar School, but despite his clear intelligence, the academic life wasn't for him and he went for a while but left as soon as he could. He was the best pig sticker in the Castlemorton area, and so was in great demand back in the day when every household kept a pig to consume household scraps and to supply a good store of meat and meat products to keep the family going through the winter. He slept in the bedroom I slept in as a small child, with his feet always overhanging the end of the bed. Each morning he would get up and empty his chamber pot out of the window, which explains why the rhubarb which grew outside that same window always produced such a plentiful and tasty crop. He wasn't the most conscientious of shepherds – his sheep strayed over quite some distance and he often had to go and fetch them back from Malvern and was fined for letting them stray so far. And, although he never married, he was quite the ladies' man, often visiting ladies who were already married and making sure, when caught out by a heavy fall of snow, to first walk back to a neighbouring farm before walking on home so that any incriminating footsteps wouldn't lead the irate husband to his door . . . All this, to an impressionable child, painted the picture of a glamorous non-conformist who went his own way, did his own thing and wasn't confined by rules, regulations, or even marriage vows!

And this was confirmed by the fact that no sooner had his mother, my great grandmother, bought a house for him over in Whiteleaved Oak, than he upped and offed to live in a remote farmhouse in the Black Mountains above Hay. There was no roadway down to the house in those days, so when we visited him twice a year, the pre-Christmas visits being to take him a Christmas cake, pudding etc, these visits were great adventures for the seven year old me. We parked the car in a layby, then laden down with food and other goodies, climbed the stile and made our way carefully down the steep slope alongside a fast-flowing mountain stream. When we made it down to the farmhouse, it was a mess, the sort of mess only a man and five or six sheepdogs can make. Great Uncle Clarence wasn't really bothered by mess, but my nan, his sister, was, so every six months she and my mum would visit and attempt to restore some sort of order – as well as delivering Christmas. The seven-year-old me on the other hand thought that being able to live in a mess was just the best thing ever – no one to insist you had a bath or tidied your room or anything. At that stage in life, I was hopelessly infatuated with horses, and my great uncle Clarence saw this and gave me a saddle he happened to have lying around. At that moment, this was like all my Christmases coming at once, and I've never ever forgotten it – even though my dream of being a rider didn't work out, that moment of being seen, understood and encouraged has stayed with me.

For a long while I had a desire to walk to Hay and then onto Capel-y-Ffin where Great Uncle Clarence is buried. To walk the mountains he would have walked, where his sheep would have roamed to their hearts' content. And here I was, finally fulfilling that long held ambition. And here he is (see fig 14), in a very old photo out on those self-same hills I was looking up at, with just a couple of his beloved dogs. He sent this out as his Christmas card in 1966!

So why did I want to follow in the footsteps of this man I had never really known? Why did I want to come to his land and walk it as he would have done? What attracted me to him was the image I have of him as a non-conformist, someone who went his own way, did his own thing without caring or probably even noticing what other people thought of him. He was definitely someone who was comfortable in his own skin. He lived his own authentic life, true to himself, not governed by the expectations of either his family or wider society. And I think, deep down, I hoped that by pushing myself out of my comfort zone so very far, in order to do this walk, that maybe just a little of that non-conformist fearlessness might rub off on me, to counteract the people pleasing conformist I had become. To get back to that seven-year-old self, that excited dreamer, to learn to live a little, to be authentic, the person I really was, to be, finally, comfortable in my own skin. Did it work? It certainly started chains of events in my life which have brought me back closer to that seven year old, and I cover this in more detail at the end of the book. I'm definitely not all the way there yet but doing

Fig 14. Uncle Clarence with dogs

the walk and writing this book made me aware of all that I'd lost by suppressing my authentic self and set me off on another journey to try to get back to her. The journey isn't over yet, and maybe it never will be, but I'm really enjoying the ride!

Having taken my break and consumed an oaty bar and some nuts and apricots, I heaved myself up and headed onwards towards Gospel Pass. Not for nothing is this the highest road pass in the whole of Wales, climbing to a height of 594 metres above sea level.

Two local legends explain its unusual name. One is that this is the way St Paul came through, preaching the gospel, guided by the daughter of Caradoc, aka Caractacus whom he'd met in Rome. The alternative explanation is that this is the way the Crusaders came through in the twelfth century to raise money and men for the Crusades. Either way you'd have had to be pretty determined or desperate to walk this way before the single-track road was built. I did love the idea of walking in the footsteps of St Paul, that made it feel very much a pilgrimage, but I did wonder what this traveller from the Holy Land would have made of the wild Welsh landscape, and even wilder weather!

As I started off again it felt like it might just be spitting with the lightest possible rain, so I plugged my iPod in and headed off along the road, dodging cyclists, motorcyclists, an army truck at one point and the occasional mad motorist. Suddenly the Archers' theme tune – Barwick Green – started playing in my ears and I started to laugh and cry all at the same time, because that tune brought my dear much missed friend Susan into my head. The tune was on my iPod because we'd used it at the very beginning of her memorial service – I'd skipped up the aisle at Hollybush Church to that tune on a baking hot day in June, explaining to those who didn't know that for Susan, everything stopped for the Archers and if you had the misfortune to be on the phone to her when 7.00 pm came round she would exclaim – 'It's the Archers' – and slam the phone down, no matter that you'd been in mid-conversation at the time!

What to say about Susan? That she was a force of nature (see fig 15), a life force, dressed like an explosion in a paint factory, yet on her it worked because she had the personality and sense of colour and style to carry it off. She accumulated clothes and accessories like nobody's business – all from the local charity shops. She had a huge talent for friendship. She was loyal and funny and infuriating and extrovert – yet she also needed time and space alone, making sure she went on the Mothers' Union retreat each year. She was a woman mighty in prayer. We held our prayer group meetings at her house every Monday night for many years until she moved into a flat in the Almshouses in Ledbury, which she loved. We missed her tremendously in the benefice – she would lead intercessions, bake for anything and everything, sometimes stocking whole

Fig 15. Susan as the Queen

cake stalls on her own – but it was her positive can-do approach to life, her sense of humour, her outrageous flirting, her strong and very much lived out faith – all these things we really, really missed. And I miss her very much still, as all her friends do. She was diagnosed with pancreatic cancer only a few months after moving to Ledbury to start a new life. She had been a district nurse and hospice nurse and, in her hospice work, she had seen too many patients put themselves through the hoops of chemotherapy and radiotherapy when she knew that it would only buy them a few more weeks of life and have a really hefty impact on their quality of life. As a result, when she received her diagnosis, she opted to reject any treatment, to just have palliative care to deal with the pain. I would take her communion and anoint her, we discussed her funeral and sorted out hymns and readings, what she wanted and what she didn't want – no crying, no dressing in black, it was to be a celebration. So that's what we did, even though our hearts were breaking at the loss of her.

She always used to say that no one is indispensable, that when she was gone it would be like a stone thrown into a pond, a few ripples and then it would be as if she'd never been there and we'd all carry on without her. Well, in one sense that's true, we have carried on as best we can without her – but our life is poorer for the loss of Susan, gone from technicolour to black and white. We miss her fun, we miss her outrageousness, we miss her laughter and her outfits, we miss her warmth and her ability to befriend those in trouble and help to guide them onto safer ground. We just miss her and we always will.

Having her in my mind was a source of pain, but also of huge pleasure and thankfulness. I wouldn't have missed being her friend for the world, it was an honour and a privilege, and she was instrumental in bringing me back to the church and the priesthood. The way in which she greeted and befriended me when I did rock up at a Hollybush service meant that I kept on coming back for more. And she was a huge support through my training and development as a priest, the cassock and surplice that I wear to this day came from her, and when I was down or nervous about a service, somehow she'd know and would just appear in the pews to give me a boost and help me through. She would have thought I was completely insane to be doing this walk – she thought all exercise was bonkers and hated vegetables – but she would also have been incredibly proud and supportive. Yet another important person in my life lost to cancer – yet another reason to keep on keeping on, raising that money for Macmillan. Thank you, Susan, for everything.

It was all road walking now up until almost the end of the day's walk, when it all went a bit off piste, but, putting that firmly to the back of my mind, I trudged onward in the mizzle feeling, if I'm honest, a little bit sorry for myself – but also rejoicing that I could relax in terms of navigation and simply enjoy the magnificent scenery all around me. It could have seemed bleak and threatening, and certainly it wasn't to be treated lightly – I could easily see that if the mist came down and you lost your way you could end up in considerable difficulties – but I loved it – it was remote, mountainous and magnificent, no sign of human habitation apart from the sheep – and the traffic. Huge amounts of green space, mind space, thinking space – it was in the biblical sense truly awesome, and I got a sudden insight into what had drawn Great Uncle Clarence to this place and kept him here until almost the end of his life.

However, as I rounded a bend in the road, I saw up ahead of me someone coming down a quite steep mountain path with a bright orange rucksack – so far, so not unusual. The eye-catching part was that they were running – pretty much sprinting – down this precipitous path while carrying what seemed from a distance to be quite a heavy load. As someone who had grown up not a million miles away, my immediate thoughts were – 'Either this is a very keen/suicidal Duke of Edinburgh participant, or it's squaddies.' The fact that I'd been passed by an army lorry not that much earlier in the day made me think army training was the most likely answer, so I wasn't altogether surprised when I rounded another bend in the road to be confronted by this (fig 16).

I was particularly impressed by the communications vehicle with its tall masts. The closer I got to it, the more comically incongruous it looked – particularly when, as I was walking past the vehicles, I coincided with a soldier completing his run, coming down off the mountain quite close to me, which enabled me to see that he was not only burdened down with a heavy pack but was also carrying a gun as he ran. My admiration for what the men and women of our armed services put themselves through

Fig 16. Army trucks at Gospel Pass

in order to be in peak condition to defend us and to assist other countries grew even more. Although they were hogging the parking place, which meant I was glad I'd stopped when I did and made do with a boulder rather than hanging on and hoping for a bench – although maybe they'd have let me hop up on the tail gate of one of the trucks, rapidly filling up with returning soldiers in various states of undress . . . I don't think so! Averting my eyes, I hurried on past, hoping I wasn't threatening national security by taking pictures – it was just such an extraordinary juxtaposition of war and peace, beauty and the beast.

Which got me thinking about how we can romanticise places of great beauty despite the fact that to exist on this terrain is hard. For farmers to make a living is tough and requires a lot of dedication, blood, sweat and tears. For every hill walker rocking up in their 4x4 with their hi-tech boots, GPS guidance system and all the latest kit, there's also a hill farmer in wellies, woolly hat and overalls, hanging on by his fingernails, just about surviving year after year, yet what they do keeps the countryside accessible and available for all of us. And in the same way, you could say that the army doing its training exercises here spoils it for the walkers and cyclists, creates a bit of a blot on a beautiful landscape. But without men and women prepared to give their all, prepared to put themselves through great physical and mental trauma, we wouldn't be able to enjoy the peace and freedom to come out and take a walk in the hills.

People often diss the Old Testament, some churches avoid reading it altogether because there's a lot of blood and guts, a lot of smiting, of wars, of vengeance as well as a lot of love, creativity and miracles. But isn't that life, life in all its richness and fullness, its tragedy and its triumphs? We can try and ignore the nasty bits, the bits we don't like, the bits that make us feel uncomfortable, but in the end, we're all going to have to deal with heartbreak, with the death of a loved one, with our own illness and mortality, with a bend in the road revealing to us a twist or turn we weren't prepared for and don't quite know how to handle. A global pandemic being the plot twist which really nobody saw coming! And none of us will know how we're going to react, how we're going to cope until it happens to us. But one thing I do know is that ignoring it, sticking your head in the sand and pretending it'll go away isn't going to work. I'm as tempted by that as the next person, and often find myself doing it, but sooner or later, you have to face up to the fact that there are situations in the world where we need to deploy force, and that we're jolly lucky that there are still men and women prepared to take on that role. They need somewhere to test themselves and stretch themselves to the limit, so it's good that the mountains are there for them – a worthy and strong adversary – as much as for anyone else.

And to some extent that's what this walk is for me, a challenge, a test, pushing myself to my limits and beyond. I don't think I've really adequately expressed my absolute and total amazement that I'm doing this. That I've walked to Hay – that just seems frankly incredible – I mean it's miles! As the discerning reader will have picked up, I've got all the usual hang-ups and neuroses around body shape, weight and physical fitness/ability and additional doubts about my map reading and way finding ability – somewhat addressed by Dave's expert tuition but still lurking there in the back of my mind. And it's amazing how long lasting these perceptions of ourselves are. My hang ups around exercise, like I suspect those of many other folks, go all the way back to school days. When you're always the last to be picked for anything sporty and don't really enjoy team games – I mean lacrosse for heaven's sake, what sort of a game even is that? – you start to just assume that sport isn't for you. This leads you to pin all your self-worth and self-esteem onto the academic side of things, where being fortunately gifted with a good memory I did tolerably well.

And thinking even further back, my parental role models weren't that great in sporting terms. Don't get me wrong, I'm totally blessed with the most wonderful loving parents in the whole wide world – but although my dad has always been a keen sportsman, played rugby until I was born and cricket for a while thereafter – he even taught PE to begin with – my mum always said it was a waste of time, for example tennis was just running around after a little white ball. Which is strange when she tells stories of what a great athlete my grandad, her father, was, particularly skilled at tennis and bowls – anything involving hand/eye co-ordination. Mum was a keen dancer in her younger days and does still love to swim, as do I, but swimming isn't that great for those of us who are already rather self-conscious about our shape and size and have it in our heads that we are slow and lumbering, likely to be an annoying obstacle for all the slim, fit people. And even my amazing, long-suffering husband has unintentionally reinforced my image of myself as slow and unfit, because when we go walking together on holiday his pace is so much faster than mine that I'm always at least ten feet behind him on any walk we do and he's inevitably in charge of navigation given his much greater expertise and mastery of technology.

I hold my hands up and agree that the blame lies fairly and squarely at my door – I've allowed myself to be de-skilled in the art of navigation, in fact rather enjoyed not having that responsibility. Although I was shocked to read in Annabel Abbs' book *Windswept* that it's the navigational hub which is the first part of the brain to fray and fade from Alzheimer's disease, a very good reason to have learnt all that good navigational stuff from Dave. But it struck me afresh on this walk how much power the voices in our head have over us, and how much more likely we are to listen to the negative rather than the positive ones. The small amount of research that I've done on this revealed that in fact our brains are hard wired to hang on to criticism and the negative stuff as a way of trying to protect us – which is not great! My negative Nagging Norah internal voice had got me to cast myself as fat, unfit, flabby, slow, lumpen – a plodder – and someone who couldn't navigate her way out of a paper bag. Whereas, looked at from a more positive standpoint you could say I do an outdoor, physical job for at least two days a week so I can't be that physically inept. I may not be the fastest walker or runner on the planet, but I have always had a lot of stamina and stickability, always been the tortoise rather than the hare. A rare positive sporting memory from school is of when we were told to run 800 metres round a track. I set off at a pace I was confident I could sustain, which meant I was last by a long way, and yet as the second lap of two unravelled, I found myself passing some of the other girls. I didn't win but I didn't come last by any means. And further back, when at primary school, I loved sports because we played hockey and rounders, both of which I really enjoyed as opposed to the netball and lacrosse of secondary school. It's so easy to get out of the exercise habit – frighteningly easy really. And to become disconnected from your body, to take it for granted, use and abuse until it begins to fail, and then it's too late. So take this as a clarion call and a wake up call in two ways. Get outside and move your body, in whatever way brings you joy- use it or lose it. And yes, we do all have a negative voice in our heads – but we don't need to always be listening to her or letting her spread her negativity unchallenged – we can fight back with a very rational counterargument – or just politely say, thank you so much, Norah, that's all really interesting, but I'm not going to take any notice of you today.

Meanwhile, back at the walk, my brain may have convinced me that I was physically incompetent and incapable, but here was my body proving my brain wrong. I was strong, I was determined, I had an average level of fitness, and I had the Lewis/Prosser cussedness and determination – not to say stubborn bloody mindedness – to keep me going. Above all, I was enjoying this whole new world, this simplified stripped back world where all I had to do was get up, get out walking and keep going until I reached my destination for the day and then stop. No other responsibilities, no decisions to be taken, it was all laid out for me and I was loving it! Another lesson about the joys of being embodied. Letting your body get on and do its thing without the overprotective brain holding you back.

As I carried on down into Gospel Pass, the weather suddenly improved and you felt like you were entering a different world, lighter, brighter and full of life, a very different feeling from the lowering mountain tops of the previous part of the walk. Now life in the shape of wild ponies and loud sheep was all around me, it was downhill all the way and soon I was marching along at a good pace, swinging my arms and generally having a good time when I heard a car horn beep behind me. Turning around, what should I see but the trusty Skoda, this time with a bike on top of it . . . It was of course Mike who had just been on a bike ride to Talgarth and back, somewhat further than he had intended . . . He stopped, kindly refolded my map for me and we arranged that he would go ahead and check in at the monastery and I would carry on walking and meet him at the Church, my destination for the day.

Ah yes, the monastery . . . I'd been looking for somewhere we could stay in Capel-y-Ffin but the closest I thought I could find was Llanthony Abbey which I'm sure would have been fine except for the fact that you had to climb stairs to the rooms and make your way along a corridor to get to the bathroom. This was entirely understandable given it was a medieval stone building, you can't be expecting en suites. But when I was looking to book the accommodation before the walk began, I really wasn't sure what sort of a state I'd be in by the end of each day so the thought of staggering to and from a shared bathroom for a hot bath to soothe my aching limbs was not particularly attractive. Then I remembered that Sara, a fellow Open the Book volunteer and friend, had talked about family holidays in Capel-y-Ffin and how they'd stayed at the old monastery and had a fantastic time. I googled more specifically and there it was, Capel-y-Ffin Monastery, literally just up the road from the church, which couldn't be better. The slight fly in the ointment was that it didn't look like they did just one night stays. My hope was that if I dropped them a line and explained why I was doing what I was doing they might be prepared to let us stay for just the one night – also, as it was one night in the middle of the week before the school holidays started they might well have a free property and better to get some income for it than none. They couldn't have been nicer or more helpful, booking us in and sending the details for which cottage we were in and how to let ourselves in.

Mike went ahead with the lunch and the ice, and I followed at a much more leisurely pace, passing a very cheery bearded farmer driving the traditional beaten up old Landrover with a gorgeous sheepdog trotting alongside. Then I arrived at the cattlegrid and realised that this was where I needed to veer off the road and take the bridleway down into Capel-y-Ffin because the road after the cattle grid became narrow with steep banks and fences either side so it was tricky for a walker to avoid the cars which would be using the road, however infrequently. I must confess to having a few doubts and misgivings as I launched off into the unknown – no path markers to guide me, deep dense bracken and more mountain springs than you would expect, creating rocky and muddy areas which were tricky to cross – more than once I was glad of my trusty walking pole! I tried to keep track of where I was by using landmarks and cross checking with my phone but the landscape, being totally bracken covered, could be misleading and this last bit felt like it was taking forever – partly end of day syndrome again and partly it was much tougher walking than the easy bit all along the road.

And it strikes me now, reflecting back on Susan and on Great Uncle Clarence, that both these big characters, both hugely influential and significant in my life, have something in common. They both had the courage to veer off road, to make a huge left turn into the unknown, to take life changing decisions and head off down another pathway which was little used, had no markers to guide them and might well have had multiple trip hazards underfoot. For Great Uncle Clarence it was moving to the Black Mountains, for Susan it was deciding to move out of the marital home in her sixties and into her own space, somewhere she could serve God and follow her vocation as an evangelist and a provider of amazing hospitality more easily. They both trod the steep and rugged pathway rejoicingly – would I ever be able to do the same? Yes, I think, in my own sweet, limited way, I've at least taken several more steps into the unknown since the walk, if not yet quite gone the whole hog as they did – but there's still time!

Meanwhile, back on the walk, I still wasn't sure I'd got it absolutely right, even when I found the steepish rocky descent roughly where I thought it should be, but I followed it on down to be greeted by the very welcome sight of a way-marked stile. Although it did lead me straight through someone's front garden again, complete with a group of statues which unnerved me initially. I would have liked to stop and take a photo, but that felt just too intrusive, so I carried straight on and over another stile into the final field of the day which gave me great views down to the church, tucked away amongst the trees at the bottom of the valley and across to the monastery, our base for the night, an impressive looking set of buildings which I couldn't wait to explore. Well, I could wait until I'd arrived and had a nice cup of tea and some lunch . . . Even more welcome was the sight of Mike waiting for me at the bottom of the field, so that we were able to walk to the church, where he took the end of day photo.

I had made it all the way from All Saints Hollybush to St Mary the Virgin Capel-y-Ffin, from where my nan, Monnoa Grace Lewis was buried to where her brother, Clarence Frank Prosser was buried – though we don't know quite where. I had made enquiries via the church website, but I'd received no response. Something which, as a priest myself, I totally understood. It would be one of those nebulous enquiries which was always going to drop off the end of the to do list. And it seemed very in character for Clarence

Fig 17. Capel-y-Ffin church

not to be easily found, even in death, just as in life he avoided lazy stereotyping and easy pigeonholing. I would like to find his grave one day though and put a proper headstone up for him, a memorial to someone who has influenced me greatly. Arriving here felt like journey's end in one sense. I'd managed to visit all the ancestors, now there was just the return journey to do – even though the return journey would take many more days of walking to complete.

From the church, we walked on up to the monastery and to

Chapel flat, which was lovely. The owners had very kindly left a donation for the walk. It was now a gorgeous day, blue sky and sun so we sat outside on a bench adjacent to a large statue of the Virgin Mary – slightly off putting – and ate our lunch, me with my feet in the traditional washing up bowl of iced water. It was only 2.30 pm and my walking day was over. The rest of the day lay ahead of us, in this beautiful, peaceful setting looking out across the valley to the mountains on the other side, a couple of very contented horses grazing in the paddock on the other side of the fence.

A car drew up and a mother and son got out and came over for a chat. The Mum had been coming here since 1971 and loved it, always returns and had recently moved nearer to make it easier for her to visit. This place was clearly very important to her. Part of its charm and peace comes from the fact that it has absolutely no communication connections to the outside world at all – no wifi, no phone signal, no TV, no radio – so perfect for anyone wanting to rest in peace and beauty – and places like this are increasingly hard to find.

However, we did need an internet connection so that I could do my blog post for the day, if nothing else to reassure my mum and dad that I was still okay. Which meant that after lunch we decided to head back into Hay in search of WiFi. As we were leaving, more visitors arrived, this time two chaps in a pristine Morris Minor. One was a GP who lived in Abergavenny and had been brought up at the monastery, the other an old school friend of his who used to visit him here. The GP had lived here in the 1970s, and both remembered games of football when the Virgin Mary doubled up as goalkeeper – which explained why some of her finger ends were missing!

It took an insultingly short time to drive what it had taken me over four hours to walk and soon we were back in Hay, holed up in Shepherds, the wonderful ice cream parlour where all the ice cream is made from their own sheep's milk – it is fab, and I'd been really looking forward to this as a celebration of making it all the way to Capel-y-Ffin. Unfortunately, they'd stopped doing the waffles and ice cream which I'd been dreaming of so I was forced to make do with just the ice cream – one scoop each of strawberry, rum and raisin and toffee and honeycomb as you're asking – plus a cappuccino, while Mike contented himself with a brownie and a cup of tea. He watched the end of that day's Tour de France on his iPad while I tapped away on the laptop to get the blog post up there – just about got it all done before closing time and made sure to give Shepherds a plug in exchange for use of their wifi.

Then it was back to the monastery where I had a soak, Mike had a snooze, he cooked pasta for tea and we sat in the lounge while I read a little about the history of this amazing place, of which more later. Then I poked my head out of the door and saw the swifts doing an amazing aeronautical display so we went and sat on the bench in front of the flat watching the evening go by. A good day.

Day Eight Stats

    Start time – 9.23 am.

    Finish time – 2.01 pm.

    Duration – 4 hours, 33 minutes.

    Distance walked – 8.5 miles.

    Total ascent – 6,896 ft.

    Total descent 6,168 ft.

    Avg. speed – 2.0 mph.

Day Nine: Capel-y-Ffin to Pandy
Keep Right on to the End of the Road

9 July 2019

We were up and out bright and early the following morning, and it was another glorious day. Capel-y-Ffin Monastery is not an ancient foundation, in fact it was built – not very well – in 1870 at the instigation of the self-styled Father Ignatius, a man called Joseph Leycester Lyne originally, who had a vision to restore monasticism to the life of the Church of England by founding a new Benedictine monastery, a Llanthony Tertia. The first Llanthony Abbey is an ancient impressive ruin further down the valley, whilst the second is in Gloucester. Father Ignatius couldn't find a bishop willing to ordain him, but he was apparently a man of great charisma and raised the money to build the monastery through speaking tours and donations. Sadly, the work to build the abbey church, where Father Ignatius is buried, was not done to the highest of standards. The staff quarters where we stayed are very sound and comfortable, but the church is now considered too dangerous to enter and parts will probably have to be taken down entirely to restore it to its former glory.

In August 1880, three boys connected to the monastery saw a bright light which took on the form of a woman in a flowing dress. They followed her across the field until she disappeared. She appeared twice more to a variety of people, including some of the monks, and is believed to be a vision of the Virgin Mary. The goalkeeping statue was erected at the spot where she disappeared. Every August there is a pilgrimage from Llanthony to Capel-y-Ffin, the only Marian pilgrimage in this country.

On the death of Father Ignatius in 1908, the monastery passed to the monks of Caldey Island, but then in 1924 it was sold to the controversial stone carver, engraver and typeface designer, Eric Gill. He and his family lived here until October 1928, and were often visited by the artist David Jones, of whom more later. The fonts Gill Sans and Perpetua, still very much in use today, were designed by Gill whilst living at the monastery.

Mike and I headed back down to the church and I was off on the next part of the walk by 8.30 am, which was undoubtedly the earliest start to any leg of the entire walk. However, before filling you in on the endurance test of border walking which was to come, let's spend some time on the little church of the Black Mountains because it is a very special place.

The current church was built in 1762, replacing an earlier fifteenth century building. The name Capel-y-Ffin means 'chapel of the boundary' as it lies close to the boundaries of the ancient dioceses of St David's and Llandaff, these days Swansea and Brecon and Monmouth. The church is dedicated to St Mary and was originally a chapel of ease to the main parish church in Llanigon, but these days is a parish church in its own right. With dimensions of eight metres by four metres it is one of the smallest chapels in Wales. Reverend Francis Kilvert in his diaries describes the church as 'squatting like a stout grey owl amongst its seven great yews.' But for me, it's not so much the history which make this a special place, it's partly the family connection and the knowledge that Great Uncle Clarence is buried here, apparently very close to one of those seven great yews. Mum can remember his funeral service and the clunk clunk of the farmers' boots as they climbed the stairs to sit in the gallery of this tiny building, but it's mainly the place itself which has such a feeling of peace, love and care. This church is so much a part of its surroundings that it feels like a place of worship which has organically grown here rather than something imposed upon the landscape. I'm particularly fond of the artwork in the church – the David Jones painting of Christ of Capel-y-Ffin for example, a depiction of the crucifixion set against the backdrop of the Black Mountains with the wild ponies, the mountain streams and the swifts and even the church itself featuring in the background. Then there is the icon of the Blessed Virgin, Our Lady of Capel-y-Ffin, which depicts the Virgin Mary with Capel-y-Ffin Church on one side and the monastery on the other and in the foreground the children she appeared to in that vision back in August 1880. But there are also kitsch touches like the pew full of teddies and the carved mouse on the lid of the font. All these special touches are true to the unique spirit of this place – quirky and very craft driven, a throwback to Gill and Jones and the Arts and Crafts movement.

And that made me ponder awhile on the nature of sacred space – what is it, that special something that draws us back to a place, makes it distinctive to us, grabs us in a spiritual way? As a five-year-old child I can remember moving house for the first time and vowing that one day I would return and live in my childhood home again some day – and that's where I live now, in a house which has been in my family since 1920. But why did I feel so strongly about this place at such a young age? What was it that drew me, bound me to this place and made me so upset to leave it and so determined to return? I only realised this was unusual when I went on one of those dreadful management courses and they asked us to draw our life plans as we saw them. Everyone else drew a straight line, but I drew a circle because I knew I wanted to come back to where I felt I belonged. Maybe that was only because I knew that I could, that it was here waiting for me to return – but I don't think so, I don't think a child of five would have reasoned like that. I believe that it was something deeper, something instinctive, something you can't rationalise. Maybe it's to do with people you connect to a place, memories of times spent with those you love, but I also think certain places reach out and speak to something in us. As a garden designer we were told to always honour the *genus loci*, the spirit of the place, and I suspect it is just that which speaks to us in certain places that then become important just to us. It doesn't have to be a sacred space, or a well-known landmark, it can be a place which is meaningful only to an individual, where there is a connection on some unspoken, unconscious level, deep speaking to deep.

There has been a lot of literature written about sacred spaces, not least by the current Bishop of Worcester and the previous Bishop of Dudley, now Bishop of Norwich. And places like Iona and Lindisfarne have their history and spiritual tradition, that liminality of the island with all the saints and their faith stories. Is it something about beauty, about majesty, about remoteness and isolation? Can we only truly come close to God when we have no distractions, no noise save for the sounds of nature, no sights save for the beauty of creation? No, I really don't believe that. God is everywhere and anywhere, in the inner city as much if not more than in a remote rural valley. But I do think there is something in us which is drawn to places like this to seek peace, restoration, renewal, inspiration and/or consolation.

Not everyone will feel that way. For many people, the city is the place to be to find stimulus, bright lights but also culture – museums, galleries, theatres, libraries, universities – and other people. I know that my training incumbent, an extroverted introvert, got his energy from being with other people, loving a big crowd that he could draw upon as source of inspiration and encouragement.

Whereas I am a classic introvert, large crowds scare me, whereas two or three gathered together in the peace and tranquillity of a medieval stone building – perfection. However, I would definitely encourage everyone to at least try coming somewhere like Capel-y-Ffin where you can't get phone signal, you can't get WiFi, you are thrown back on your own resources, forced to confront your own thoughts, hopes and fears – not always pleasant, but sometimes necessary. For people of faith, it's a time to listen to God, to seek his voice, his vision and guidance for the future – which again can be challenging. I would never have sought out the priesthood willingly, and there is still a large part of me that doesn't understand why me? I guess I just have to try to make peace with the fact that God's ways are higher than our ways and sometimes we may not fully understand but we can still follow and hopefully be of some use in his glorious plan for the good of humanity.

But I do also think there is something unique about places of worship, places that have been sacred for centuries, where the prayers of past generations have soaked into the walls, the trees, the very ground on which we stand. You can't buy that, you can't fake it, you can only experience it in the peace and quietness of place – and I see that reflected in the visitors book of All Saints, Hollybush, which stands open for visitors 365 days of the year in daylight hours, thanks to my feisty friend Susan and our friend Shirley who has been locking and unlocking it for many years. Now we have an automatic locking system, so it can be open 9.00 am to 5.00 pm every day of the year – global pandemics permitting. That's why I definitely think it's worth fighting to keep our old and long-established buildings up, running and open to anyone and everyone who wants to come to them, whether that's for historical curiosity or to find a space where they can just be. Space which is peace filled and timeless is harder and harder to find – another reason to support the Quiet Gardens Movement too.

But enough of these meanderings and ponderings, let's get back to the walk. I headed out into the bright morning, blue sky and sun my companions, and the first part of the walk was fine, all along the side of the valley, passing close by what looked like a couple of unoccupied large holiday cottages, and then onto farmland. I was conscious that I needed to keep an eye out for the turn up the hill and I did go slightly astray once, including leaving my trusty walking pole propped on a fence while I consulted map and phone and walking on without it. Luckily, I realised before I'd gone too far and doubled back for it. I managed to find my way onto a farm track, as per the map, and then discovered the waymarks – but only after I'd gone through the gate did I see the way mark that told me I needed to go back through it and up the side of the hill. I think the path might have been diverted to avoid walkers having to march through the farm buildings, a diversion I definitely approve of! This was the Vision Farm, renamed as such after those appearances by the Virgin Mary, but now equally famous for being owned by Monty Don, he of *Gardeners World* fame. Sadly, I did not come across Monty on my travels but that might have been a good thing as the incline had now become so steep that I wouldn't have had any breath with which to exchange witty badinage – in my dreams. I really should know by now that contour lines that close together equals much huffing, puffing and many pauses to look back down into the valley at the fabulous views.

From up here you could really get a sense of the length of the valley and almost see the glacier moving slowly carving its pathway through the mountains. Onwards and upwards I went, following the path clearly cut through the sea of bracken and even waymarked at certain key points. It was hot, sweaty work and at times the gradient meant I could hear my own heart thumping so loudly that it seemed to drown out all other noise. At one point I even thought that if this was to be the place that I was going to drop dead of a heart attack, it wouldn't be a bad place to die – if somewhat inconvenient for whoever came looking for me and was tasked with lugging my body all the way back down the mountain. Such are the thoughts which cross the mind of the sweaty walker . . .

I don't think it's a spoiler to tell you that I survived the climb, though emerging from the bracken onto the open hilltop proved slightly more confusing and I joined up with the main pathway a little further back than I thought but soon found the reassuring Offa's Dyke pathmarker, which felt very much like greeting an old friend. Grateful thanks to all who maintain the path so well even in very exposed places like these hilltops. Given the strenuousness of the climb, it was slightly disconcerting to come across three wild Black Mountain ponies at the very top of the hill, contentedly munching away without a care in the world.

Although it was another welcome reminder of Great Uncle Clarence who loved these wild Welsh Mountain ponies. I wonder if, like the ponies, he felt he belonged here, that this place spoke to him as it has spoken to so many other people in the past and will continue to down the ages. When he lived at The Plough, where I live now, he was, in worldly terms, a successful sheep farmer, running a herd of about one thousand sheep in partnership with his mother, my formidable great grandmother. But he doesn't appear to have been a particularly keen or conscientious sheep farmer. And while his single status wasn't due to any lack of interest in the opposite sex – quite the reverse – it maybe did indicate a man who didn't want to commit himself to any one woman when there was a wide selection to choose from. Not one to be tied down my late great uncle. Interestingly, looking through some old papers recently, his mother left this house to her daughter, my grandmother, rather than to her son who had been her business partner. She specified that there would always be a room kept for him in the house, a room which later became my first ever bedroom, but she left the house and orchard to my nan for her lifetime and then to my mother. Maybe she could see a way of securing the property long term and was pretty sure Clarence would never settle down and have children. He never did. Maybe she realised that being tied down to a property and responsibilities wasn't his thing. He stayed in the house after her death just long enough to buy The Penant at Llanigon, the remote, inaccessible property which I described earlier. And there he lived the life he wanted to live, enjoying his own company or finding other company when the mood took him – apparently, he used to have long conversations with the playwright Arnold Wesker who lived along the valley from him – oh, to have been a fly on the wall! He lived his life on his terms, running wild like the ponies. He was a maverick, a one off, didn't care what other people thought, just did things his way. For a self-conscious people pleaser like me, that's a challenging ancestor to have – but challenge is good, challenges like this walk for example. It reveals to us that we are capable of so much more than we think we are.

It was beautiful – though a bit windy – walking along the tops. Which was just as well, as it turned out I was going to be walking along this ridge for some considerable time. Bleak but beautiful, just me and the mountain top and the big, big sky – lots of time and space to think and be up here.

I was aware that I was walking along the border with Herefordshire on one side and Monmouthshire on the other – the county of my birth next door to the county of my schooling. And I also realised that I was walking above another area we had stayed in – Longtown with its wonderful castle and fab village shop and Michaelchurch

Escley with its very good pub, The Bridge, right by the river, where we'd once had to get our feet wet walking back across the eponymous bridge when the river was in flood. We'd climbed up this hill from the Longtown side many moons ago and seen hang gliders throwing themselves off and floating high on the thermals. No hang gliders today, but lots of other walkers – this was probably the busiest bit of the walk for seeing other walkers, and they were all, without exception, walking in the opposite direction to me – I was clearly doing Offa's Dyke the wrong way round!

Fig 18. View back to the Malverns

The views were terrific, and you could see for miles all the way round. The problem was you could also see exactly how many miles you still had to walk – and there were no benches of any sort anywhere for the weary traveller to rest and take their ease. Which was totally understandable given how exposed it was at this height – who wants to lug a load of materials up to construct seating which will either blow away or rot within a season? However, I quickly discovered that trig points could be used as stopping places – they gave you a raised platform to sit on, somewhere dry to put your rucksack and you could shelter from the wind behind them – perfect. I therefore took my first stop of the day at a trig point at 610 metres above sea level, which I suddenly realised gave me a great view back across to the Malvern Hills, their distinctive silhouette outlined on the horizon.

It was a sobering thought – on the one hand I'd walked all the way from there to here in eight and a half days, what an achievement. On the other hand I had to walk all the way back in another six and a half days . . . still quite a bit to do then! As I sat looking back to the Malverns, it seemed to me that a really bright light shone from them, a discreet point of really bright light shining like a beacon. I'm sure there is some sort of rational explanation, but I couldn't think what it was – fancifully I saw it as a beacon calling me home, rather than another vision of the Virgin Mary, so got up and got going again.

The weather seemed to be clouding over, causing me to put my raincoat on for the first and only time during the walk and plug myself into the iPod to distract me as I plodded on. This was the one and only time on the walk when knowing exactly where I was going and seeing how far I still had to go was a bit of a motivational problem. I knew that I just had to keep putting one foot in front of another, which meant that there weren't going to be any unknown twists or turns in the road, no navigational challenges, no danger of going wrong. But on the other hand, there were also no changes of scenery, nothing to engage me or keep me alert and motivated during the hours ahead. Interestingly, when I was exchanging notes with my friend Nick afterwards, as he'd been doing the Camino at the same time I was doing the Amble, he commented that it was the straight, flat roads which were often the hardest to walk. We think that's want we want, the easy life, no hills, no hidden turnings, but in fact it can be mentally much tougher to deal with. Kind of like a metaphor for life I guess, we think we want an easy trouble-free existence and when we get it, we're bored. In reality, we need to be stretched and challenged in order to grow, however painful an experience that might be.

I'd never say I was bored during the walk – I had my iPod to keep me entertained and with shuffle I've got plays mixed in with music folk have chosen for funerals, Christian music and hymns and then rather a lot of secular rock and pop music from Billy Joel to Squeeze. Music was a big help in lifting my mood whenever I was feeling tired or down or out of sorts during the walk. It can cheer you, transport you, even give you a fresh rhythm to walk to, or get you singing along like a madwoman – excellent! And the hymnody has lots of walking lines to stick in your head – at the moment it was 'Not for ever in green pastures do we ask our way to be, but the steep and rugged pathway may we tread rejoicingly'.

Onwards, ever onwards, I tramped, tramped, tramped – saying 'Hi' to the people passing by, and trying not to keep looking at the map and working out how much further I had to go. Eventually the path got a little more twisty, swinging round in what seemed to be a big arc. I had targeted another trig point for my second stop of the day but as I came up to it, I could see another couple had had the same idea. Luckily there was a hollow on the other side of the path where I could duck down out of the wind, have my snacks and re-fold the map before continuing on, confident that surely I must be nearly at the end of this bit of path by now. Finally, I made it, voyaging over Hatterrall Hill and coming right off the hills altogether down a steepish slope past some walled sheep pens, then through a gate and onto some good old fashioned lane walking. As arranged, I texted Mike to let him know I was back on tarmac, but for once I didn't get a speedy response. I kept on walking and after seventeen minutes of no response, tried again. I was fast reaching the point at which I'd only got another couple of fields to cross before the rendezvous point and was starting to catastrophise as only the overimaginative can. I even had enough signal to try phoning him but it just went to voice mail. Across the field I went, then the final bit of road walking and I knew I just had to cross the railway line and I'd be virtually there.

At last, thirty-one long minutes after my original text came the reply 'Just about to pay at Waitrose'. Apparently the Abergavenny branch of Waitrose is a signal free zone, yet another reason to go there! Reassured that there would be food to eat and that Michael was still in the land of the living I pressed on more cheerfully until I encountered my final obstacle of the day . . . a large sign instructing me to Stop, Look, Listen and Beware of trains. This did not bode well. I'd assumed there would be some sort of bridge to get me across the railway line, but instead, I rounded the bend to see what looked like a few gym mats which British Rail had laid haphazardly across the tracks to help the unwary walker wander across. This was definitely not the sort of challenge I wanted after over five hours of walking – although monotonous it certainly wasn't. Here was something to get the heart pumping again! I stopped, I looked, I listened and I scurried across as swiftly as my weary walker's legs could carry me. However, as I crossed the River Monnow almost immediately afterwards via the handily placed bridge, I heard a train come tearing past – it was a close run thing . . .

Then it was just round the edge of a playing field and over a stile and there I was at the rendezvous layby, and with a screech of tyres and brakes applied, the trusty Skoda just about made it at the same time as me – another close run thing! End of day photo taken and that was leg nine of the walk completed, exactly eleven miles walked in six hours and twelve minutes. I had turned the corner; I was heading for home.

Day Nine Stats

Start time – 8.27 am.

Finish time – 2.39 pm.

Duration – 6 hours, 12 minutes.

Distance walked – 11.0 miles.

Total ascent – 1,293 ft.

Total descent 1,965 ft.

Avg. speed – 2.1 mph.

Day Ten: Pandy to Llantilio Crossenny
Day of Castles and Churches

10 July 2019

Day ten dawned fair and bright yet again. The weather was in fact stupendous – blue sky and sunshine – so instead of sporting my fetching purple raincoat from the day before, today the overly floral but very effective French sun hat was making a comeback. On the minus side, it definitely made me look slightly deranged but on the plus side, would save me from getting sun stroke, which I'd had once whilst walking in Italy and wasn't keen to experience again. I couldn't believe it was the last day of week two – that meant that by the end of the day I would have completed two thirds of the walk – it just didn't seem possible.

I was dropped off back in the layby by the long-suffering Mike at just after 9.00 am and he took the start of day photo, which shows what a very nice day it was and me as a result looking very happy – deranged but happy! And as an added bonus I only had about eight miles to go and most of it was still on my old and reliable friend, the Offa's Dyke Path, so although it involved a lot of field walking, I felt a lot more optimistic than I might have done about the prospect of arriving at my destination in one piece. The first challenge was to make it across the A465, the main Hereford to Abergavenny road, which I managed and then followed the waymark which directed me along the side of some houses and into the relative comfort of a field, walking along the hedge line towards an easy to spot waymark into the next field. The next sign was slightly ambiguous, but I understood that I needed to hang a right up and round and diagonally across the field to find my next stile and this little bit of height allowed me to pause and look back to the hills I'd been walking in the day before.

It was a pretty idyllic view back over the Monmouthshire countryside – picture perfect. However, I couldn't linger for too long admiring the view behind me, I needed to crack on towards my destination but the view in front when I got over into the next field was also rather striking, a distinctively shaped hill lay ahead – I wondered whether it was Skirrid, famed for being the home of the Garden in the Clouds. When I got home and checked the mountain, it was definitely Skirrid, a name derived from the Welsh word 'ysgyryd' meaning to shake or tremble, and it's easy to understand why the hill would be called this given the massive landslide which has caused one part of it to separate from the rest. It is still prone to small mud flows and landslides to this day. It is also known locally as Holy Mountain, a name which may have derived from one of two sources. The first is more immediately provable, there is a ruined chapel, dedicated to St Michael, right on the summit of Skirrid, which was used by Roman Catholics as a place remote enough and hard to get to that they could continue to worship as Catholics after the Reformation. The second source is a local legend which tells how the dramatic landslip shown above was caused by an earthquake or lightning strike at the exact moment when Christ was crucified. The more pedestrian but factually accurate explanation is that the upper slopes of the hill are composed of Devonian age sandstones, with weaker mudstones of the St Maughans Formation beneath, which would obviously contribute hugely to the instability of the steep slopes.

However, I much prefer to focus on myths and legends!

Apparently, there is a distinctively shaped piece of sandstone known as the Devil's Table, but on the other hand, there's also a local tradition that earth from Skirrid was holy and especially fertile, so it was taken away to be scattered on fields, on coffins and in the foundations of churches. Most interesting to me on the walk, the summit was a place of pilgrimage, especially on Michaelmas Eve. The hill has been owned by the National Trust since 1939, and one day I will make a pilgrimage of my own up to the summit, but meanwhile, back to the walk currently in hand.

I continued onwards and upwards into the next field, which turned out to be full of cows, but once more, cows far more interested in the tasty grass than they were in me. I must admit after that close shave with the galloping bullocks in the field outside Monkland I never had cause to worry about cows again. They were very docile and disinterested, which was great. Checking the map, I found that I had one more field to go, then a little bit of lane walking and then I'd be heading back across fields again. The only disadvantage of the phone tracking my walking was that on the odd occasion when I found myself in the middle of a field with buildings quite some distance away it tended to ping over to those buildings as if seeking company. However, in the middle of this particular field was a very helpful and reassuring signpost, which kept me heading in the right direction, onward, ever onward towards Llangattock Lingoed which I could see had a church so was hopeful that there might well be a bench which I could use for my first break. It was a little early, but I couldn't see any other obvious stopping points for a while so decided to learn from previous mistakes and take a break while I had a potential bench on offer.

Soon I was walking on a narrow path with a field on one side and houses on the other, until finally I came out into a lane which led me to the church. Offa's Dyke Path actually went through the churchyard, so I decided to stop and have my two hourly rest and possibly take a look inside the church – though from the outside it looked fairly insignificant. How wrong can you be? As soon as I stepped through the door, I could see that I was in the most beautiful and ancient building.

There was so much to take in in a relatively small space that it was difficult to decide where to look first. This place had everything – ancient wall paintings, a medieval ornately carved bressummer (or load bearing beam), some medieval stained-glass fragments,

Fig 19. St Cadoc's interior

some very ornate gravestones and last but by no means least, a fully functioning kitchen. This last was not a thing of great beauty by the standards of the rest of the church but it enabled them to have functions and provide hospitality which would have been vital in securing the future of this amazing building. I can't begin to tell you what an impact the beauty of this place had on me – not least because the exterior was so unassuming that I'd nearly walked on by. Talk about a lesson in not judging a book by its cover.

The guidebook was extremely well produced in full colour

with excellent photographs, so for once I splashed the cash which I carried in case of emergencies and took a copy home with me. What I later read in the introduction only served to make the building even more remarkable. It was Grade I listed – which didn't surprise me – but in the summer of 2002 the nave roof moved to the point of collapse and the village was faced with the decision of whether to attempt to raise the considerable funding which would be needed to restore the church or to simply let it fall into ruin and disuse. Bravely the small community bit the bullet, raised funds, successfully applied for grants and work began. As is so often the way with projects on ancient buildings, things got worse before they got better. The removal of the roof showed the full extent of Deathwatch beetle and rot, some of the masonry was unstable, the electric wiring dangerous and the organ and bells unplayable. Thanks to the work of very skilled craftsmen, using traditional techniques, within an incredible fifteen months the church was restored to its former glory. Greater than its former glory in fact, because the work revealed the existence of treasures like the Rood staircase and the wall painting of St George and the Dragon which had probably remained hidden for 450 years. In all this the aim of the community was to make the building safe and usable for generations to come, and then to 'make it the finest possible example of a quintessential country church in its largely unchanged setting.' I would say that they have succeeded magnificently and should be very proud of what they have achieved.

The Church is dedicated to St Cadoc, one of the most important of the early Welsh saints who lived between approximately 497 and 577. He was a contemporary of St David and St Columba and lived before St Augustine came to Britain to convert the Saxons – so we are looking once more at a Celtic rather than a Roman form of Christianity. The name of the settlement within which the church stands derives its name from this sacred space. Llan indicates a sacred space, perhaps granted by the saint himself, and the earlier name for Lingoed was Cellenig, meaning 'woodland grove', which gives a derivation of the monastery/cell of Catwg in the small wood, Catwg being the name Cadoc was known by in South Wales. So possibly this magnificent building began life as a simple beehive type monastic cell, made out of timber, wattle, daub and thatch, used by a resident monk who would have led services outside and performed baptisms in the nearby stream. The church stands on a hilltop overlooking a fertile valley – the traditional features of a Celtic monastic outpost. St Cadoc founded a monastery at Llancarfan and travelled widely to spread the good news of Christian hope during a dark period of British history. He visited Scotland, Ireland, Cornwall and even ventured as far as Brittany where several churches are dedicated to him. He was famed as teacher, devoted to serving his community and was a strong contender to be patron saint of Wales.

And I'm ashamed to say that until visiting this church, I had been blissfully unaware of his existence. Funny how the saints of Ireland and Scotland and places like Iona and Holy Island dominate our view of Christianity during the Dark Ages and we forget that in Wales and in Cornwall clearly much good work was being done. Memo to self to read and research more widely and to always keep my eyes open and not ignore the chance to learn and to be surprised by beauty and community, as I was in Llangattock Lingoed.

All too soon, it was time to tear myself away and continue with the rest of my journey, despite the obvious temptation of the village pub right next door to the church. I put my rucksack back on my back, plugged in the iPod, realised I'd left my stick in the church, so went back for it and eventually headed on across the churchyard and out the other side. I traversed a lovely easy bit of downhill going down and across a field, then bypassed a house and emerged onto the lane for a bit of road walking. Eventually I found the correct turn off the road and down a field to cross over a river and headed on up a pretty overgrown bit of path towards a farmhouse. Happily, the path then took me off down a green lane, and on across fields of pasture to a mainish road by a small group of houses at the wonderfully named Caggle Street. Cars were zipping along at a good pace but I only had to navigate a short stretch of road before finding the waymark I was looking for and heading on into a field of crops, where the farmer had very kindly left both a margin and a clear way across right where it should have been. I then rocked up at an interesting, if narrow bridge, one plank wide, fenced in with chicken wire above the vertiginous drop to the water below and with ivy slowly but surely starting to cover the scaffold pole and chicken wire balustrading on each side. I crossed it successfully and headed on up the field towards the opposite boundary, knowing that the White Castle, my next major landmark, wasn't far away.

I climbed up the next field, pausing as I spotted a bird of prey hovering. I fumbled with my phone, trying to take a photo, but as I looked away trying to focus it, suddenly the bird was gone. I can only assume it had dived down upon a hapless rabbit, but it had totally disappeared. Which was a lesson for me in staying in the moment, rather than trying to view life through the lens of a camera on my phone. Some experiences are there to be captured by the naked eye and remembered, not uploaded to a cloud somewhere.

And while I was faffing about, a couple of walkers appeared behind me, so I pushed on rapidly to the end of the field, through a gate and then turned sharp left along the hedge line to emerge right next to the castle, walking down one side of it before emerging onto the lane which runs alongside it. I confess this was a slight diversion from the route Mike had indicated, but it did mean sticking with Offa's Dyke Path and avoided getting up close and personal with some farm buildings. It also meant I approached White Castle from the rear and was very impressed by the scale of the castle and by how much of it was still standing.

Further research has only made this place more fascinating. The Welsh form of its name was Castell Gwyn, said to derive from a local ruler of Norman times called Gwyn ap Gwaethfoed, but its original name was Llantilio Castle, which is logical as it stands on a hill only about a mile away from the village of Llantilio Crossenny, my destination for today. The name White Castle first appears in the thirteenth century and must refer to the white rendering which is still visible on parts of the exterior walls and must really have made this place stand out in the surrounding countryside.

Originally the castle would have had defences of earth and timber, and at this time you would have entered the site from the south, the direction from which I approached it. But in the thirteenth century, when most of the stone defences we can still see today were built, the whole castle was turned around by 180 degrees and a new gatehouse was built, which now forms the entrance to the castle.

White Castle, along with Grosmont and Skenfrith Castles formed an important strategic triangle, designed to control this area of the southern Marches. All three were royal castles in the later twelfth century and in 1201 were granted to Hubert de Burgh by King John. In 1254, all three castles passed to the king's eldest son, Lord Edward, later King Edward I and in 1267 to his younger brother Edmund, then Earl of Lancaster. At this time the threat posed by Llywelyn the Last was at its height, so it was probably then that a gatehouse and circular towers were built to shore up the defences. Even if attackers had managed to overcome the outer defences they then had to get across the moat, which still remains, and you go over the drawbridge to get into the large inner ward of the castle. It is easy to imagine how people would have lived in the castle, because the ruins are so intact, and stunning to think that they are still standing after hundreds of years.

The castles saw a brief revival of fortunes during the Glyndwr uprising of the early thirteenth century but were largely abandoned after that crisis had passed. Luckily all three were still used as local centres of estate management, administration and revenue collecting throughout the Middle Ages, which meant that money was spent on maintenance and repairs, which probably goes a long way to explaining why this castle in particular is still in such a good state of preservation.

I had actually worked at a castle similar to this one as a gap year job between school and university – Goodrich Castle – which I would see on one of the next stages of the walk. It was a really good way for a shy teenager to be forced to interact with the great British public and did force me to come out of my shell a little before heading off to university. I enjoyed my time up there in the little ticket office on weekends and bank holidays. I also wondered whether this might be a taste of the future for our churches. This ancient castle had outlived its purpose – thankfully England and Wales are no longer at war, at least for the moment – and had now found a new purpose as a site of great beauty and historic interest. Would many of our churches soon be of historic interest only? And if so, who would pay for their upkeep and repair? One of our benefice churches, Pendock Old Church, is now cared for by the National Churches Trust, but they are struggling for funding and volunteers just as we are. It is a conundrum which we really need to get our thinking caps on about, as the volunteer pool is shrinking as fast as our congregations, yet our buildings have great value and historical significance and need to be looked after – answers on a postcard please!

I made a mental note that I would love to return one day to explore the castle itself properly and to do the Three Castles circular walk involving Skenfrith, Grosmont and White Castles which the map showed me I was heading towards. The traditional 'I'm almost at the end of the walk' text was soon winging its way off to Mike, letting him know that I'd arrived at the final big landmark of the journey and would hope to be with him in about half an hour. I headed on down the lane, resolutely ignoring the onward sign for the Three Castles Walk and sticking to good old Offa's Dyke which took me off to the right, down a track/green lane which made for lovely walking. Absolutely no danger of oncoming cars and no chance of getting lost, so I could just keep walking and enjoying the wonderful weather.

Eventually I emerged onto the road between Tre-Adam and Great Treadam, the latter looking like it had been turned into a wedding venue. When I checked up later, I found that Treadam Barn was indeed a wedding venue, a superbly restored fifteenth century oak-framed barn, situated on the Offa's Dyke Path between Abergavenny and Monmouth. What a very beautiful setting for a wedding, though obviously nowhere near as beautiful as our own, our very own, Birtsmorton Court. I obediently followed the waymark along the side of the venue and then into the last set of fields of the day – the end was in sight – hoorah! There was just one final curve ball in store, again caused by crops in fields and me not quite being able to work out where my actual route lay and how far it might have been diverted to take care of and not damage the crops. This necessitated a bit of walking up and down field margins and making sure I really was where I thought I was, until the route finally revealed itself and I was heading down a path left through the middle of the final field of the day towards the final stile of the day, with the tower of the final church of the day clearly visible in the not too far distance. Once I was out onto the road, I just had to hang a left, walk a little way along the road, turn right and then left along the road signposted to the very magnificent church of St Teilo, Llantilio Crossenny, which is absolutely huge and which feels even bigger when you get inside, like a little cathedral.

When I did some research, I discovered that as it was such a large church for such a small village, it's been suggested that the Bishop used it as a sort of cathedral as he progressed between manors collecting tithes. The original church would have been a wooden building and was replaced around the end of twelfth or early thirteenth century with stone – about the same time as the castle was updated – I wonder if the same firm of builders did both jobs? They did a lovely job of building a central 'early English' tower, some sixty feet high, which would originally have had a parapet and probably a flat lead roof. It is dedicated to St Teilo, because in 550 AD the Saxons were plundering in the area and a local king, Iddon, asked Teilo, a holy man staying in Llanarth, to pray for him. Teilo raised a cross on the ancient pre-Christian mound and the Saxons were repelled. In return, Iddon granted the mound to Teilo, who later became Bishop of Llandaff and a saint. The present name is a corruption of 'St Teilo at Iddon's Cross.'

Beautiful but vast, and somehow didn't inspire and delight me in the same way St Cadoc's had – but what an amazing treat of a day to have two such beautiful yet contrasting buildings in just a few short miles of each other. And the purity of the white paint and the stone arches, and the soaring height of the building were stunning. Although I must admit I did also fall for the very jazzy stained glass (see fig 20).

I noted it was donated in 1960, hence the fab colours and the kind of sixties vibe to it, but I've only noticed while writing this that it was given in memory of the Johnson family of Treadam –

Fig 20. Stained glass window at St Teilo, Llantilio Crossenny

the place I had just walked from. I loved it because it was so bright and vibrant and full of life, and the faces are very modern day faces somehow. I could easily imagine the Apostle Luke turning up as a handsome new surgeon on Holby City for example, but I'm sure that's sacrilegious and not at all what the artist intended. Or perhaps he did want to make the point that all those figures from the bible were flesh and blood just like us. And I also found more of the very ornate gravestones, like the ones at St Cadoc's.

Clearly the folk in these parts have always had a great sense of style and panache, going back to medieval times and beyond. And have had access to very skilled craftsmen who were able to carry out their commissions – and long may that continue. I also discovered that major restoration work on this Grade 1 listed building had been undertaken in 2012/13, including the removal and replacement of 12,000 oak shingles. Lots of grants were used to fund the work, but if the local community don't get behind a project like this, it doesn't get very far, so again, huge respect and thanks to the people of the village for doing their bit to preserve such beauty for future generations. I think the whole day showed me that there are treasures all around us, if only we open our eyes and look for them. I had no idea any of these places existed but now I'd love to return one day and take a proper look at all of them. And maybe that's also a metaphor for appreciating what is local to us, right under our noses, not always trying to push onward to the next thing and the next and the next. Sometimes, beauty and wonder are right there waiting for us, and we just need to open our eyes and our minds to take them in. And it also reminded me that all our ancient buildings, especially our churches, contain stories of lives and communities gone by, which have a value all of their own, and we need to get better at telling those stories, sharing them more widely. Because if a community takes a church to its heart, if it continues to earn its place in local affections, it is that much more likely to survive, to become a prized asset rather than a forgotten burden.

Homeward bound we went, to rest and recuperate over the weekend. I was looking forward to plunging my feet into the final ice bath of the week and not having to worry about finding my way for a couple of days. On the other hand, it also meant that the walk was now two thirds done, I was already part of the way home and in five days' time I would have completed the full 150-mile challenge. Which I definitely found difficult to believe!

Day Ten Stats
    Start time – 9.06 am.
    Finish time – 1.33 pm.
    Duration – 4 hours, 27 minutes.
    Distance walked – 8.3 miles.
    Total ascent – 669 ft.
    Total descent – 814 ft.
    Avg. speed – 2.3 mph.

Day Eleven:
Llantilio Crossenny to Monmouth
Homecoming Queen

11 July 2019

Monday of my final week dawned with blue skies and sun – just like all the other days so far. I really had been exceptionally lucky with the weather. I'm sure it would have been much harder to keep going if it had poured with rain every day. As it was, I was feeling quite sad at the prospect of reaching the end of this mad undertaking. Something I never really thought I could do was now two thirds done and I was fast approaching the home straight. And it really would be the home straight as today I would be heading into very familiar territory because this leg of the walk would end at Monmouth, the place where I had gone to secondary school. It's where I'd learned to drive, practising hill starts on the road I now take to the local branch of Waitrose. It's where I made a bunch of good friends – eventually – some of whom I'm still in touch with to this day. It's where I started going to the pub – the Nag's Head, on Old Dixton Road, allegedly the same pub in which Robert Plant, lead singer of Led Zeppelin, occasionally drank. I think there was one time when he was in at the same time as us, but as I was hopelessly uncool – something which has never changed – I don't think this had the same impact on me as it did on the savvier members of our all-girl gang.

It was an all-girl gang because we all attended Haberdashers' Monmouth School for Girls, a single sex school, one of the many reasons I objected to going there. I also resented it because none of my friends from primary school went there, no, they all went to sensible mixed schools in Ross – where I wanted to go too, and should have gone to, having passed the eleven plus. But instead, I ended up catching the bus to Monmouth every day wearing a stupid girls' school uniform – stupidest feature of all, the headgear. A beret in the winter, a boater – yes, incredibly, your eyes do not deceive you – a boater in the summer. And they didn't even play hockey, which I loved and was mildly good at. No, they played lacrosse, which is a ridiculous apology for a game, and which I hated. Cue a lifetime of believing that I was no good at any type of physical exercise and being the last to be picked for any type of sports team. It's amazing how influential these youthful stereotypes can be. There was a definite dichotomy at school – you could either be nerdy, swotty and no good at games or brilliant at games, cool, confident and popular with boys. To be clever and sporty was just not a thing. Which is bonkers and damaging, and I suspect part of the reason I just assumed I could never do something as physically challenging as the Amble. Always good to confound your own expectations . . .

The first year or so at the new school was pretty miserable. Whereas at primary school I had been confident and outgoing and had loads of friends, here I was a lonely swotty nerd who really didn't fit in, so much so that I was subject to some low level bullying at break times. It was nothing major, I don't think I told anyone else about it, name calling and a bit of pushing and shoving at most, but it did make me feel very isolated and alone, out of place in this new and strange environment. I took to heading off on my own to find some out of the way place to be – or haunting the library when we were allowed to, books having always been my friends. I think this is probably when I began to lose track of me, the real me, and started pushing her down, suppressing her, so that I could fit in, be acceptable, be liked. Of course, that never works because people can spot lack of authenticity a mile off. But then I met a group of other swotty, nerdy, bookish girls, who I could be myself with and we formed our own little gang. They were all in the other half of the year from me alphabetically so we didn't have lessons together but that was okay. As every slightly bullied person knows it's the break

Fig 21. Marianna

times when you need to have mates to hang out with and finally, I had found my tribe. There were two Susans, Jane, Sara, Marianna and me. But it was Marianna with whom I established the closest friendship (see fig 21).

The two of us had a lot in common – both only children, both voracious readers of anything and everything, both with a seriously uncool love of the works of Barry Manilow . . . Our musical tastes did develop eventually – in very different directions. Marianna graduated to a love of heavy metal and fast cars whereas I was drawn to the clever lyrics and jaunty tunes of the mighty Squeeze and the even mightier Manchester United. However, our love of books remained constant and formed the foundation of a friendship which lasted until her untimely death from breast cancer in May 2001. As the years went by we inevitably drifted apart a little. She and Sara went off to Cambridge together, I didn't, so we formed different sets of university friends. We still took holidays together, the six of us, Sara and Steve, Mike and I, Marianna and Martin, including a particularly memorable boating trip to the South of France when Mike and I woke up to find our cabin flooded, and a Lake District holiday when we scaled Scafell Pike. But it took her diagnosis with breast cancer to wake me up to what a big and valued part of my life she really was. Her lovely husband Martin was an absolute star, doing things like organizing a special thirty-fifth birthday party for her, instead of the fortieth which, very sadly, she didn't make it to, dying at the appallingly young age of thirty-seven. Even worse than that was the fact that while she went through her treatment for breast cancer, Martin became ill with Hodgkins Lymphoma, a blood cancer which is generally curable – except in his case it sadly wasn't and he died in October 2000, six months before Marianna's death. This meant that her mum and dad moved into her house in Newport to take on the main responsibility for her care – how they managed to deal with caring for a dying child I have absolutely no idea. During those last six months of her life, I would go over most Saturdays which enabled her mum and dad to go back to their home, pick up changes of clothes, and just take a break. But those Saturdays also gave us the opportunity to rediscover something of the closeness we'd had as teenagers. I remember lots of laughter, a few tears, and the privilege of being able to take her for a last trip out to see the sea. And I remember the Macmillan nurses who visited and were so caring, kind and practical – a huge support, not only to Marianna, but also to her family and her friends.

After her death, I knew I wanted to do something to raise funds for the wonderful work which Macmillan Cancer Support does. I'm just sorry it took me so long to get around to doing it. Marianna's influence continued to shape my life long after her death. She wanted to change direction, change careers, do something more creative than accountancy and she definitely had the intelligence and creativity to do great things, but sadly her time ran out before she was able to make that move. It was thanks to that urge to make the most of whatever time we have – almost to live the life she never got the chance to live – that meant I took a deep breath and leapt into a career as a garden designer/gardener and later on a priest.

You see she also brought me back to my faith – a faith which developed in childhood as my mum and dad were always regular church goers – and continued at university. I first met Mike properly when we attended confirmation class together. But what with moving away for work, and not really finding a new church in the big city, faith had become something that existed on the periphery of life, not at the centre. It was only when Marianna became ill, in fact when she lay dying in St Anne's hospice, that I was driven back to faith, to pray, really pray, that God would take the pain and fear away and give her a peaceful death. The last words she ever said to me were 'It's alright, it's okay' and my belief has always been that he answered my prayers and sent his angels to comfort and to reassure her, to help her on her way. Maybe they were just angels in the form of the hospice staff, who were so kind to me when I went down with a bout of food poisoning whilst staying over with her. I don't know whether you've ever tried to vomit quietly in a hospice to try to avoid disturbing the properly ill patients, but it's not easy. To add to the general Greek tragedy of it all, her mum, Margaret, died the day after Marianna's death, from an angina attack. Which was why there were two coffins at the funeral you read about at the very beginning of this book. Their graves are side by side in Abergavenny Cemetery. Reading out that last message from her at the funeral was one of the hardest things I've ever had to do, but later on that moment made me think that if I could stand up and read something so emotionally charged and poignant for me and do it well, then it meant that I had a voice, that was my talent, nurtured at home, in school and university for reading aloud, and this was the seed which would eventually lead to ordination. I owe Marianna so much. This walk is just the latest, and in many ways greatest of her many gifts to me – but nothing will ever be quite as great as the gift of her friendship, which I miss so much.

Mike dropped me off back at the massive church at Llantilio Crossenny, took the start of day photo and then I headed off down the road, looking to meet up with another old friend – the Offa's Dyke Path. Today would be almost my final day of solo walking – tomorrow Simon would be returning for another leg and Mike and Ruth were due to walk with me on Thursday with just Mike and myself completing the final leg on Friday. I decided that I should make the most of the solitude while it lasted. I picked up a cut through along the bank of a stream which ran along the backs of a row of houses – always interesting for a gardener to see how other people design and plant their gardens. Then it was out onto a quiet lane for quite a long stretch of road walking. This is good in one sense – a chance to let your thoughts wander, to dream dreams, to soak up the views and the countryside all around you – but if you're me, you do need to keep one eye on the map and on the names of the passing farms to ensure that you know where you are, know which way to go when the road splits and where to look out for the waymark telling you to leave the road and head off across the fields. Dave would have been proud – he had taught me well!

I successfully navigated my way to the first bit of field walking of the day which turned out to be orchard walking – lovely but not as relaxing as you might think. All the trees in their neat and orderly rows mean you're unable to spot your exit point from the field. However, I checked maps and the general direction of the waymark and followed the way I thought I should be going and arrived at another waymark on the far edge of the orchard – result! It directed me uphill hugging the field boundary and then continued uphill diagonally across a couple of fields. Looking back the way I'd come I saw yet another magnificent view over the beautiful Welsh countryside.

I carried on over a stile and out onto a farm lane. The path took me around the farm and its buildings, thankfully, and into a field which had a large hand painted notice asking walkers to please stick to the path. It was at this point that I came across my second lone female walker of the trip, heading, as ever, in the opposite direction along the Offa's Dyke Path. She was young and fit and a proper back packer, judging by the size of her rucksack, and I rejoiced to see her striding out across the field, doing her own thing. We smiled and nodded as walkers do and carried on our separate ways. I stuck rigidly and self-righteously to the path, which meant walking all around the field edge, rather than cutting diagonally across the middle of the field. Clambered out over a stile back onto the road, heading onwards and upwards towards Pen-pwll-y-calch Farm where I encountered yet another very friendly farmer, who'd come out to check on one of his ewes. He was a little bemused by my journeying, but he wished me well and I headed on downhill across his fields. There I encountered a German couple walking the other way along the Dyke, who stopped me heading off in completely the wrong direction.

I was now heading for the hamlet of Llanfihangel Ystum Llywern which I could see from the map had very few houses but did have a church. Hopes were raised of an interesting diversion to look inside and maybe even a bench in the churchyard where I could rest and have my first break of the day – a little early but none the worse for that. Imagine my disappointment then at not only finding no bench, but finding the church itself locked and, to add insult to injury, a message on the door, just above the padlock, which said 'Thank you for your generous donation which helps towards the upkeep and survival of this precious church', with a helpful arrow pointing down to a slot in the door to push your money through. The juxtaposition of a plea for money next to a padlocked door spoke volumes, but not in the way I suspect the congregation intended. The subtext – at least to my mind – was 'We don't trust you enough to actually let you have access to our precious church building, but we'd like you to give us some money to fund its upkeep anyway.' Now, maybe the parishioners had had to deal with the aftermath of thefts or damage being caused to the church – I don't know. Maybe in such a small hamlet, they lacked volunteers willing to come and unlock in the morning and lock up again at night – it is a commitment and a tie. Although the noticeboard stated that the church was open at weekends, so they clearly had no objection to opening per se. What I did find harder to forgive was the locked door combined with the request for money – that really didn't sit well with me. I headed off towards the road, but then had second thoughts. The porch had stone benches, I could sit on one of them and take my break. Except by the time I'd doubled back, those benches were occupied by a very nice couple walking the Dyke from Chepstow who were taking their mid-morning break and who were as unimpressed by the locked door with its slot for money as I had been. I didn't feel I could gatecrash their break, though they did very kindly offer to make space for me, so I left them to it and continued onward, mulling as I went.

Every other church even vaguely on the Offa's Dyke route was not only kept open, but also made a real effort to offer hospitality to walkers – facilities to make yourself a drink or have a snack, and even, memorably, the toilet at Gladestry. Yet here, where the Dyke path ran literally right past the door, it was locked, and instead of offering help, they were asking for help. Maybe the parish was in a financially precarious position, maybe the church was under threat of closure – I do realise that I was totally ignorant of the pressures on that local community of parishioners. But I did know that locking the door to visitors wasn't the way to engage with people nor to get them to offer to help you. And it has since struck me as symptomatic of a wider problem within the Church – the fact that money has become such a central theme. We're always discussing money at our PCC meetings – lack of it, how to raise it, how we can pay our parish share to the diocese, how we can increase the level of giving, how we can fund the almost constant repairs and maintenance needed on our beautiful church buildings. But we follow a Saviour who said sell all your possessions and give the money to the poor! And we want to be talking about how we can play our part in helping those who need it within our communities and how we can share our faith with them – not how we can wring an extra few quid out of everyone or how we can continue to do everything we do now but with substantially fewer paid clergy.

I continued on down a track, through a gate and into a long stretch of meadowland with the path clearly mown through the beautiful long grass, first of all alongside a stream and then on across a flat, open meadow – stunning. My equilibrium was restored. Eventually the waymarks pointed away from the River Trothy and across fields back onto the road. Time was passing and I was really keen to find a stopping place. As I set off on my next bit of field walking, I held out some hopes for the ruins of a Cistercian Abbey – Grace-Dieu Abbey according to the map – but they were either non-existent ruins or too far off the path to be seen. I continued doggedly on – even braving the stile blockaded by a small herd of cows trying to soak up the shade of an overhanging tree. As I followed the path around some farm buildings, I came upon a Portakabin with a sofa plonked outside it. It was very, very tempting to take my break there in comfort, but it just felt too intrusive, the sofa must surely belong to someone?

Onward and upward, I thought to myself as I climbed up the field and out through a gate onto the road. I even considered plonking myself down in the gateway, but there were a few houses nearby and I still yearned for a proper seat. So on and on I tramped, up the road, past farms and B & Bs and then down a track between fields, heading for a long stretch of woodland walking. Then, on the side of the track, set back and nearly submerged in the undergrowth, there it was – a bench! A proper, sit down, take a break bench – an oasis in the Monmouthshire seating desert. I don't know when I've enjoyed a break more – and I provided some midday entertainment for some friendly and curious cows as well as watching mystified as someone drove past up the track and then reversed all the way back down a few minutes later.

Writing this now makes me realise how lucky I am that the search for somewhere to sit and be isn't part of my normal every day. That I have a comfortable home to return to and people who love me. But it also illustrates the stripped-down nature of real pleasure which the walk revealed to me. When finding a bench to stop and rest is the highlight of the morning, that really demonstrates the importance of rest, food and water – all things that I know I am lucky enough, privileged enough, to take absolutely for granted. They've always been there and so I assume they always will be – but I know many people are on the edge of existence, just about getting by, but only a washing machine breakdown or an MOT failure away from losing that security.

On the walk, life is somehow boiled down to its essentials, so that rest/shelter/food and water become the highlight of the morning rather than taken for granted, and a curious cow becomes an object of wonder and beauty, whereas normally cows are things we whizz by or walk straight past without a second glance. Going on a long walk sharpens the senses and gives you a heightened awareness of plants, birds, animals and insects with whom we share the planet. It gives you more of a perspective – a big view across open countryside shows you how very small and insignificant you are – whereas most of the time we are the leading actor in our own drama. In the same way in which going into ancient buildings and churches reveals to us that we are a millisecond blip in the narrative of history. This sounds as if it should be depressing, but in fact it's refreshing. It punctures the ego and provides a reality check. I'm not nearly as important as I think I am – and neither are you. How liberating.

So, refreshed and restored, and knowing that I was two thirds of the way towards my destination for the day, I set off up the track towards the woods. I very much enjoy woodland walking. To be surrounded by trees, bathed in green, surrounded by all that verdant life, is very heaven. Shade and sounds, birds flitting from tree to tree, ferns unfurling their fronds, to walk in a wood is to find solace and shelter, refreshment and renewal. Forest bathing is all the rage in Japan, and there is now an Institute of Forest Bathing here in the UK, with sessions being hosted by Kew and the Forestry Commission to name but two organisations who are spreading the word about how beneficial it is to spend time with trees. My only worry, as ever, was that it's even easier to get lost in a wood as everywhere can look deceptively similar and there's no view out to distant landmarks to guide you. Maybe that's a sign that I'm still a bit of a control freak, still anxious and lacking confidence in my way finding abilities, because actually there is something to be said for getting lost from time to time, following the unknown path rather than sticking to the known, safe, waymarked route. We often find things we didn't even know we were looking for when we allow ourselves to get a little lost. But I was still following my old reliable friend, the Offa's Dyke Path, so the waymarking would be good and my phone map would tell me if I wandered off course, so all would be well.

I loved this brief walk through the middle of the woods, dappled sunlight and shade, emerging into paths along field margins and then suddenly a glorious vista of blue, a whole field of borage, as stunningly beautiful as it is surprising. Across a footbridge and alongside one last field margin and then I was out onto a road on the very outskirts of Monmouth. As ever with the final part of a walk, I hugely underestimated how much further there was to go. I mean, the walk ended in Monmouth and I was – just about – in Monmouth, so that meant I was nearly there – right? However, I

Fig 22. Monnow bridge

was at one far end of the town and the walk was due to end at the diametrically opposite end of town at the Church of St Peter's, Dixton. So, I kept on keeping on, buoyed up by the soundtrack of my iPod, the walk also now enlivened by being able to look at the houses and gardens lining one side of the lane. Eventually I reached the main road and then, slowly but surely, approached the main part of town, starting to pass shops and pubs as I went. Then came the left turn up and over the Monnow Bridge where I just had to stop and take a photo to prove I'd made it.

It's a magnificent and unique structure – the only remaining fortified river bridge in the whole of Great Britain with its gate tower still standing tall. It's now a Grade 1 listed building but has been used for many purposes since its original construction in 1272 – a jail, a munitions store, a lodge, an advertising hoarding, a focus for celebrations and, most significantly, as a toll gate because tolls and taxes largely funded the development of medieval Monmouth. However, to me its major significance was as a major test of my nascent driving abilities. In the days when I was learning to drive, the bridge was still open to traffic, so the novice driver had to work out how to drive up to it and time it to get through its single-track opening, teaching both good driving manners and how to do a hill start all in one. Now it's for pedestrians only and was looking good in the sunshine against the backdrop of a gloriously blue sky.

I have to confess that it did feel rather surreal to be walking up the main street of a busy market town in my full walking gear. Particularly having spent the rest of the day in splendid isolation in the midst of nature. But on the other hand, it did mean that the end of the day's walk was getting steadily closer, and, for a short while, I knew exactly where I was going! Up Monnow Street, along Church Street, past Rossiter's excellent bookshop and the wonderful Savoy Theatre and then hanging a right by St Mary's Church to head for the underpass under the A40 and thence to the River Wye and Monmouth Rowing Club.

But, more importantly, I was bidding a fond and final farewell to the Offa's Dyke Path, a trusty companion and guide for many days, and saying Hello to the Wye Valley Walk, a new companion, who I hoped would be just as good to me as dear old Offa had been. For now, I was confident in my new way because all I had to do was walk along the river to the church. And it was strange to be walking by the river when for so many years I'd looked down on it from a car whizzing along the A40 or sat in a car idling in the queue to get across the traffic lights, or on a Friday afternoon on my way to a retreat at Llangasty stuck in a long queue of traffic. It was nice though to be down by the river – busy and very popular with dog walkers – and fairly soon the river was hidden from sight as I plunged into a path with fenced off fields on one side and riverside scrub on the other. There was slight trepidation in my heart, just in case I managed to miss the turn off to the church, but Mike had assured me that this was impossible and so it proved to be. The path took me into and through the churchyard of St Peter's Dixton, a beautiful, white painted building, kept open by the use of an automated locking/unlocking system – thank you parishioners!

Inside it was a spare, sparse even, but in a good way, good clean space, uncluttered. A good place to just rest and be. It was light, bright and white, with a beautifully carved wooden gallery and a challenging and striking artwork. Almost austere in its bareness but beautiful and welcoming. I sat outside in the shade, content and happy that the day's walk was done and that I was back on home territory, places I knew, places which felt reassuringly familiar. Mike arrived and took many end of day photos, and that was it, final Monday done, now onto Tuesday with Simon.

Day Eleven Stats

    Start time – 9.30 am.

    Finish time – 2.51 pm.

    Duration – 5 hours, 21 minutes.

    Distance walked – 11.0 miles.

    Total ascent – 8,878 ft.

    Total descent – 8,822 ft.

    Avg. speed – 2.3 mph.

Day Twelve: Monmouth to Bishopswood
Walking through My Childhood

12 July 2019

We picked Simon up from his house in Coombe Green and headed off back to St Peter's Church, Dixton. I don't really need to tell you that it was sunny with blue skies anymore – you can almost assume that, and I was certainly beginning to take it for granted, but looking back now I still can't believe how blessed we were with the weather. 'What will you do if it rains?' was another common question pre-walk, to which 'Get wet!' was the only possible answer. I'd have had to keep walking no matter what, but how lovely was it to be walking in these beautiful places in such wonderful weather.

Simon was once more resplendent in his umpiring hat and sporting his England Cricket World Cup winners T Shirt. I was in my walking gear, complete with absurd flowery hat, bought from a market in France, which continued to do an excellent job of shading me from the sun.

We headed off back down through the churchyard towards the river and picked up the Wye Valley Walk path which led us out across some fields, a lovely expansive start to the day. We had a slight blip as to which way we should be going through a gateway but were soon back on track, the Wye Valley Walk already proving herself to be a good companion, as was Simon. It's interesting that when you walk with other people they notice different things to you – part of the joy of accompanied walks. What Simon noticed was the noise of the A40. Initially that wasn't surprising – from the field we climbed up into woodland and were now walking a path very much sandwiched between dual carriageway and river – discovering some very well-hidden away houses along the way. But even after we'd crossed the border back into England and followed the river in taking a 90 degree turn right, heading away from the road, it was still audible for a long while afterwards. Every now and then Simon would say 'Can still hear it', as we were passing through woodland and past all these very lovely houses hidden away in the depths of the countryside, yet the traffic noise was ever present. It struck me, thanks to Simon, how easily we have given up the gift of silence.

I didn't always feel this way. Silence used to scare me. Who knew what I'd have to face up to or confront about myself if I wasn't continually distracted by some sort of noise? Radio for me, usually, an ever-present background sound, comforting and reliable if not always comprehensible. And I know that this isn't unique to me as quite often, when doing baptism and funeral visits to people's homes, there will be a ginormous TV talking away to itself in the corner of the room, white noise for the twenty first century. But part of the training to be a vicar is to go on a silent retreat – terrifying, I know. And the first one I ever went on also included a bonus of watching a film about a monastery of Trappist monks, also silent, obviously. I went in dreading it and came out loving it. I loved my tiny room, just slightly bigger than a cupboard. I loved the lake, right next to the retreat house at Llangasty and found myself reverting to childhood and leaping and jumping about like a mad thing while out walking around it out of the sheer joy of silence. Although there were downsides – eating toast during an otherwise silent breakfast is possibly the noisiest thing in the world!

After that I just fell more and more in love with silence and noticed more and more how hard it is to come by these days. We are lucky enough to live in the middle of beautiful countryside where you'd think it would be much easier to find silence – and it is – but even so there are always cars and other machinery – tractors, JCBs, our neighbour's band saw, planes overhead and even the occasional drone. And whenever we go to stay with friends in London, you are very much aware that it is a city which never sleeps with traffic noise, ambulance sirens, the noise of people in the streets, some sort of soundscape pretty much every hour of the day or night. Nearly every activity we undertake nowadays creates noise, even in gardening we have chainsaws, leaf blowers, lawn mowers, hedge trimmers and rotavators – all really useful and labour-saving pieces of kit but all noisy. And we're now able to carry our own noise with us to screen out the noise we don't want to hear by filling our heads with the noise we do want to hear – our own selection of music, radio or podcasts carried round on Ipod or phone, to wash our brains with sound. Something I too was guilty of for at least parts of this walk.

But silence is never really complete and total silence. There are always the birds tweeting, or even just the sound of our own heart beating and blood thumping round our bodies. So why do I think silence is so important for our mental, physical and spiritual health and wellbeing – important enough that I put my money where my mouth is and take myself off to have a Quiet Day each month and a silent retreat over near Brecon every year? Because it teaches us to just be. Call it meditation or contemplative prayer or whatever you like, but to sit in silence and breathe, to feel the air fill your lungs and leave your lungs and to just focus on that, to still that ever-whirling chatter in our heads, that mix of thoughts, hopes and fears which rushes around all of our brains most of the time – that is a joyous and a glorious thing.

I remember sitting outside while on my pre-ordination retreat – a time of great fear and trepidation for me – and becoming transfixed by the beauty of a fly, just a normal everyday fly that landed on my arm and that nine out of ten times I would simply have jerked my arm to get it to fly off. Have you ever looked at a fly, I mean really looked, seen the iridescent blue colour, the hairs on its fine legs, the veins running through its translucent wings? In the silence, you become aware of your surroundings, aware of nature in all her glory. Suddenly you hear the things which the noise has been screening out – birds singing their hearts out, lambs calling to their mums, things you wouldn't even have noticed in your rush through life become things to notice and give thanks for. Being silent makes you stop. Relax those tensed up shoulders, and just be. If you're a person of faith you can pick a phrase from scripture as a mantra to give your silence focus – 'Be still and know that I am God' is a favourite of mine. If you aren't a follower of any faith, a word or a sound, or simply the resolution to notice when your mind is drawn back into the chaos, notice it, accept it and then draw your attention back to the silence, to the fly, to the daisy, to the sound of a babbling stream, to the texture of the grass beneath your feet. Being silent means that you stop trying to do a million and one things and just focus in on one thing, the one thing needful, being here now, being present wherever you are and being thankful.

Of course, it takes some time to get into the flow of it, and even the best laid plans for silence can end up going hideously wrong – I well remember attempting to conduct a silent vigil for Maundy Thursday one night at Birtsmorton while there was a wedding disco going full blast and very audibly next door. My lovely meditative Taizé chants stood very little chance against Tony Hadley giving his all to singing 'Gold'! However, silence is well worth persevering with – don't be scared, give it a go. To me, entering into silence now is like sinking back into a warm relaxing bath, it embraces me and supports me and sends me back out renewed to face the day. It's definitely not for everyone but for me it's a lifesaver, and I wouldn't be without my times of silence and solitude.

Back on the Wye Valley Walk, I considered myself blessed to be walking with someone who also had an ear for silence, even the lack of it. I suppose, being a baker by profession, Simon had been used to being up and working in the wee small hours, when silence is at its most prevalent – maybe that explained his sensitivity to noise. We emerged from the woodland into some flat and open walking along the riverside at Wyastone Leys. Mike had wondered whether this might have provided an alternative pick up/drop off point for the end of yesterday/beginning of today's walk but judging by the number of notices we saw telling us that this was private property, and we should not deviate from the designated path it was clear that we'd made the right choice in opting for St Peter's instead. This was very much a place where walkers were tolerated rather than welcomed.

Then it was back into woodland, lovely and shady, but you needed to keep an eye out for rogue tree roots acting as trip hazards. Fascinating to see what looked like a cliff face in the middle of the woods at Seven Sisters Rocks and then suddenly we were in the middle of an emerald green playing field, bright green well mown grass and even some toilets – open and available. We'd arrived at the Biblins and the first of our three bridges of the day, a chain bridge built by the Forestry Commission. This magnificent structure is built on the site of what was originally – back in 1919 – a winch point for moving logs across the river. In 1924 it was converted to a footbridge and then in 1957 upgraded to the wire mesh suspension bridge we had just used, although much of that original construction has since been repaired and replaced. It comes complete with a notice warning of grave consequences if it was misused – no running, bouncing or swaying allowed!

Simon remembered camping there and crossing the bridge as a small child. He took a photo of it on his phone and sent it off to his brother who identified it without any help in moments. Looking at the photos I took on the day it seems a phenomenal piece of bridge building and engineering – since adapted to make it wheelchair accessible too. Though on the day I remember being slightly nervous and glad to get safely across. Also, a bit shamefaced and surprised that I'd never been here before. That all this gorgeousness was literally just down the road from where I'd lived for ten years or more and I'd never experienced it until now. Better late than never I guess but thinking back on those childhood times, I was very bookish, lived a lot in my head, although I did still climb trees and go for walks, even the odd run. But going for a walk together wasn't really part of our family dynamic. I guess there was always other stuff to do. Mum and Dad were both holding down full-on full-time jobs, looking after parents and a stroppy teenager and a massive garden. So maybe it's not that surprising. But I still felt more than a little ashamed of this omission. Then again, I do remember being dragged on a couple of walks as a teenager and being a sulky nightmare – so it's no wonder Mum and Dad didn't feel up to giving it a go. I think I'm transposing me now back to me as a teenager and that's just not realistic. Which is good – right? Means I've made some progress somewhere along the line.

Anyway, having crossed the river we were now on a very well used three lane highway equivalent of a path. Lovely to walk along, no danger of going wrong, meeting and acknowledging dog walkers and joggers as we went, the river now accompanying us on our left-hand side.

In a relatively short time we arrived at Symonds Yat East, with its hotels and boat trips and general touristy stuff. It was busy with people and a great contrast to the greenness and peace and quiet we'd just walked through. This was getting to be quite the day of contrasts. Despite being full of hotels and cafes and coach parties – or maybe because of that – there were very few places you could actually just sit and eat and drink your own supplies, but we managed to find a place to hunker down overlooking the river and all the pleasure boats awaiting their first trip out of the day. We could survey the very nice-looking houses over the other side of the river with their gardens running down to the riverbank itself and we got a bird's eye view of the hand pulled cable ferry, being operated by an obviously very fit young man.

This is one of two hand pulled ferries on this short stretch of the River Wye, but back in the early nineteenth century it is reckoned that there were twenty-five of them between Ross and Chepstow, many of which would have been similar to this one operating from near the Saracen's Head today. The ferryman uses the overhead tensioned cable to pull himself and his passengers across the river, with the boat being attached to the cable by a rope to prevent it from drifting away downstream. It's a great tourist attraction, but also a very useful and important part of local life for those wishing to travel between Symonds Yat East and West. Their only other options would be to walk the three miles back to the Biblins Bridge which we'd just come across or to take a five mile road trip upstream to Huntsham Bridge. So much easier to just pay the small charge which goes toward maintenance of the ferry and payment of the ferryman, and people, animals and bicycles can get pulled across the river in a trice.

We don't really think much about bridges now, unless they are closed like the one near Welsh Bicknor or impassable because of flooding. Only then do you realise how relatively few crossing points there are of the Wye and the Severn, and how vital they are to just getting around. I suspect that historically, especially in medieval times, people would have been much more aware of the vital role which rivers and their bridges played in day to day life – for example the multipurpose Monnow Bridge I'd walked over the day before.

But there are also life bridges which get us across from one phase of life to another, and our walk today through landscapes familiar to me from childhood and teenage years made me think about that crucial transition from shy, bookish, uncommunicative teenager to the slightly more confident adult I was to become. University played a key role in this, giving me a whole new bunch of friends, broadening and deepening my faith and enabling me to transition from living at home to learning to look after myself, do my own laundry, manage money, cook for myself – all those key life skills I was able to pick up with the safety net of coming back home for the holidays. Oh – and yes – got a degree as well! Plus, far more crucially and importantly, university was where I met and got engaged to Michael the love of my life, and the hero of this story really in terms of all the planning and logistics.

I went to Brasenose College, Oxford, a fact which I rarely speak about, simply because being an Oxford graduate makes people think you are either rich and/or clever and I'm definitely neither. I tried out for Oxford using the attitude which has taken me to so many challenging and rewarding places – didn't think I could do it, so let's give it a go and find out! And the decision to put Brasenose as my first preference college was again down to sheer stubbornness. My single sex school advised applying to single sex colleges, but after five years at an all-girls school I had had more than enough of that and would rather have not gone to Oxford at all then ended up with more cloistered living.

And so, I ended up moving from a rural area to the centre of

Oxford, meeting and making friends with an eclectic bunch of Northerners and experiencing a faith community full on for the first time in College Chapel and the Christian Union. Up until now I had been a cradle Christian, finding faith from parents, school and the local church. Now, for the first time, I was meeting folk from a wide spectrum of the Christian faith – Catholic, high Anglican, Evangelical – it was fascinating and stimulating and made you actually think about what you believed in. I was and remain a faith mongrel – happy in the middle ground, appreciating the beauty of a High Anglican service, the energy and biblical knowledge of an evangelical service, and loving the community which formed around college chapel. Our chaplain at the beginning of our college years was Father Jeffrey John, later to become famous for sadly not becoming Bishop of Reading, yet another example of the Church of England shooting itself in the foot over same-sex relationships. His ferocious intellect made for some fascinating and challenging sermons, and he prepared Mike and me for confirmation into the Church of England – which was also when we got together as a couple.

University was a great bridge from childhood to adulthood in so many ways, but it definitely moved me from a childlike faith – no bad thing – to a more adult, expansive, curious faith. Foundations were laid that would bear fruit much, much later in life, and help me cross another, much scarier bridge, from member of the congregation to priest. If you'd told me that back in my college days I'd never have believed it possible. Then again, I wouldn't have believed I could walk 150 miles and here I was, nearly having done just that!

Having eaten and drunk to restore ourselves after the first couple of hours of fairly flat and easy walking, Simon and I set off again onto a more challenging section of today's walk, already challenging enough in that it was set to be a long day – at fourteen miles or so one of the longest of the trip. And there was added jeopardy thrown in, all to do with those vital bridges. Our next target was the bridge at Welsh Bicknor, known as the Black Bridge or Stowfield Viaduct, vital to enable us to cross the river once more. However, this bridge had been found to be structurally unsound and so had been closed and barricaded off for over two years. In fact, a couple who I know who had been doing the Wye Valley Walk leg by leg had been caught out by the closure and had then had to walk many miles out of their way to get back on track. Luckily, my parents gave us insider knowledge, and were sure they had seen on the local news that the bridge had been temporarily repaired and re-opened to walkers. We researched this online, and it definitely seemed to be true. However, being a natural born worrier, I was still worried! We had now reached the point in today's walk where we had to make a choice. We could stick with the Wye Valley Walk and assume if there was still a problem with the bridge, there would be warning notices alerting and diverting us. Or we could make a fairly major diversion via Huntsham Bridge, which would land us securely on the other side of the river, but which meant a long stretch of boring road walking and took us well out of our way.

We stuck with the Wye Valley Walk – I'm not sure Simon and I even discussed it, though I do remember making sure I read a notice fixed to a post as we crossed the road and headed up into the woods – but thankfully it was nothing to do with the walk. Simon now expertly took the lead as we embarked upon paths which took us deep into woodland, had lush summer growth alongside them and didn't appear to have been much used – which could well be due to the previous path closure. They were also single person tracks and pretty up and down in their gradient so that you needed to stay alert to both the rocky terrain underfoot and to brambles and other vegetation flopping over the path. It was pretty tough going and I was very glad I had turned down my dad's request to walk this bit with me, as although he was at this time a very fit eighty-four year old, this was challenging walking for someone thirty years his junior, let alone for him. There were some bright spots! It was very beautiful, and very tranquil to be walking through this verdant greenness – I've been reading a number of books recently about the beneficial effects of being in nature on both physical but primarily on mental health, and the detrimental effects of being separated from nature by our current, increasingly urban lifestyle. On this part of the walk, it felt as if we were being embraced by nature, engulfed by it really. One of my favourite quotations is from a poem called 'The Garden' by Andrew Marvell, a seventeenth century metaphysical poet and it goes 'Annihilating all that's made to a green thought in a green shade.' That's what it felt like to walk in the midst of all this beautiful green.

And then there are the places that you find walking these paths which you would never come across any other way. We had circumnavigated Huntsham Hill and were once more walking alongside the river when suddenly the path opened up to reveal a house – a Hansel and Gretel cottage in the woods – with the most amazing garden with tree house and den and swinging tyres for whichever lucky children were growing up here. I really wanted to take a photo, but felt that this would intrude upon private space, so refrained and now I begin to wonder if it even existed at all. Yet the memory is very strong, the envy of those children growing up with such freedom in such a beautiful space and also the wonder of how on earth one accessed such a dwelling in the middle of winter with snow and ice on the ground. I have hunted for this place on maps since and can only think it is in the middle of Elliot's Wood, some distance from any roadways. Maybe they go in and out via the river on their doorstep – again what a fairy tale place to live and to be.

Whatever the hardships of winter, in summer it was truly magical.

On we walked, through Elliot's Wood and were now heading for Symonds Yat Rock. There was an amazing flight of decking stairs in the middle of nowhere to assist us up a more or less vertical incline, with reassuring Wye Valley Walk signs, and also signs pointing off to the Rock, but we were on a mission and not in the mood for detours so kept on keeping on along our set path – thanks to Simon's assiduous navigation, reassuring me that we were indeed still on the right track. Finally, we came to a particularly rocky bit of walking, which turned out to be Coldwell Rocks, and a challenging descent around the back of a new or renovated house where we heard other voices for the first time in a while. Not for the first or last time on this walk I was grateful for my sturdy walking pole, providing extra stability and support. Once we were back on blessedly flat and open ground, it was a longish but pretty straightforward walk along by the river until the bridge of destiny which would decide our fate that day. Would we be able to get across, as I hoped and prayed we would, or would we have to turn tail, retrace our steps of a couple of hours walking, and then walk the whole thing all over again on the other side of the river. I really didn't think I could cope with that! On the other hand, if the walk had taught me anything it was that one's body is capable of amazing feats provided one's brain doesn't get in the way . . .

We continued on across fields and grassland, the river a constant and tranquil companion on our left-hand side. And we did come across some cyclists travelling in the opposite direction, which gave me a little more hope that our bridge would be open. Soon we came up to the stretch identified on our map as 'Dismtld Railway', which ran straight and true, right along the riverbank. Simon picked out what looked like a massive old house up high and set back on the other side of the river, and we speculated for some time about what it could be. On the map it looked as though it must be The Green, possibly a big old farmhouse, and another building set in the midst of fields with no apparent means of access – a very impressive sight though, particularly given the distance we were viewing it from. This was a very pleasant distraction, but, bit by bit, little by little, we were approaching the point of no return – or potentially the point of immediate return. . . .

What really astonished me and what I'd been totally unprepared for was the sight of a massive disused factory in the middle of what felt like nowhere, but then did make sense of the railway, and indeed the bridge, which I only now noticed was down on the map as Viaduct (FB). We agreed to stop for our break just short of the bridge, but walked on to it just to make sure that it was really open – although from a distance it did look promising . . . and to my immense relief, new temporary boarding had been installed on the walking surface of the bridge itself and on either side and it was very much a fully functioning bridge to get us across the River Wye and onto the next phase of our journey.

What about the massive, abandoned factory in the middle of nowhere though – what was that all about??? Some research revealed a fascinating history, and a timely reminder that the beautiful Forest of Dean area also has a strong industrial heritage. It all began back in 1912 when one Harold J. Smith bought land at Stowfield, close to the River Wye and the steam railway junction, and erected the Lydbrook Cable Works, employing a modest forty people. The outbreak of the First World War led to them being kept busy making the cable needed for field telephones, about 15,000 miles of it, and the workforce expanded to 650 but with the end of the war, business slumped and went into the hands of the official receiver in 1920. However, in 1925 the Edison Swan Electric Company bought the business, and used its greater resources to expand the factory, which again played a vital role in the Second World War as they possessed one of only four machines in the world needed to make lead alloy tube which was required for Petroleum Lines Under the Ocean aka PLUTO which was what allowed the Allied Invasion Force to be kept supplied with fuel as they advanced through Europe. In the late 1940s, Edison Swan became part of Siemens Cable Works, and by then about 1,100 people were employed at Stowfield. In 1966 the factory was bought by Reed Paper Group, and was closed down and abandoned in 2003. However, since our passing by, and while researching the site's history, I came across a report dated February 2021 saying that the site was then being renovated and split into work units and warehouses, good to know that it may well be back in use by now and a really beautiful spot to work from.

Strange to think that cable made in this isolated, beautiful rural spot played a key part in both World Wars, but when we returned to the small slipway, opposite a little hut, where we'd decided to sit and have our break, there was a somewhat spikey, warlike notice warning us off 'Keep off the boats. Surviving Trespassers Prosecuted.' – definitely a territorial mood being struck here! Clearly the natives were not entirely friendly in these parts, but we were able to sit and enjoy a well-earned rest safe and undisturbed by any irate owners of riverbank or landing stage. Although we did see a couple of canoeists float past, and as we crossed the blessed bridge, a few more floated by. Then it was farewell faithful friend of a bridge, and many, many thanks for being open and safe to cross.

And onward, ever onward to the final part of our day. After a very short walk, we emerged once more into open grassland, with masses of people in it – a great shock to the system when we'd been pretty much on our own for most of the day. It was a gang of young people – doing the Duke of Edinburgh's Award I think

– all congregating in front of the amazing looking Welsh Bicknor Church. I took photos and wondered about stopping to visit but the final stretch of the day didn't really permit it.

This was the point of the walk at which I texted Mike to let him know we'd made it across the Black Bridge and were on our way to the pickup point at Bishopswood Village Hall. As we walked once more along the riverbank, but this time with the river on our right, we encountered more groups of youngsters with large rucksacks, getting to the end of their D of E expedition. Some of them were in better shape than others, including one girl who was carrying her rucksack in her arms rather than on her back!!! Across the river I began to notice familiar landmarks. As we walked the final big loop of the river, I could see the Lydbrook Hotel with its car park opposite which I vaguely remembered coming to as a teenager with my mates to park up and do what teenagers do – generally just hang around, waiting for something to happen!

We were now literally on the home straight, walking across open grassland, and I could see the caravan park – static caravans really – with its garage and shop run by a friend of my mum and dad's, and knew that opposite was the road that led up to Bishopswood Church and Bishopswood House. It really was a case of so close and yet so far, which made the final bit of the walk agony as we plunged once more into woodland, but woodland with waist high nettles and brambles and many roots to trip the unwary – a trip hazard I fell foul of on at least one occasion! I think it was being so close to the end of the walk, yet it feeling still so far away which made it such tough going for me – Simon was very much his usual enigmatic self! The woodland closed in around us, apart from a little bit more Dismtld Railway, so we just had to keep keeping on, trusting and knowing really that we were on the right path and that there really wasn't that much further to go. Very much like a journey of faith really. Those times when you can't see the wood for the trees, don't know where you're headed or how to keep on going, it's faith, hope and trust which enables you to keep putting one foot in front of the other, keep believing, keep on keeping on. Faith, hope, trust and good companions, encouraging you and leading the way as Simon had done for me all day long. Finally, we emerged from the woods and could see ahead of us that blessed sight on a hilltop – Goodrich Castle – which meant the end was almost in sight.

The Castle has a special place in my heart as I was, during that time between school and university, deputy weekend custodian of this very lovely ancient monument. There I earned my first ever pay packet for working weekends and bank holidays taking ticket money and only occasionally having to race out to chastise folk who had attempted to climb up the tower . . . The sight of the castle always brings back happy memories, but never more so than on this occasion as it meant we really were nearly there now!

We just had to cross the field, avoiding the large plume of water being pumped out of the river to irrigate the crop – although by this stage of the day both Simon and I were so hot, dusty and sweaty that a good dowsing would actually have been quite welcome! We hauled ourselves up the steps and across the stone magnificence which is Kerne Bridge – a bridge I had crossed daily for more years that I care to remember on the way to and from school from the age of eight to eighteen. I'd hardly ever walked across it though, but at that precise moment I was more focussed on simply getting to Bishopswood Village Hall rather than savouring the final bridge crossing of the day. Over the bridge, turn right, down the road a little way and suddenly there we were, and there the trusty Skoda was to whisk us home in air-conditioned comfort at the end of a long hot day.

We'd crossed three bridges, and one national border. We'd revisited both our childhoods to some extent and above all, we'd had a great walk. And I had definitely discovered the other great benefit of a walking companion – they ensure that you keep going and, if they have Simon's navigational skills, they keep you on the straight and narrow, heading in the right direction – something I was to find myself sorely in need of the following day – but that's for the next chapter. For now, I'd just like to thank Simon for being my walking buddy on one of the longest, most challenging days of the walk – couldn't have done it without you, my friend.

Day Twelve Stats

Start time – 8.39 am.

Finish time – 2.59 pm.

Duration – 6 hours, 20 minutes.

Distance walked – 14.5 miles.

Total ascent – 925 ft.

Total descent – 896 ft.

Avg. speed – 2.6 mph.

Day Thirteen: Unlucky for Some
From Bishopswood Village Hall to the Appropriately Named Moody Cow

13 July 2019

Day thirteen, a Wednesday in case you're losing track, dawned bright and sunny, just like all the previous days. However, a cloud had appeared for consideration upon the horizon – the forecast for Friday, due to be the final day of the walk, was for rain – heavy rain. Bearing this in mind, we were mulling over whether it would be either possible or advisable to turn the two shorter walks planned for Thursday and Friday – a nice, easy gentle finish to the expedition – into one final mega walk to get me over the finish line before the rains came. Let's wait and see what actually happened, but in the meantime, all was set fair for day thirteen, and my parents came along to see me off at the start.

They had wanted to join me for at least part of the walk – and could easily have done so being wonderfully fit and well – but the way the schedule of walking had panned out, I was doing this leg on a Wednesday, the day when Mum runs a monthly lunch club, better known as The Oldies Lunch – an ironic name given the vast majority of those attending are probably younger than her ... Dad goes along to help put up tables so they weren't able to walk the first part of the day with me, although it was lovely to have them there to offer moral support and to see me on my way, even if the directions they offered were somewhat confusing ....

What can you say about the two people who gave you life and so

Fig 23. Mum and Dad

much else? They brought me up to know that I was loved, absolutely and unconditionally. The longer I live the more I appreciate what an amazing and vital gift this was. They taught me so much between them – my dad was literally my teacher at primary school level, ensuring that I was stretched and challenged. My mum taught me to cook and to sew, vital life skills. Her attempt to teach me to drive ended after one lesson – wisely for both our sakes! They demonstrated to me what a long and happy marriage looks like.

My mum worked as a teacher all her life, once I was old enough to go to school, so it never occurred to me that women didn't have careers. We always ate our evening meal together, round the table, a meal cooked from scratch, using vegetables grown in the garden, and though as a teenager I hated the 'how was your day' chats, it meant I never had any doubt that they cared about me, how I was doing, and that I could always talk to them about anything, anything at all.

Family was vitally important to them. They moved house and job to be closer to both sets of parents as they started to age and succumb to illness. My mum moved in with my grandad at one point when my nan was in hospital, leaving me and my dad to fend for ourselves, which we managed rather successfully! And in later years, they would care for my gran, commuting between home and The Plough, giving so generously of their time and care because family was important, and looking after those who had given so much to them was simply part of who they were and are. They worked hard, always. Looking back, they made the transition from working class – daughter of a carpenter, son of a gardener – to middle class – head of home economics, head of a primary school – but they never forgot or were ashamed of their roots – rather the opposite. Roots were really important to them, especially my mum, and the fact that we now live in the house where she was born means an awful lot to her.

And faith was always a part of life. They got me baptised at All Saints Hollybush, a church which remains important to them. Mum would always do flower arrangements, run flower festivals, bake for whatever church function was happening, Dad would read the lesson and attend regularly, taking me along as a child and teenager. It laid the groundwork, started the habit, made faith and church a normal part of life. This is something which is now worryingly rare amongst children – and parents. Sunday is a family day with so much activity to fit in, and church is not first on the list at all. Yet church attendance, and going to church schools, gave me a rich biblical heritage, a familiarity with hymns which I love, and got me used to being in the building, following and taking part in the service, knowing when to stand up and sit down – all these things are such barriers to those who don't have the grounding which I was lucky enough to have, thanks to Mum and Dad.

I have so much to thank them for – just being the amazing, wonderful pair they are today is enough – funny and busy, amazingly fit and well for their ages – but the gift of knowing that I am loved and the gift of a thorough grounding and foundation in the faith which we share – those are two fundamental strands of my character. Without those, I wouldn't be the person I am today, and I definitely wouldn't be embarking on day thirteen of a fifteen-day walk, as stubbornness runs in the family too!

I clambered up and away from the village hall, whose sloping surrounding banks I had been responsible for planting – a Herculean task which it now seems madness to have undertaken, but not doing too badly. Crossing the road, I followed the footpath signs which led up between the houses. As I passed close by the door of one house it opened and a man stepped out – I don't know who was more surprised, him or me, but he was very kind, asked where I was walking to and checked that I had enough water with me, before entering the door of the house opposite. I climbed up, and up and up, ascending Leys Hill towards Leys Hill Farm. Up past all the houses, then along the enclosed edge of fields on a very well-marked path, which was still my old familiar friend the Wye Valley Walk which had got me from Monmouth to this point and which I was aiming to stay on for most of the day. The trouble would come when I had to leave it, but more of that later.

The walk then levelled out and was good walking along clear wide tracks, often skirting houses or the bottom of gardens, and giving good views out across the countryside, at one point looking across the village of Walford where I'd spent most of my childhood, towards Walford Church. Like many villages in the three counties, Walford has seen a lot of changes over the years. It now has a real mix of old and new houses, many sporting solar panels which would have been unheard of when we first came to live in the village, and at that time there was a garage and a post office/shop, both long gone. The school, opposite where my parents live, has expanded, community activities have contracted – although the newly built Bishopswood Village Hall does buck that trend, being a centre for many classes, meetings, lunches and even a popular venue for wedding receptions. But it has also become necessary to drive in order to live in the countryside, given the dearth of bus services and the closure of the rail lines I'd walked along yesterday, back in the 1960s. Folk have become much more individually minded, much less community minded, something which you could say will have been exacerbated by the isolation caused by the Coronavirus crisis we are living through as I write this. However, there are signs of the opposite occurring, signs that folk are reaching out to help and to get to know their neighbours in a way they didn't before, some silver linings which may help us as we move into an uncertain future.

All this would never have crossed my mind as I ambled along the forest track. I was just enjoying the experience of being surrounded by trees, yet not having to fight my way through nettles and brambles – although tree roots were still a hazard! I couldn't recall walking this path as a teenager, but as I moved from Leys Hill over onto Bulls Hill things became more familiar – although I confess I did have a bit of a losing my way moment at the transition point around a house called The Rock. Luckily there was no one home apart from a ginger and white cat who regarded me curiously but did nothing whatsoever to help guide me on my way. Eventually I worked it out and continued on along familiar paths on Bulls Hill, coming out by a little group of houses which I had to circumnavigate and then started downhill towards Howle Hill when I came upon a most unexpected planting. A vineyard of all things! I knew we had vineyards in England – we buy wine for our holiday cottage from Lovells Vineyard just down the road from us in Welland – but I had no idea an optimistic person was attempting to grow wine on a hillside in Walford. Wondering whether it was for public consumption or private pleasure I walked on down the hill, over a footbridge, round a house and crossed a lane to begin my ascent of Howle Hill. This was good walking along a track used to access several houses – I remembered tracks like this with many hidden houses from my teenage activist days when I delivered leaflets for the Liberal party as it was then, Lib Dems as they are now. Until then I had no idea how many houses there were up tracks and along rough roadways on these hills.

Walking reveals things about place and person. You find things like this vineyard which you would only find by walking through it – it's not visible from the road and would probably even be tricky to pick up from the air now that we live in the age of the drone. And walking reveals things about the person doing the walking, the limitations of the imagination, the things that you can do if you dare to dream, the way your mind can float free – provided the path is well marked and you know where you're going – while your body takes care of the rest. The fact that the old cliché of one step at a time is really very powerful. How many times have I allowed myself to be put off doing something – like writing this book – because of the size and scale of the task. How many years had I failed to get around to doing a walk like this because of so many very good reasons/excuses – no time, too unfit, too difficult to organize. Yet the whole thing had fallen into place very quickly and easily, in a matter of months from Valentine's Day that February until the 1 July start date – four and a half months had been time enough to set it all up, to get most generous support and sponsorship, to book accommodation, buy boots, practise long walks and phone usage and above all, to have the support and encouragement of husband, family and friends. And now, July 2020, I thank God for whatever pushed me to doing it then, as I'm not sure how long it will be until I would be able to do a walk like that again, how long it will be before any of us can freely undertake this sort of expedition in our current situation. So, if you are contemplating doing something but think there is all the time in the world for you to get it done, think again. I'm not saying a global pandemic will get in your way, but there are always so many good reasons not to do something, but only one incontrovertible reason to seize the day – we none of us know what the future holds, so carpe diem, take heart, take courage and step out in faith.

And stepping out in itself sorts you out –*Solvitur ambulando* – it is solved by walking. Knotty problems and difficult dilemmas can somehow sort themselves out as you walk, the solution dropping into your mind as if by magic, some sort of alchemy between being outside, being in nature, letting your mind float free and your feet do the worrying. What I had been worrying about was missing the point at which the path headed off this very convenient track and plunged straight down a quite precipitous field. Finally, I'd started being able to read contours, Dave would have been so proud! However, I didn't miss it and set off down the field, aided by my trusty walking pole. As I crossed over a track, I was brought up slightly short by a sign stating there was a diversion to the path, but I decided that this was an out-of-date notice and carried on, emerging triumphantly onto the Coughton road for a short while. The signed route then took me nervously through a farmyard, which always worries me, but no problems here and then I was climbing up through a field towards my next set of close together contour lines which would take me up and into Chase Wood.

However, as I climbed I espied up to my right that nirvana for all walkers – a bench – and so headed for it right away as I had learned my lesson on never walking past a bench when it's coming up to break time as you never do know where your next bench is coming from . . . Brilliantly, as I came up to it, I saw that it was a bench with a name – Bob's Bench. A great boon for the weary walker, and with a fabulous view to sit and contemplate while eating and drinking.

As I got ready, reluctantly, to leave this haven behind, a man came through the gate I was about to go through, heading in the opposite direction. He was clearly a local and let me know that the bench had been placed there in memory of Bob, father of the current owner of the farm, who was very fond of this view. It reminded me of Bob James, husband of Revd Julie James, our incumbent, and a great walker and climber in his day, still very involved in scouting and in supervising Duke of Edinburgh expeditions – a real outdoors man and so an inspiration to me as I plugged myself into my iPod ready to journey on.

And fairly shortly, I needed all the inspiration I could get as the path was as steep as the contour lines suggested – funny that – and pretty overgrown in places. But there were two positive factors to hang on to – it was fern fronds and bracken rather than nettles and brambles, and the path remained clear to follow even through the undergrowth. I made good use of my trusty multi-purpose walking pole to clear the way and eventually emerged onto a wider path at the top of the hill, having circumvented some interesting looking earthworks which the map tells me was a fort, with a trig point of 203 metres. The path was now wide and true and reassuringly free from undergrowth so I could easily follow it past Hill Farm, through Merrivale Woods and out into fields with a lovely view over the town of Ross-on-Wye. Not Ross from its best side though. Like most towns it has a commercial, industrial estate side and a more scenic touristy side – here I saw the vast expanse of industrial units and housing estates stretched out before me. And while it may not have been exactly scenic it was a very welcome sight, as getting to Ross marked the halfway point on today's walk for me and I was due another break, plus being my home town, I knew where there were some handy public toilets – or very convenient conveniences.

However, as is so often the way on this trip, no sooner was an end in sight than I contrived to get lost. I wonder why this happens so consistently. Is it that I relax and stop paying attention, or on this occasion was it because I assumed being on the outskirts of town meant I knew where I was? Anyhow, I made the rookie error of seeing a stile in the hedge and assuming that's the way I was meant to go, whereas a proper study of the map showed me that I should be on the original side of the hedge where, once I looked in the right direction, my onward passage was screamingly obvious. How often are we seduced by the open gateway, the tempting stile, when our way lies along quite another route?

Anyhow, philosophical questions aside, I made it into the outskirts of Ross, wound my way up through the town, daring to not always follow the Wye Valley Walk as this time I really did know where I was going. I paid a visit to the public toilets and very clean and tidy they were too – many thanks to Ross Town Council – and headed for the river to resume my acquaintance with the Wye, and, hopefully, find a pleasantly situated bench for my lunchtime break.

Initially I walked along a path through pleasant open parkland, with spectacular sculpture to enjoy. There were empty benches along the way, but the path and surroundings were quite busy with walkers, dog walkers, buggy pushers and other good citizens of Ross, taking the air, so I plodded on. The rowing club doesn't like visitors, so forced me to take a detour path around it, which didn't endear the rowers to me . . . particularly as I was becoming increasingly desperate for a sit down. To distract myself, I looked back towards the town and saw the more scenic side of Ross-on-Wye, beloved of a thousand post cards, with the church spire as a landmark giving height and grandeur to the composition. However, trudging onward ever onward away from the town I came to the bridge carrying the A40 dual carriageway over the river, and there, on the handily placed pile supporting the bridge, I sat and took my ease. It was a somewhat noisy ease as the traffic thundered above me, but it does mean that every time I drive over this particular bit of dual carriageway I am reminded of that day and that short break which the bridge afforded me, and I am grateful.

And I guess it's also a reminder that as we motorists whizz past at increasing speeds in our hermetically sealed vehicles, we miss out. Sure, we can still take in the view if it is safe for us to lift our eyes from the road for a moment and we're in the mood to appreciate it. If we aren't too absorbed in our own thoughts, our phone conversation (hands free of course), our road rage or our sat nav instructions. But what about all that lies beneath us, that we never see? The river, the fields, the farmers working to grow food for us to eat, the canoeists or rowers giving it their all, the birds and the bees working away – we miss all those sights and sounds and smells which are freely available to the walker. And because we don't see them, we think they are of no consequence, that our environment will keep going whatever, but it won't and it doesn't and unless we stop and take notice then we are heading for an even bigger crisis than the one we currently find ourselves in.

However, enough of that, I picked myself up, sorted myself out and headed off on the last leg of today's walk, the last bit of solo walking I would do on this trip. And given I'd got lost slightly twice in the morning and was to get lost more seriously twice in the afternoon, the joy of solitude was this time outweighed by how handy it would have been to have had a trusty navigator with me.

At first, all went swimmingly, with straightforward field walking along by the river. Then the river turned away and I continued straight on along another bit of dismantled railway. I was worried that I might miss the point at which the path left the disused railway, but that was straightforward, along another field margin but blessedly easy walking – although any field margin brought back memories of earlier in the walk! I nearly re-joined the river at Backney Common but the path skirted past it, across a farm track and into more fields. I was making good time and heading towards my next big waymark – the wondrously named Hole-in-the-Wall. This is one of those intriguing names of villages which I'd often seen on a signpost on the old road from Ledbury to Ross-on-Wye but never visited, so I was looking forward to finally seeing what the village was like. Onward ever onward on the clearly marked path, but then I hit a snag and couldn't quite work out which way to go. I headed one way alongside a crop of maize where there appeared to be a path but when I'd got all the way along the field, I arrived at a fence with no apparent onward route despite looking every which way. And I'm always so reluctant to admit defeat and turn back – walking back over ground you've already walked always feels like such a lot of wasted effort.

Yet again, I think I was heading for a wooded area, knowing that woods were part of the next phase of the journey, but I think what tripped me up here was that I was looking out for a field boundary, clearly marked on the map but which had since been grubbed out. Of course, once I got myself back on the right path, it all fell into place and was very obvious, but it took a little time and I felt rather foolish as I walked alongside the wooded plantation, now magically restored to its correct place on the map. Then it was over a very definitely still in place field boundary, passing a large number of cows on my way across a couple of fields – thankfully they remained scornfully disinterested in me and mainly lying down, and then up into another patch of woodland where I met a man walking the Wye Valley Walk in the opposite direction – first person I'd bumped into doing that. Eventually I emerged out onto the road opposite Orchard Cottage and felt a sense of relief as all I had to do was turn left and keep going on along the road and I would fairly shortly arrive at Hole-in-the-Wall. I resisted the temptation to detour off across Foy Bridge to Foy Church as it was getting late in the day and long in the walk and arrived at the charming hamlet of Hole-in-the-Wall in good spirits. The village noticeboard proudly proclaimed the unusual name of the hamlet, just in case visitors were in any doubt.

However, my good mood at being at the final waymark on today's walk – the point at which I texted Mike to let him know to start thinking about leaving home to come and pick me up – soon changed because at this point I needed to leave the Wye Valley Walk and join the Herefordshire Trail and do you think I could find that Herefordshire Trail – if so, think again!

Throughout the walk, I'd been using my mobile phone as a tracker, recording where I was walking in real time so that it now provides a record of where I was, times I got lost or took a wrong turn, and was helpful at the time in showing me that I was not yet on the right track. The problem, yet again, was assumptions. I was tired, I was hot and sweaty, I just needed to find the right path and as Mike unwisely put it in a text back to me 'It should be all Herefordshire Trail looking at map. See you at Moody Cow.' That text is timed at 2.53 pm to which I texted back 'Lost already so not great.' And if you look at my track on the phone map, it looks like a toddler has taken a pen and moved it back and forth, back and forth over pretty much the same piece of ground. I'd stood at that noticeboard and seen a footpath sign pointing the way up and to the right. I knew that that was what I was looking for – a right turn to take me off the Wye Valley Walk, onto the Herefordshire Trail – so I obstinately persisted in trying to make it the path I wanted and needed it to be. I tried about three different pathways and driveways and tracks up to field gateways, luckily each time having the sense to see from my phone map that this wasn't the way but not having the sense to work out where the path I actually needed was. I must have wasted a good twenty minutes on trying to make the path I needed materialise in a place it wasn't meant to be. And so, in my terms, God sent me another set of guardian angels – don't know whether you remember my previous guardian angels – the farmer mowing a path through his crop of potatoes and the man who had cleared the very overgrown path for me literally just before I needed to walk along it – but the third lot were a couple out walking their dog. I had fortunately decided to give up this siren wrong path as a bad joke and returned to the noticeboard which was the last place I felt secure in knowing where I was. As I did so, a couple emerged from a tall mass of shrubby undergrowth BEHIND the Hole-in-the-Wall sign, and suddenly there also was the waymark for the Herefordshire Trail. Alleluia, praise the Lord! But I also felt like a total idiot, and I think shared some of this with the couple as we chatted, and they couldn't have been nicer, kinder, or more interested in what I was doing. Walkers are good people in my experience, engaged, interested, always ready to stop and chat – or even just a nod or a quick Hi or Hello as you pass – it's a lovely way of saying Yes, I see you, I acknowledge your humanity and your equal right to walk these ways and to exist on this planet – or maybe I'm reading too much into it!

So, I embraced the Herefordshire Trail and headed off across the fields of quiescent cows, happy in the knowledge that all my problems were at an end and it was now to be all plain sailing . . . If you've read this far, you'll know by now that this portends disasters yet to come. Hold that thought, as at first it really was all good. Clearly signed, good walking across fields alongside a woodland plantation, Eaton Park. I could see on the map that I then needed to take a sharp right turn along a track, followed by a left turn onto another farm track, leading to a gateway out onto the A449, the Ledbury to Ross road. Then all that I needed to do was cross straight over the road, walk around another couple of fields, down what looked like a track on the map to Wobage Farm, from there onto the B4224 to Upton Bishop and my day was done. Had I been able to fly a drone up and see what was to come I would have stuck to the busy A449 and the less busy B4224 and so arrived at my destination in a much better mood . . .

As it was, the first indication that this wasn't going to be an altogether straightforward final part of the walk was that the waymarks disappeared totally as soon as I'd crossed the road. Nothing daunted, I continued down the first field margin, taking in a very beautiful view of distant hills across a cornfield dotted with bright red poppies, those same hills I'd been walking along earlier that day. I carried on following the map I carried, backed up by the phone tracker which confirmed that this time I really was heading the right way – right into the next field hugging the boundary, then a left still in the same field down the long boundary

– Dave's voice in my head telling me to look at the map, see which side of the boundary the path went and stick to it. All good so far. And then, disaster struck in the shape of a very overgrown green lane, just about passable, but with brambles to snag you as you went and grass grown so long that it hid the pitfalls and potholes, and the brambles grabbed at you and tripped you up. Nowhere near as bad as what Julian and I had encountered on our way to Bromyard, but, at the end of a long hot day, on the final part of this leg of the walk, it wasn't what I needed. I battled my way through in high dudgeon and emerged at the other end in a state that my grandad or my mum might have described as tamping – cross, frustrated, cheesed off, railing against landowners who didn't keep footpaths in better shape, and against myself for having the damn fool idea of doing this walk in the first place. It might have been around now that I received what I now see was a lovely encouraging text from my dear husband, telling me he had arrived and was parked in a bus stop, so I just needed to turn left at the pub crossroads, and I'd see him. My reply was short and to the point 'Fine. Will be there in about three days.' In fact, it took me about another half hour to reach my goal. Once I'd emerged from the green lane, I had to circumnavigate the buildings of Wobage Farm, a well-known local pottery and art gallery. Normally I would have felt a bit nervous and inhibited about this, but I was so mad at myself and the world in general by now that I just stomped round the buildings – following some signs I might add – and down the farm track to the road.

Once I had achieved the B4224, it was indeed plain sailing although in the mood I was in I bitterly resented the fact that it was quite a stiff climb up to the crossroads upon which the Moody Cow pub sits. Along the way I waved a not at all fond farewell to the Herefordshire Trail, and upon arrival was not at all impressed to see parked in the bus stop not the trusty Skoda which had seen me through so much, but the much more flighty Morgan. Now, you may say, how wonderful, how glorious, what an exciting romantic end to the day to be driven home in style in a racy, open topped sports car. What may not be immediately apparent is that the Morgan is a low slung vehicle – all part of its charm and style – but when you've just walked thirteen and a half miles and got really rather grumpy towards the end of said walk, having to bend down and contort your aching limbs to enable you to even get into said beautiful hand built car is not necessarily going to improve your mood . . . poor Mike. And then it started to rain on the way home . . . just a few drops though, and by then I was starting to see the funny side.

Needless to say, the end of day thirteen photo shows a very moody cow at the Moody Cow. I'm attempting a smile, but frankly it comes out as more of a grimace. However, to be fair to myself, I had stuck with it. Each time I'd got lost, I had worked it out, found my way, got back on the horse – that's what I should have done, should have had a horse! – and I'd made it almost to the end of the whole thing. Whether there was only one more day's walking to be done or two – depending on the weather – it really looked like I might make it. Unbelievably, I was going to succeed at walking 150 miles – and if that didn't cheer me up, nothing would.

Day Thirteen Stats
  Start time – 9.04 am.
  Finish time – 4.31 pm.
  Duration – 7 hours, 26 minutes.
  Distance walked – 13.6 miles.
  Total ascent – 1,358 ft.
  Total descent – 1,152 ft.
  Avg. speed – 2.2 mph.

Day Fourteen: The Final Countdown
From the Moody Cow Back to All Saints Hollybush

14 July 2019

Day fourteen dawned so fair and bright that it was hard to believe the forecast of heavy rain for the following day could possibly be correct. As it had worked out the last two days of the walk as originally planned were nice and short – a mere sevenish miles each day – so it was theoretically possible that we could just keep going and finish the whole thing a day early. With this in mind, Mike decided he would accompany me on the Thursday when he had only planned to do the Friday – thanks to the lovely Julian offering to do drop off and pick up so that we could walk together. Our only other concern was that Ruth, who had kindly offered to do another day with me on the Thursday, might end up walking twice the distance she'd originally signed up for. Fortunately, she is a very fit person, but also very easy going and accommodating, and was happy to go with the flow. We decided we'd complete Thursday's walk, which happily was due to end at a pub around lunchtime and then see how we were all feeling and decide whether to push on or to call it a day and let Mike and myself risk the Friday deluge together.

So, the three of us reconvened back at the Moody Cow for the start of day fourteen. No flowery sun hat today but at least it was a sincere and genuine smile as I transformed from the moody cow of yesterday to the refreshed and rested let's get going walker of today. At least I didn't have to worry about getting lost as the man who had masterminded the entire route would be leading the way – what could possibly go wrong?

And talking of that man, now might be the time to pay a small but heartfelt tribute to he who has shared my life for the past thirty-five years of marriage and a few years leading up to that momentous day in October of 1988 when we plighted our troth to one another. Reader, I married him and how lucky for me that I did. I know that I say on every marriage prep day we've ever run that my husband is from the north and therefore not given to public displays of affection, to showering me with extravagant showy gifts or bunches of flowers or making grand romantic gestures – although to be fair he does do all those things from time to time. But what he is truly brilliant at is the important stuff, the day in day out stuff, the being there for me all those times I really need him, for putting up with my complete lack of competence at the technical, the financial, the practical because he is omnicompetent in all these things. I love to walk with him, to spend time working alongside him in the garden or orchard, to go out for a meal with him, to spend time sitting in silence with him, basically I just enjoy being with him and feel so blessed and lucky to have him in my life. His contribution to this walk had exemplified all that is so brilliant about him, and kind of illustrates our relationship and why it works. I had had the mad idea of walking 150 miles in a circle, visiting the ancestors, he had knuckled down and worked out how I could actually do that. He'd found the footpaths, he'd designed the route, he'd worked out the drop off and pick up points, set me up with a blog page, given up his time to drop me off and pick me up resulting in hours spent driving around the countryside . . . and much more than that, his loving, practical support gave me the confidence that I could maybe pull this off, that if he thought I could walk 150 miles then it must be possible. I am a stronger, more confident, more generous and

adaptable person because of spending my life with him. He inspires
me to be a better version of myself – not to change to fit in with
him, but to be more me – which I think is how all relationships
should really work. I hope we build each other up and support each
other in all our various wild and wacky endeavours – but you'd
have to get his opinion on that . . . He is so generous with his time
and talents, not just to me but to friends, family and neighbours.
True he can be a grumpy old git from time to time, but then again,
at times he has good cause to be. Basically, I love him, he loves me,
and that love has continued to grow and develop down all our years
together, and that is something astonishingly precious for which
I am eternally thankful.

Right, enough of the schmaltz, back to the walk. The three
amigos headed off briskly walking down the road, away from the
pub. I couldn't believe I'd been at the Moody Cow twice and both
times it had been shut. Although an 8.37 am pint would have been
pretty keen really. We walked along the road leading out of the
village of Upton Bishop, and then hung a right down towards the
church. We came across a very impressive lych gate first – although
the tree behind and beside it and towering over it was in many ways
even more impressive. As we took a detour through the churchyard
we also discovered a very excellent information board, which did
a great job of providing lots of interesting facts and figures about
the church and its surroundings, giving Ruth and myself ideas and
inspiration to take back to our own churchyards. For example, St
John the Baptist, Eldersfield has a very lovely churchyard with many
interesting old tombs and other features, while St Faith's, Berrow
is an exquisite circular walled churchyard with fabulous cowslips
in the Spring and amazing acrobatic swifts in the summertime, so
both could benefit from an information board like this. We carried
on round to the church door, but sadly found it locked. Probably

just as well as it was very early in the day to begin church crawling – but it's always disappointing to find a church locked up.

Nothing daunted, Ruth and I re-joined Mike on the road and continued on our merry way. At a T junction we turned left and carried on along the road – truly it was a very nice easy start to the day and even when we turned off the roads and into some woodland, the tracks were lovely and wide and relatively flat so Ruth and I were able to chat as we walked along while Mike the route master strode off into the distance. Now far be it from me to say it was really irritating that Mike had decided to join me for by far the easiest and most straightforward day of the walk so far – but it was, a bit. However, it being easy for him did also mean it was comfortable for Ruth and me, so silver linings. We followed a footpath along the boundary between Linton Wood and Dymock Woods, skirting the M50 which was to be a feature of the first part of the day, and then turning away from it and heading through the Michael Harper Reserves. These are split over eight fragments of Dymock Forest, an ancient woodland within the modern-day Queen's Wood, particularly rich in flora and fauna. My research tells me that over 470 species have been recorded in this forest, including many local and national rarities. For some species this is their only recorded sighting in the whole of Herefordshire. Dr Michael Harper, a local GP and entomologist, identified these eight areas as being habitats of importance for moths and butterflies way back in the 1960s. He organized a working party of volunteers from the Ledbury Naturalists' Field Club to come out to the woods every Thursday and undertake small scale coppicing and clearing. Just shows you the power of one individual to notice, inspire and organize others to ensure the survival of species. Yet again I was walking through an area of great beauty and huge importance in the natural scheme of things, just a stone's throw from home, and

I'd had no idea it was there, nor would ever have thought to get in the car and drive over here to walk it. The things we miss out on through lack of awareness.

Something I wasn't about to miss out on was the moment at which I clocked up 150 miles. For some time now it had been apparent

Fig 24. One hundred and fifty miles and not out

that my darling husband, so brilliant in so many ways, had got his calculations slightly wrong. No criticism intended. He'd done a totally fabulous job of stitching together this custom route for me and 99.9 per cent of the time it had worked brilliantly – and you really can't hold him responsible for poorly maintained paths or me getting lost. However, the fact remained, I was definitely going to be walking over 150 miles and it was while we walked through these woods that I hit my mileage target – 150 miles walked to celebrate 150 years of Hollybush Church – and this is the moment captured for posterity.

It still seems frankly incredible that I could have travelled all that way under my own steam. Once again, kudos to my amazing body, capable of far more than I had ever imagined.

Sadly, there was no champagne or fanfare – that came later, much later – and after taking the celebratory photo we carried straight on with the walk. Just as we were about to emerge from the woodland onto a road, we spotted a picnic bench and decided to take our first break of the day and very pleasant it was – the first table with benches either side of it that I'd come across on the whole walk and perfect for the three of us.

All too soon we were back on the road – literally – but after only a short period of road walking we headed back into the woods – the border between Dymock Woods and Oxenhall Wood. We were now in Gloucestershire as Dymock Woods is a Gloucestershire Site of Special Scientific Interest. However, way more important than that, I was about to meet up again with an old foe – The Three Choirs Way! Remember what a dance this route had led Julian and myself on day two of the walk, well day fourteen it was back but it looked very . . . different. A totally clear, wide, well-kept path through glorious woodland. So of course, Mike just had to take a photo of how totally fine, un-overgrown and eminently walkable it was so that we could show Julian when we got back . . . We continued on along the virtually unrecognizable Three Choirs Way all the way through Dymock Woods along the road which took us over the M50 by bridge for the first time. Then at a T junction as we turned left and continued on along the road, the Three Choirs Way headed for Hereford by way of Betty Daw's Wood – who was Betty Daw I wondered? I'd love to know, how wonderful to have a wood named after you! But there was also a road sign which had a personal significance for me and for Mike – it directed you to Dymock and to a place called Normans Land – Norman being the name of Mike's father, my father-in-law.

We continued along the road for a short distance, sadly not reaching Normans Land, and then really did double back on ourselves through a hamlet called Four Oaks, ironic really as we live in a hamlet called Eight Oaks, and then back under the M50 via a not very decorative underpass and so we picked up The Daffodil Way as we were entering the Gloucestershire Golden Triangle, an area famous for its poets, particularly Robert Frost and Edward Thomas, and its wild daffodils. Initially we walked alongside our old friend the M50, but then we turned from the motorway for a prolonged period of quieter, very pleasant field walking. It was then that we caught our first glimpse of the Malvern Hills and knew we were very much on the home straight.

Those blue remembered hills drawing us home, still some way in the distance, but giving us a real incentive to keep on going. We continued on across the fields, viewing from afar what looked like a magnificent old building fallen on hard times, which I can now identify as Boyce Court, a Grade II listed building. Emerging onto a country lane I actually got the navigation right – which was so unusual that I remember it – and guided us onto the next part of the Daffodil Way which took us alongside a very disused bit of canal. Another fascinating part of the industrial heritage which surrounds us but which is often concealed unless you happen to be walking past it or looking it up on a map. We emerged out into more open fields, and the spire of Dymock Church was now within sight – hoorah. Crossing an orchard, we passed through a group of new build houses and came out in the centre of Dymock, right across from the Beauchamp Arms, our end point for this part of the walk. We'd walked just over seven miles in a whisker over three hours arriving at the pub at just before 12 noon – and glory be, it was open! So, in we went, treated ourselves to a lemonade and lime with ice in my case and a packet of crisps, and then went out and took our ease in the really very lovely beer garden out the back. I would highly recommend the Beauchamp Arms and would like to return one day to sample their menu.

As we sat in the garden, we held a council of war – or should that be a council of walk? The day was still young, we were all still feeling pretty fit and well and it emerged that we were all still game to continue with the walk. We did it on a bit of a suck it and see basis, agreeing that we'd walk as far as Bromsberrow Church and then reassess.

So, at 12.30 pm on Thursday 18 July, we headed for home – the sun had come out and the sun hats were on – Bromsberrow here we come! Off down the B4215 we made our way, pausing only to stop and look at a place which converted Ford Transit vans into campervans. Ruth is the proud owner of two classic campers, to whom she is devoted, so this was definitely an allowable stop! Mike strode on ahead and was soon leading us onto Poets' Path Number 1. I think on the planned route we were due to take Poets' Path Number 2 but we opted for Number 1 which also proved troublesome. Once we'd managed to find our way around a very snazzy cricket ground with brand spanking new pavilion, we puzzled for quite a while over how to get out of the field we were in and onto the lane below. Mike did eventually find the stile, somewhat overgrown by hedge, and we were on our way once more along a road taking us past The Pound – a farm not a mint. The path then veered off across the fields once more, taking us across the River Leadon – for we were in the Vale of Leadon – and dangerously close to some farm buildings only to take a sharp right and take us back to our friend the M50, walking alongside the banks of the Leadon. Back under the M50 we went, walking gingerly on a raised concrete walkway alongside the river and then we knew we needed to turn left and go up and away from the river but we were faced with one huge piece of meadowland with no discernible path leading us through it. Mike strode boldly forward, we trailed in this wake, hugging the field boundary to begin with as that seemed the safest thing to do. Mike then called us over to nearer the middle of the field and then, growing in confidence, he spotted the stile which would take us out of this field, onto a farm track and then straight over and into the next set of fields. The final glitch of the whole walk had come and gone and we were still up and running – well, walking by this stage, very much walking.

The lovely thing was that as we headed across a couple of open fields of grassland, with the M50 on our left, I recognised where we were. It was an area I had looked down on many times while driving back and forth along the M50, that road linking me to my mum and dad's house, and in earlier days, the route I would have taken when going down to see Marianna on my weekly visits. It feels like a road I've known all my life, so made a good if noisy walking companion. And it also made me feel very much homeward bound. Emerging out of the fields and onto the road, we knew it was virtually all road walking from here to Bromsberrow and once I was in Bromsberrow I really did know the way home – I'd walked all round there while doing my practise walks so that really would be familiar territory. The excitement grew!

We turned right, away from the motorway and then left, heading for the village of Ryton, pausing only to let an argument between a lorry and a bus sort itself out. Taking the right hand fork out of Ryton we started to climb the hill towards Bromsberrow Heath. True a hill of any sort was not all that welcome at this stage of the walk but at least it did give us glorious views back over the way we'd come. Gosh we'd come a long way!

Past the sand and gravel works at Bromsberrow Heath, over the motorway for the final time, past the Sewage works, take the right turn – not straight on as I'd tried to lead us astray and we were at the A417 – a home road! Pick up the path, head across a couple of fields and there we were at Bromsberrow Church for a very well-earned break. The church has a gorgeous porch, is really well worth a visit and is kept open. It has a special place in my heart as, for reasons which need not detain us, I conducted my first ever baptism in Bromsberrow Church and to my own astonishment didn't drop the baby by the cunning ruse of never picking her up but getting Mum or Dad to hang onto the babe throughout the actual baptism, a stratagem I still employ to this very day.

Another short discussion ensued in the porch which ended with three-way agreement that we'd made it this far, we might as well see it through to the end – very game and noble of Ruth I felt, as this was pretty much double what she'd signed up for. She texted ahead to let Mel know that we were, after all, going to be finishing that day and would hopefully be arriving at All Saints Hollybush at about 4.30 pm. We crossed one final field and came out onto the Bromsberrow Road just up from the school. Now I really did know exactly where I was and where I was going. Follow the road up to the war memorial, take the road up towards Toney's

Farm and then take the path across the field, with a view over to Bromsberrow Place, towering above its lake, which enables you to cut the corner off the road. Go down the road past Hayes Coppice and then suddenly there we were at Chase End – we'd made it to the Malverns! Chase End is quite deceptive – it's a long slow haul up to the Trig Point – but it is a long haul, especially when you've just walked the best part of twelve miles to get to this point. Even Mike was feeling it, and he had a little lie down when we reached the top, while I took some photos of the fabulous views, looking out over Worcestershire and Gloucestershire – what a very beautiful place we are lucky enough to live in. Also, don't we owe a lot to our farmers who care for the land – looking out at that patchwork of fields, it would all revert very quickly to woodland were it not for our farmers who keep cultivating it.

As we recovered at the top of Chase End, a debate ensued about the very last part of the walk. Mike had deliberately designed the route to take in every hill in the Malverns range, so he was very much of a mind that as our finale we should climb Raggedstone Hill, as Cathy, Simon and I had begun by climbing Midsummer Hill way back on 1 July. Ruth and I were more of the view that Raggedstone was a step too far. I knew the hill very well having climbed it many times during my practise runs and so was aware that it was a tough ascent but a really hard on the knees descent particularly coming from Chase End and down into Hollybush. Whereas if we took the path which skirted round the hill we could be at All Saints Hollybush in no time at all without risking further damage to our knees. Ruth was very much of my opinion – and who could blame her being on the verge of completing a walk double the length of the one she'd signed up for. She'd already been terrifically accommodating so the least we could do was accommodate her wish not to have to drag herself up Raggedstone Hill!

The majority won out – although I do still feel a bit guilty that we didn't absolutely fulfil Mike's route and could see his point about covering all the Hills – but then again, I had already walked way more than the 150 miles I'd originally set out to walk, so maybe I don't feel that guilty after all. We descended from Chase End and entered the hamlet of Whiteleaved Oak. Named after an ancient and sacred oak nearby – sadly destroyed by fire – allegedly from a portable barbecue – in 2020. This was an ancient tree, said to have variegated white and green leaves, and also thought to be at the centre of a series of ley lines which linked Stonehenge, Glastonbury and Avebury. I had been to see it years before and found it festooned with ribbons and other offerings, apparently placed there for the solstice. A reminder that places of worship very much pre-date our Christian churches and are still venerated and visited to this day. And it is in the quirky and original hamlet of Whiteleaved Oak that my great grandmother bought Cider Mill Cottage for my great uncle Clarence, but he never lived there. Instead, on my great grandmother's death in May of 1955, he sold it and used it fulfil his lifelong dream of living in the wilds of the Black Mountains; a life free from family obligations. I always think of him as I walk through this village and wonder if he ever had any regrets about leaving. I suspect not.

Up the track out of the village, we ignored the stone marker pointing us up the Raggedstone and took the lower path along the wooded lower slopes of the hill and very cool and pleasant it was too. I looked out for the footpath across a field and found it – the very last field to be crossed on this walk. Then it was just a matter of turning left along the lane, past Sue Cosker's old house, onto the main road where we turned right past the old tin hut, scene of so many Hollybush Church Fetes, then past Shirley's house and she came out to join us for the very last part of the journey. Down the main road along the Common, and then suddenly we were there, it was over.

There was a lovely, if slightly embarrassing welcoming party, waving flags, blowing little trumpets and offering a very welcome glass of champagne – it was so kind of them all to turn out. Julian arrived to give us a lift home and said that I must be feeling very

Fig 25. End of day fourteen

proud, very satisfied, but that wasn't it. I think I was just stunned, just couldn't yet take it in.

I had started walking at about 9.00 am on Monday 1 July 2019 at All Saints Hollybush, I'd gone via Malvern, Bromyard, Leominster, Kington, Hay-on-Wye, Capel-y-Ffin, Monmouth, Ross-on-Wye and now I was back here on Thursday 18 July having walked 169.7

miles in fourteen days and raised the frankly astounding sum of £5,200 which was divided up between Macmillan Cancer Support and All Saints Church, Hollybush. Oh yes, and it did pour with rain on the Friday after the Thursday when we decided to keep going and finish the walk a day early – so a good decision made! Even now I still can't quite believe I managed to walk the way of my life – so I've written this book to convince myself that it really did happen – and to ask myself – what next?

Day Fourteen Stats

First part of walk:

    Start time – 8.37 am.

    Finish time – 11.58 am.

    Duration – 3 hours, 21 minutes.

    Distance walked – 7.3 miles.

    Total ascent – 223 ft.

    Total descent – 440 ft.

    Avg. speed – 2.4 mph.

Second part of walk:

    Start time – 12.32.

    Finish time – 16.31.

    Duration – 3 hours, 59 minutes.

    Distance walked – 7.7 miles.

    Total ascent – 666 ft.

    Total descent – 479 ft.

    Avg. speed – 2.3 mph.

Part Three
Revelation

Making All Things New

It took a while for the impact of doing the walk to really make itself known. Not so much an instant revelation, more a gradual unveiling of all the different ways in which walking 150 miles was going to change me and way I lived my life. Initially, the answer to that 'what next?' question was a return to normality, to the everyday, to continuing to juggle multiple responsibilities in the way in which most people have to – work, church, friends and family. However, in the reflections I wrote immediately afterwards there was one part which I highlighted, drew a border round, and clearly wanted to emphasise to myself. Here it is in full:

> Don't want to just go back to normal life – life as it was before. Want these three weeks to have been some sort of watershed – turning point – for both of us.

Re-reading it today, I'm particularly interested by the both of us bit at the end, telling me that I clearly felt both Mike and I needed a change of some sort in our lives. But this didn't happen immediately. Whether it was that I needed time to process the walk, or whether it was just our old friend, Nagging Norah and her self-limiting fear, life carried on, as it always will unless we/I decide to change it.

And then of course the biggest enforced change ever in our

lifetimes happened with Covid, lockdowns, churches locked, services suspended. We were forced to live in splendid isolation and we loved it. I know, I know, we were very very much the lucky ones. We had space, we had work we could still do – yes, my gardening work ceased for a while, but actually re-started fairly swiftly as you know what those weeds won't weed themselves! We were able to sort out grocery deliveries for ourselves and for parents, and of course with Zoom and phones we could stay in touch. It was terrifying initially but to suddenly have a totally blank diary was so liberating, it was amazing. I read, I gardened, I walked – guiltily I was definitely living a version of my best life whilst others were going through hell, not able to be with beloved family and friends whilst they were dying, not able to have a full funeral, that was very distressing. Revd Julie bore the weight of those curtailed funerals – until her mother-in-law, then she and Bob went down with Covid. That was very concerning, and sadly Bob's mum died from Covid, and we had a couple of weeks of being very worried about Julie and Bob, but I'm delighted to say they pulled through and are hale and hearty once more.

You would have thought the experience of walking with others through a global pandemic, keeping services going, building an online community, reaching out to others, participating in getting masks and scrubs made, would have triggered some sort of change in me, but no, still not.

Earlier on in the book, I described how our eldest niece, Bex, played a key role in getting me back into church attendance by asking an innocent question. Enter niece number two, Hannah, who sent us through a cheery Happy New Year email on 15 January 2021, letting us know, amongst other things, that she'd finished all her training and exams to become a personal trainer and was just waiting for her results, to get insurance and for the gyms to re-open so that she could set up her own business. I'd known for some time that I needed to do something about my physical fitness, for health rather than aesthetic reasons. I had been steadily gaining weight – I never weighed myself but could tell from the tightness of clothes – and knew that at my age I was on a one-way street to ailments and illness unless I took action. So, I asked Hannah – or not even as definite as that actually, here's what I replied in an email;

> If you ever want a real challenge of a clapped out, flabby unfit fifty-six-year-old to train remotely, I'd definitely be up for being a paying client, but I guess you need gym machines and things which has never really been my thing – way too intimidating.

Almost wriggling my way out of it even before I'd properly got into it. Luckily, Hannah was having none of this, and so, despite emails going into spam and other delays which meant I didn't really get started on my fitness journey until March of 2021, when we began slowly and gently, building up gradually as my fitness improved. Hannah is an outstanding personal trainer, both online and in person, so if you're in need of her help go to @hannahcharlottereilly and drop her a message. If she can sort me out, she can help anyone!

Two years on, and my relationship with my body has been transformed. I've completed a hilly, Malvern Hills Trail Half Marathon – accompanied by my fabulous niece number three, Lydia and her wonderful cowbells, completed a sprint Triathlon, the really lovely friendly and gorgeous Newent Triathlon, and cycled thirty miles in a Sportive with Mike. One of the best things Hannah did for me was to get me back into swimming, so I started going to Halo Leisure in Ledbury as soon as Covid permitted. Then I decided if I was going to attempt triathlon, I needed to swim front crawl so enrolled in their adult swim coaching sessions with Callum. He is an amazing coach! I can still vividly remember the joy of coming out of my first ever session with him going, I CAN swim front crawl. I've also taken up yoga, pilates, and strength and mobility training, involving lifting weights, something I never, ever thought I'd be able to do. This year's challenge has been an Olympic length triathlon involving open water swimming, something that I love doing in the sea, but had never thought I'd attempt under race conditions. Thanks to finding Lenches Lake over near Evesham, with the lovely Amanda being so kind and encouraging, I was able to swim 1k front crawl in open water, and had a blast completing the triathlon – with my PT Hannah doing the longer version, and members of our family coming along to cheer us on – a great day! So my understanding of what my body can do has been revolutionized. I've amazed myself and others – as my gorgeous sister-in-law Sharon, the sporty mother of an incredibly fit, active and sporty family put it – 'Who would have thought of all of us it would be Anthea who was the first to complete a triathlon??' I loved that comment sooo much – and it all began with the Amble.

My relationship with how my body looks has changed too. I've lost three stone in weight. I've gone to a personal styling session in John Lewis Cheltenham and absolutely loved and enjoyed it, when I thought it would be awful, embarrassing and humiliating – shout out to Dorothy Marsden, part of the amazing team of personal stylists there. And it feels as if I've become far more me again, both physically and mentally. Stairs which I used to puff and pant up I now take in my stride, clothes which used to pinch are now so big I've had to replace them, I can look in the mirror without pausing to count my double chins – I have a neck again! In a post-Covid world, when we know being overweight heightens the risk factors for that disease as well as many others,

I've now moved out of the obese BMI scale and into the merely overweight – and I haven't finished yet.

Even more importantly though, it has shown me that I am capable of way more, way way more than I had thought. That by getting the right help, and being held accountable, I can achieve things I truly still can't quite believe I did. It's not easy, I can have down days, days when I whinge and moan to Hannah like a trooper. But it's also meant that I am more confident, more resilient, more determined, and more willing to become the architect of my own life. I chose those challenges for myself – I signed up for the Half Marathon which involved running up and down most of the Malvern Hills, I then signed up for the triathlon which meant I needed to learn to ride a proper drop handle barred bike – borrowed from niece Bex, delivered by niece Lydia, taught to ride it by Lydia's now husband, the incredibly patient Ewan. Another team effort – thanks gang!

Was I scared, did I have huge doubts and fears and insecurities about completing them? Yes, absolutely. But did they also give me immense highs and feelings of achievement which will live with me forever. Hell yes! What I hadn't realised is that it's a mental battle just as much if not more than a physical one, and it's been an education in coming to understand myself more and in understanding to learn how to change. 'I am not my thoughts' has been a pretty radical revelation for me, helped by the amazing Hannah Almond-Barr, yoga teacher extraordinaire. If you're ever in need of an amazing yoga teacher, she's @halmondbarr. And of course, taking the time to do the exercise, particularly the running and cycling, has brought me head space, time outdoors, time to think, time to be, time alone. Time in fact to be once more that tom boy running wild -literally – that the walk made me realise I was missing so much.

I am, as we all are, a work in progress. I still find it hard to break out of my socialized shell, to think of what *I want* to do and be and go for it. Because actually that's a hard thing to do. Going along with what others want and need you to be, that's easy street in a way because you never have to draw the line, never have to disappoint, never have to say No, just go with the flow. You'll be busy, the days will be full, but is this really what you want to do with your one wild precious life, with your last thousand weeks?

I'm writing this as I come to the end of a sabbatical, a three-month break from church work taken at least in part in order to finish this book. I doubt I would ever have had the courage to ask for, let alone take, a sabbatical if I hadn't asked Hannah to hold me accountable for doing it. Am I just going to go back to 'normal' life once more, or am I going to take some tough decisions, make some changes, disappoint some people by putting my needs and those of Mike and the wider family first? I don't know. But at least I'm asking the question, at least I've claimed this time and space for myself, at least I can see now that I have a choice, I've always had a choice, I've just chosen not to make it – but not making a choice *is* in fact making a choice. And that is a revelation to me, and maybe to you too.

And where does the spiritual fit into all of this? Doing the walk definitely expanded the breadth of my spirituality. I keep coming back to the 'My church and my gym' comment from the man on Hergest Ridge. This can leave me frustrated by the structures and all the rules and regulations within the Church, which, after all, is a large bureaucratic organization as well as a force for good and a spiritual haven for many. And the obsession with money, the cutting back on priestly resources in the rural areas, the unwillingness to try new things – all these factors do leave me feeling tired and disillusioned with the organization.

But the people we serve – they are amazing and brilliant, hard working and dedicated, and it is and remains a privilege to serve them and to be alongside them at tough times and joyous times. And we can try new things locally – we've had a couple of Walking Church sessions which have been brilliant – small steps, but if the Amble taught me anything it's that any step forward is a good one.

So, have I made it back to being that fearless, outdoorsy tom boy of a girl who loved to use her imagination and creativity and didn't care what anyone else thought about that? Not quite yet, but I'm an awful lot closer to her now than I was four years ago. At a time of my life when I could be in decline, going to seed, to use some gardening terminology, I am in fact blooming and blossoming in ways that I wouldn't have believed possible, and I am learning so much on every level, which is such a buzz. And I know that she is my trajectory, that fearless outdoorsy tom boy, my role model, my true authentic self, so in walk terms I know where I'm headed. I'm not there yet, but I'm on my way and you can be too. So here are my final top tips, my takeaways to set you off on your journey, your own personal songlines pilgrimage.

- Dare to dream, but then do something about it.
- Be the change you want to see in the world, but start in your own life.
- That first step is the hardest, vocalize your needs and dreams then go ahead and seize the moment.
- You are entitled to follow your dreams and to make them into reality.
- Find your tribe, find the help, support and encouragement you will undoubtedly need to keep going – there will be ups and downs, highs and lows, mountain peaks and valley floor troughs.
- But better to try, fail, try again, fail again, fail better and

then succeed than to wind up on your death bed never having tried at all.

Good luck, let me know how you get on by emailing me at rootsandboots@eightoaks.com.

For further reflections on what I've learned from the walk, see the Epilogue which follows, and I've also put in a list of the books which inspired and challenged me both before, during and after the walk.

Fig 26. Start of half marathon

Epilogue
Reaping the Harvest

I wrote some reflections on the walk in the immediate aftermath of it, picking up on some threads which, hopefully have been woven into the fabric of this book, but nevertheless, I think it would be good to reiterate them here, just to give you some takeaway, a reward to fellow pilgrims who have made it this far.

The amazing feat of engineering and creativity which is the human body.
Or to quote from Psalm 139 – 'I praise you because I am fearfully and wonderfully made'. This is not how I used to think of my body. In fact, in the first draft of this book, it was generally referred to using some quite derogatory terms, which reflected how I thought about it then. When I thought about my body, if I thought about it at all, it was in terms of how it looked, not what it could do. Pretty much all my adult life, I have been self-conscious about my body, worn baggy clothes to try to disguise it and been lucky enough to have the good health to be able to ignore its existence. As I said earlier, it felt to me like a means of transport for my brain and that was it.

This walk, and what has come after it, have changed that. And changed it for the better. I was amazed and impressed by what my body was capable of – way more than I would ever have assumed it could do. Which in turn made me realise how self-limiting I had been about pretty much all things physical. Can't go running or swimming because I'll look ridiculous, people will point and laugh, not built like a runner, too self-conscious to be seen in a bathing costume. All the stories we tell ourselves which just aren't true.

Women, it seems to me, are or have been (please God it's changing now) brought up to be ashamed of their bodies. To be constantly striving to make them fit into some air brushed Instagram form of perfection. And God forbid we discuss menstruation or menopause – again this is slowly changing in this country, though not throughout the world. And somehow, from a very early age, it's made clear to us that we shouldn't take up too much space in the world – we need to reduce our bodies down to be slender. By far the most frequently asked question after the walk was 'Did you lose weight?'. Not 'did you enjoy it', or 'what did you learn', or 'what was your favourite part of the walk' but 'did you lose weight', 'did doing the walk help you towards the Nirvana of slenderness'? Well, no, it didn't, I lost virtually no weight, but I gained a hell of a lot more confidence in my physicality, in my right to take up space in the world. Notice the way men and women sit on a train, in a pub, even in church. Men are generally relaxed, knees splayed out, arms wide, taking up all the space they need. Women are carefully keeping all their limbs closely aligned, elbows inside the seat line, not wanting, not daring to be seen to take up more space than their allotted amount.

The church has a very ambivalent attitude towards bodies, gender and sex, going back to the split from Celtic to Catholic Christianity in this country. From a faith where men and women were pretty much equally valued to a faith where men were leaders, preachers and priests and women were pastoral workers, making the tea, tending the sick, feeding the hungry, caring for the family, knowing their place.

But you don't find any back up for this in the life of Jesus – quite the reverse. For a start, Jesus is God becoming embodied, incarnate, going through the whole messy gestation and birth thing to be fully human as well as fully divine. And, further back than that, we are made in the image of God, we are fearfully and wonderfully made. Our bodies are amazing, our bodies are things of wonder and beauty, God given, to be cherished and enjoyed, not starved and despised, hidden away. And if you look at Jesus' encounters with women – the haemorrhaging woman, clearly suffering from really heavy periods, who he healed, the woman at the well with the exceedingly dodgy relationship history who becomes the first evangelist and brings many to know and love Christ, the woman taken in adultery – funny how she managed to commit adultery all by herself – who he refused to condemn and simply told to go and sin no more, the woman who anointed his feet with perfume and wiped it with her hair, an incredibly sensuous image which clearly made the other men in the room very uncomfortable (or jealous?), but who Jesus defended because she got who he was, why he was there, and what was about to happen to him. The anonymous woman who bested Jesus in debate, unlike his clueless male disciples, in order to get healing for her daughter by stating that even the dogs get to eat the crumbs from under their master's table. And at the foot of the cross, it was the women, including his mother Mary, who had the courage and the strength to stand there until the end. And Mary Magdalene, and other women, had the courage to go to the tomb, to find the stone rolled away and then encounter Jesus in the garden, mistaking him for the gardener until he spoke. She was the first person to go and tell the good news of the resurrection. He treats the women he meets as equals – in fact more than equals, he treats many of them as friends. They certainly seem to understand more about who he truly is and what his mission is all about than most of his male disciples!

In the liturgy we talk frequently about the body of Christ, but our lived faith tends to be more intellectual, more head than heart, more words than actions. Jesus had both, he was always on the move, a great walker, someone who loved to be outside, who commanded the elements, who loved to withdraw to a quiet place and just be who he was, listen to his heavenly Father in peace and tranquillity. Maybe our faith needs to become more embodied again. Not to be a sitting down faith but an on the move faith, walking as well as talking, using our amazing bodies for more than standing up and sitting down again on very hard and uncomfortable pews. In the pandemic, holding services outside was very popular – let's not lose that, let's get back in touch with the origins of our faith – walking church, forest church, eco church – all great ways to rejoice in the physical and spiritual as well as the mental and spiritual. Remember the man on top of Hergest Ridge – this is my gym and my church. We have allowed our faith to become static, disembodied, boring. Let's change that before it's too late.

As women we should be proud of our bodies. The human race would be pretty stuffed without them. And we should appreciate and cherish them for what they can do, rather than what they look like, for their strength, their flexibility, their ability to move – run, jump, dance, swim, cycle, play football, rugby, cricket, squash, tennis. For behold we are fearfully and wonderfully made, we are powerful, we are strong, we are fit and active and we more than deserve to take up space in this world. An image that has stuck with me from the summer of 2022 is that of Chloe Kelly scoring the winning goal for the Lionesses in the European Championship finals and, in the joy of the moment, ripping off her shirt, and running to her team mates, shirt whirling round her head, sports bra proudly displayed. That's what women's bodies can do – and it's brilliant.

Furthermore, when you reach my age its very much a case of use it or lose it – keep mobile, keep flexible, keep looking after that body and it will look after you. One of the women I most admire, by the name of Mary Williams, is in her early nineties now, and has been doing yoga for the last forty odd years. She is a walking, bendy, flexible miracle. I want to be like her when I grow up. This walk planted a seed in me, a seed of knowledge that my body could do way more than I had realised or was allowing it to do. That seed germinated in the late winter of 2021, and has transformed my life, body, mind and soul. Meanwhile, onto learning point number two.

Perseverance

'Nevertheless, she persisted' is a phrase which has come to mean a great deal to me and to many other women. It was used by Senator Mitch McConnell, when preventing Senator Elizabeth Warren from reading a letter objecting to the appointment of Senator Jeff Sessions as Attorney General. He stated:

> Senator Warren was giving a lengthy speech. She had appeared to violate the rule. [A rule which prevents one Senator impugning the integrity of another.] She was warned. She was given an explanation. Nevertheless, she persisted.

Fancy that, a woman having the gall to persist when told not to by a powerful man? Unsurprisingly the phrase has become a hashtag, a meme, a poster, and, in my case, a necklace. Because it's a phrase which reminds me of a massive learning point from the walk, one that I want to keep on remembering, which was that it's truly amazing what you can achieve if you simply keep going, in my case if I could keep putting one foot in front of the other, eventually I would arrive at my destination – simple, no? Well, no, not really. Because to do that you need to overcome all those negative voices in your head telling you you can't do it, it's too hard, too difficult, too dangerous, not really worth trying because it'll only go wrong. Negative self-talk is its official title. But in my head, she's called Nagging Norah, and I've referred to her a couple of times in this book, because naming the voice can take away some of its power.

How did I overcome this on the walk? By not giving myself any alternatives, by going public with my intentions, by taking money from kind donors and sponsors to give to good causes, by committing to walk with other people, by doing the preparation so that I had no excuses. I just had to keep going because otherwise I'd have had to admit to public failure, with all the humiliation and embarrassment that would involve, and give everyone their money back.

But if I hadn't persisted, hadn't kept going even when times got tough – that day of getting lost with Julian, the time I fought my way along a field margin only to fall into a ditch, to name but two examples – I would have missed out on so much. On the joy of walking with others and alone, the highs of walking in the mountains, of remembering friends who have gone before, the happiness of completing each day and knowing that all I had to do was sleep, eat and begin again. The freedom of that constraint in a way. The stripped-down nature of a life on the move, little by little, one foot in front of the other.

Because we live in a time when perseverance and practice is out of fashion. If at first we don't succeed, give up and go and try something else instead. 'No grit, no pearl' is another slogan I've become fond of. Yes, it's hard to keep trying and failing and getting up to give it another go, but the pay off when you finally get there is immense. Plus, the most talented of people are generally also those who have put the hours in, hours and hours of keepy uppy, hours and hours of writing draft after draft, hours and hours of practising the same piece of music. When called a lucky player, the golfer Gary Player responded that it was strange that the more he practised, the luckier he became, whilst Samuel Becket's mantra was 'Ever tried? Ever failed? No Matter. Try Again. Fail Again. Fail Better.' Cultivate a growth mindset which tells you that failure is a building block on the road to success, not a reason to stop trying. No baby ever walked the first time they tried. It takes time and perseverance to get to where you want to go, but you can do it, because if I can, anyone can.

This walk showed me the power of perseverance, also the pain of perseverance, but it was so worth it. Have I got it all sussed then? No. I still struggle to keep going, still struggle to put myself through the pain barrier, time and again, still have days where Nagging Norah convinces me that there's no point and I'll never get there. But that's the power of an adventure like this one. I know it works. I lived and breathed it. I walked every step from here to Hay and back again. Amazing. Unbelievable. Brilliant. And no one can take that experience away from me. It's in me. In my body, which now knows it is capable of so much more, in my brain as a way of countering Nagging Norah. In spite of doubts, in spite of fears, in spite of getting lost and falling in a ditch, nevertheless I persisted. And you can too.

Fear

'Feel the fear and do it anyway' – easier said than done. But from the faith point of view 'Do not be afraid' is one of the most common phrases in the Bible, both Old and New Testament, normally coming up when God is about to appear and ask someone to do something really scary. Because the thing is we aren't designed to stay in our comfort zone, comfortable though it undoubtedly is. If you look at the life of Jesus, the lives of the prophets, the lives of the saints – comfortable they really aren't. What you'll see instead are people pushed to the limits, asked to do and be things they really didn't believe possible and then do that again, and again, and again.

It now strikes me that part of this walk for me was beginning to learn to live with the fear, to live with the discomfort, to hear all that Nagging Norah was saying to me, and then go ahead and do it anyway. This makes it sound easy, but bear in mind it had taken me eighteen years, yes one-eight, eighteen long years to actually screw up the courage to, essentially, go for quite a long walk.

We all have different fear buttons which are pressed for each of us. For me it's fear of failure and fear of public humiliation. I don't want to put my head above the parapet, I don't want to try something I'm not guaranteed to succeed at, I'm even less comfortable if I'm attempting it in a glare of publicity. So, you can see that for me, the walk was fraught with difficulty. And I also think that like many of us, women in particular, I want to be liked. I don't want to upset people, I want to please people predominantly by saying yes to any sort of a request, even if by agreeing to do that, I am, as a result, letting down my nearest and dearest. Because every time I take on yet another role or task, the amount of me that's available for those I claim to love the most ie Mike, my mum and dad, wider family, friends, becomes exponentially smaller. In fact, they are left to make do with the scraps, the leftovers of my time and attention, while the best of me goes into church work, or gardening work, or school governor work. Sound familiar?

The courage required to claim this time to do the walk for myself, for something I wanted, needed even, to do, something that was important to me on a number of levels was immense. And I reckon I only managed to do it because it was for chariteee, with a capital TEE. Because as women we're brought up to care, care too much maybe, care too much what others think, care too much for others and taught from early on that to look after ourselves is selfish.

Fear is the emotion which keeps us in our comfort zone, restricts us to our tram tracks, keeps us living little lives. Over and over in the planning phase, people would wish me well, but follow that up with a phrase like – I couldn't do that or tell me that I was brave to even think about walking some of the stages on my own, or, even worse, just assumed that Mike must be walking with me as obviously I'd need a man by my side to keep me – safe???? In the middle of the English/Welsh countryside?? Really???? There is a long history of women being confined, restricted, kept in their place by being physically circumscribed by society – that same history that said women weren't physically able to run marathons – hello Paula Radcliffe, that same history which banned women's football because our poor weak female bodies couldn't take it – hello Lucy Bronze and the rest of the Lionesses. But thankfully there have always been adventurous women who broke the mould, and women like the well named Jenny Tough are still pushing those boundaries out on behalf of all of us today. Do read her book – *Solo* – or see the film of her incredible expeditions around the world.

I didn't need anyone to protect me, or supervise me, all I really needed was someone to keep me heading in the right direction as you'll have seen in various chapters – but then if I'd had that for the entire walk, how would I have learned? You've got to get it wrong in order to find out how to do it right. That growth mindset coming up again, something which my nan and gran would have called 'learning from experience'. But to me the fear of getting things wrong has been, and to an extent, still is a strongly restricting fear. Because if you don't try you can't fail. But if you don't try you don't learn, you don't grow, you calcify, stuck in your old routine, never taking responsibility for your own life.

What do I mean by that? Simply that if you always let your life be dictated by the needs and demands of others – work, church, family, children – then you never have the time to do what you really want to do. Maybe you never even have the luxury of time and space to sit down and work out what it is you want to do. Maybe the very idea of that is even now making you roll your eyes and think, it's alright for her, privileged educated middle class comfortably off Oxford educated white woman. And you would be correct in classifying me as immensely fortunate and privileged. In the lottery of life, I definitely drew a golden ticket. And yet, and yet. All my life, I have wanted to be a writer, to publish a book, to earn at least part of a living from writing – and here I am, three quarters of the way through that very privileged life if I'm lucky, and I've done anything and everything except what in my heart of hearts I most want to do. Why is that? Because if I never try, I can never fail.

And then I found this Erin Hanson quotation:

> There is freedom waiting for you,
> On the breezes of the sky,
> And you ask 'What if I fall?'
> Oh but my darling,
> What if you fly?

Which made me realise what a ridiculously crazy attitude I had to trying and failing, definitely a fixed rather than a growth mindset, definitely the lizard brain in overprotective mode. And looking back I see now that all my busyness was at least in part a way of avoiding trying to do what in my heart I most wanted to do. Because I was afraid, afraid of the sheer grinding work involved – check out the perseverance point above – but mainly afraid that it wouldn't be any good. And latterly, having written over 90,000 words, afraid that what I've written reveals the real me, the person behind the people pleasing façade, and that really is a scary prospect.

I've been doing a lot of reading these past few years, and a standout book is one called Four Thousand Weeks by Oliver Burkeman which starts by reminding the reader that one fact in life is certain – our lives will end. We don't know when or where or how but we do all know that no one lives for ever. And yet most of us live as if that particular inconvenient truth applies to everyone else, just not us. We assume we have all the time in the world to get round to doing what we really want to do, we'll wait until we retire, until we've got enough money, until the mortgage is paid off, the kids have left home, the time is right. Burkeman tells us that on average we all have just four thousand weeks. And Marianna didn't get anywhere near four thousand weeks – that was a major wake up call for me. If you stop, put down this book, work out how many weeks you've already lived, how many you've still got to go – on average – you might get a bit of a shock. The time is never going to be right unless you decide it is. The time is always right. It's just waiting for you to make that leap, to feel the fear and the self-doubt and the negativity and do it anyway.

Looking back, the times I've been brave enough to push myself out of my comfort zone have generally been forced upon me – the time my A Level German teacher told me that if I didn't go spend time in Germany I'd fail my exam, so I responded to an advert in the *Daily Telegraph* and booked myself on an intensive spoken language course in Munich – never travelled abroad alone, never even been on a plane before – what was I thinking? When I made the leap from full-time, well-paid employment at Wrox Press to retrain to be a garden designer, with all the uncertainty of self-employment which that involved, it was in the immediate aftermath of Marianna's death. I had been brought face to face with the death of someone my own age, someone who had wanted to change her life, her career, but never got the chance to do so. When I offered myself up for the priesthood, possibly the furthest out of my comfort zone ever, and continues to be so, it was in response to God's call, the tug on the string, the still small voice which refused to be silenced, however hard I tried not to listen. I remember reading the first few chapters of the Book of Exodus in the Old Testament, the call of Moses, burning bush and all, and being so comforted by the fact that this great man, prophet, forefather of several faiths, tried so hard to say No to God, culminating in him saying – Please Lord can't you send someone else? This is the mood music of my vocation. I am, and continue to be, a very reluctant Reverend – sorry Lord.

This walk was a turning point though. Yes, I had to box myself in to do it, give myself permission by using the justification of charity fundraising – whilst remaining hugely grateful to all those who gave so generously – but in reality, it was something I wanted to do, something I decided to do, something I carved out the time to do. Not alone, I had tons of help and support, but the idea, the genesis, the momentum, the decision to do this thing was because I wanted to do it. To step out in faith, in the blaze of the public gaze and attempt to do something I wasn't at all sure I could do, but I went ahead and tried to do it anyway, and I didn't fail, I flew. And once you've done that once, you can't go back to a state where you are bound by your self-limiting fears because you've broken free once so you know you can do it again, and again, and again. It's still a battle, the fears and the negative voices don't pack up camp and head off into the hills, but you know you have the power within you to defeat them, albeit temporarily. And each time you do it, in the tiniest of ways, you and your self-belief become a little bit stronger, and the fears and negativity in your head become a little bit weaker.

So don't wait, do it. Whatever it is, big or small, take that chance, make that decision, start – just start. Because the longest journey starts with a single step and if you never start, you're never going to get there.

Support crew

I referred above to the tons of help and support I received and which, hopefully, I've flagged up repeatedly in the book you're reading. And my learning point here, addressed mainly to myself, as they all are, is don't be too proud or independent to ask for and, even more importantly, to accept help. My self-image has always been that of a loner, me against the world, latterly me and Mike against the world, but someone who very much keeps themselves to themselves, a listener not a talker, self-contained, happiest in my own company, not wanting to be beholden to anyone.

All of which is fine, but again, very limiting, very narrow, very insular and closed in. Because what I can achieve on my own is pretty limited – although not as limited as I once believed. Without Mike to plan the route and do all that driving I could never have done this walk. Simple as that. Without Dave teaching me the rudiments of map reading I probably wouldn't have completed the walk. Without Simon, Cathy, Julian, Dave and Ruth's company during various legs of the walk, it would have been far more of struggle for me, and I would have missed out on the joy and encouragement of their company. And let's not forget those guardian angels, the complete strangers who cropped up just when I needed them to be there – the farmer mowing off a perfectly good crop of potatoes, the chain saw wielding topless man who had made straight a way that had been impassable for years and the people who emerged from the hedge at Hole-in-the-Wall to save my bacon and point me in the right direction. Always show hospitality to strangers the book of Hebrews tells us, for you may be entertaining angels unawares. These complete strangers were all angels to me and made the journey much smoother than it would otherwise have been.

Without the support and encouragement of family, friends and the wider community I wouldn't have had the additional drive provided by their donations and weight of expectation. Involving other people, being accountable to other people, asking for and then accepting help, support and guidance from other people has been key to achieving this walk.

There is something about sharing your dreams, your hopes, your aspirations with others, making yourself accountable for delivering them, which is powerful. In some ways, the point when this walk went from dream in my head to reality was when I told Mike about this crazy idea I'd had, and he didn't dismiss it, or laugh, or tell me it couldn't be done. Instead, he took it seriously and then did everything he could to help me to actually get out there and do it. For us to be able to make the space to do what we want to do generally involves other people stepping up to take on some of the stuff we would usually do, and that's why, women in particular, don't often do this. Don't even ask. Just assume they need to wait . . . until time and space magically occur???? They won't.

This has made sense of a passage in the Bible which I'd always found difficult – Seek and ye shall find, knock and the door will be opened unto you, ask and you shall receive. Always seemed like nonsense to me because if I asked God for a Ferrari and fifty thousand pounds it seemed highly unlikely that I'd wake up the next morning to find them sitting on the drive. But then I realised that I was looking at the wrong end of each of these phrases. The point was we need to be pro-active, to take the initiative, to be demanding. Ask, seek, knock – don't just sit there, do something, anything to make things happen. It's only when you take the risk, step out in faith, start to try and make things happen that God can join in. All of which reminded me of that Richard Rohr quote which I referenced earlier in this book – 'We do not think ourselves into new ways of living; we have to live ourselves into new ways of thinking.' You're never going to find your way without seeking it, never going to find which door to go through without knocking, never going to get what you want without asking for it.

Suddenly it seems to me that this is God saying you've got to be humble enough, realistic enough, to know that you can't do this on your own, you need help so ask for it and you'll be amazed by how many people respond. Generally, people like to help. Like to feel they can do something, be involved. Don't be too proud, too arrogant, too insular to ask for help, and always, always remember to say thank you. And it's also a useful corrective to arrogance and ego. Because there is a limit to what one person knows, or can imagine, or has the vision and capacity to see and envision. The more eyes, brains and experience you can harness to tackle a problem or an adventure, the more likely you are to succeed. Don't be too proud or arrogant to tap into the expertise all around you. And here I'd like to pay tribute to my editor, Sarah Hudson, whose expertise in reading through this manuscript and making so many fantastic comments and suggestions, asking so many great questions, helped me so much and opened my eyes to the value of the editorial process.

Family

The walk was structured along songlines principles, a walk to reconnect me with the ancestors, to revisit the land where they had lived and to find out what they had contributed to making me who I am today.

What did I discover? I was reminded that I come from a line of strong, hard-working women, who have endured and overcome hardship and obstacles the like of which I have never come up against, thankfully. My great grandmother the amazing musician, turned sheep farmer, who left the property we now live in to the female line. My maternal grandmother, my nan, who coped with a gravely injured and damaged husband, taking on the tasks of supporting her own family, looking after her mother-in-law and caring for a flock of sheep and making it all look effortless. My paternal grandmother, my gran, who worked hard at tough physical jobs pretty much all her life long, who loved the sunshine, loved to walk fast, cleaned for England and brought up three amazing, intelligent, hard-working sons on not a lot of money at all. All of them lived either all their lives, or a significant portion thereof, without mains water or electricity. Also, without many of the labour-saving devices we take for granted today. Gran endured the loneliness of widowhood, kept working, kept walking and I'm so glad that she had a long, sustained period of caring and being cared for when living with my maternal grandfather – she more than deserved it.

And my own darling mother – from a working-class background she became a teacher of home economics, rising to head of department, managing a home, husband and difficult daughter in the process. And if she is a pessimist par excellence, who will always look on the dark side and expect the worst to happen, surely that's because one day her beloved father went off to work as he always had and when he eventually came back he was a changed man and their whole family dynamic and situation changed in the split second when the scaffolding collapsed and down he fell, sustaining irreparable brain damage.

All of these amazing women were the centre and hub of their families, the ones who kept the show on the road, the decision makers. The men are much more shadowy figures, apart from my dad, who don't seem to have had the same agency as the women – which is strange given the times they lived in and through.

These women kept going, endured, thrived and survived, and it is because of all their efforts that I have the privileged life that I do. And that gives me a responsibility to live it as best I can, to live it as a gift from the past, a gift from the ancestors, not waste it. To be inspired by their example to persist, to endure, to overcome.

And I come from a family of shepherds and gardeners, both definitely priestly attributes. Jesus said, feed my sheep, take care of the flock. There is so much nature imagery in the bible – The Lord's my Shepherd, I shall not want for example, Jesus the good shepherd, who goes looking for the one lost sheep, and gardens, gardens feature a lot. It all begins in the Garden of Eden, and then goes horribly wrong. Jesus is taken captive whilst praying in the Garden of Gethsemene, and is buried and seen for the first time in his risen form in another garden, in fact Mary assumes he is a gardener. So maybe it was my destiny to become a priest, shepherd of a flock, tender of gardens, learning that it takes time for a garden to grow and flourish, time, patience, tending and good care, good soil and water – living water ideally.

However, the one ancestor who definitely didn't foreshadow a future in the priesthood is possibly the one who most attracted me, was most glamorous in my eyes, the black sheep, the bad boy of the family, my great uncle Clarence. Maybe it was a case of opposites attract. Maybe it was his life of splendid isolation which appealed to me – no one to tell him what to do, make him tidy up or go to bed at a certain time – freedom it seemed to me as a child, that's what he had.

Now I think it's more the state of mind that I admire, his ability to be utterly and unashamedly who he was, no more no less. To own it as the young people say today. And to have the courage to step off the hamster wheel, to look at the tram tracks, the obvious path – a lovely house in a beautiful hamlet where he could continue to work his mother's flocks, or not as he chose, enjoy the easy life – and say, 'No. Sorry, Mum, sorry, Sis, I'm off; off to a much wilder bleaker more isolated but incredibly beautiful landscape, off to be me in splendid isolation because that's what I want to do. This is what you want for me, but it ain't what I want for me.' He claimed the space he needed and wanted for himself, totally and unashamedly – and that's rare.

And it's also a hard thing to do. To go against family, friends, expectations. To potentially disappoint and hurt those who love you the most, and who you love in return. But the truth is, as Glennon Doyle, author of *Untamed*, would say, you either disappoint others or you disappoint yourself, and, given that choice, may you always have the courage to disappoint others. Because if you aren't living an authentic life, a life which is true to your values, your dreams, your desires then slowly, little by little, day by day, year by year, something important and vital inside will shrink, diminish, and eventually, wither up and die. You can call it spirit, or soul, or true self, call it what you will but if you are currently crushing your authentic self down, contorting it to fit into cookie cutter shapes or pigeonholes designed by other people, you will know exactly what I'm talking about.

And I think that's the real reason for doing the walk. Yes, I wanted to raise the money, yes, I wanted to test myself, body, mind and soul, but more than that I wanted to find my authentic self. I wanted to go back, back to the people and the places I had known as a child, before all that other stuff got overlaid on top of who I was – the wife, the daughter, the friend, the priest, the gardener – somewhere in the mix, I'd lost track of myself. I'd been so busy trying to be perfect, trying to be all things to all men and women, to fit into so many pigeonholes. I was second guessing all the time what everyone else wanted from me, how they wanted me to be, but what did I want, how did I want to live out the last quarter of my life, that last thousand weeks as Oliver Burkeman would describe them? Did I want to carry on with the fruitless quest to be a perfect shapeshifter, or did I want to take what felt like the final opportunity to be the real me – otherwise what was the point?

God knows us and loves us from cradle to grave, and he alone knows the real us, the good stuff and all the not so good stuff which we try to conceal. But he wants us to have life in all its fullness – surely that means an authentic life, a life being who he made us, designed us, called us to be? A life lived without fear or limitation, a life where we make the most of all the amazing gifts which he has given to us – our bodies, our brains, our health, our strength, our intelligence, our talents, all the things which make us the unique human being each of us is. Why then would I try to be someone I'm not, simply to try to gain approval or avoid disappointing folk? Worse than that even, to avoid disappointing folk who don't really care that much about me anyway, and in the process letting down and disappointing those who care about me the most. Be more Great Uncle Clarence going forward, always remembering to draw strength and inspiration from those amazing strong women who have gone before – as I might well need the latter if I'm going to be the former.

Nature

Or creation, or the environment, call it what you like but get out there and be in it, appreciate it, cherish it or within a generation or two it will be gone. I now know that I have a deep-seated need to spend at least part of each day outdoors. Being a gardener definitely helps as at least two days a week, that's exactly where I am, head down weeding, or planting, or pruning. And no, I don't just mean when the weather is fine. As I'm out more, in all weathers, I find that there is a joy to being out on a wet and windy day, particularly as normally there are very few other people mad enough to be out in it. There is nothing like being buffeted by the wind, and soaked by the rain, to make you feel most fully and gloriously alive, part of nature, part of the whole eco-system.

The joy of walking is that it slows you down. You walk at nature's pace almost. Okay, okay, I know, there are very fast animals and birds and for all I know fish in nature that whizz around the place. What I'm trying to say is that when you walk you see things, hear things, smell things, notice things that you miss out on when zooming past in a hermetically sealed car. You get to places that you would only be able to reach on foot. You have the time to look around you and appreciate the beauty of the countryside, the fields, the skies, the trees, the birds flitting in and out of the hedgerows, it's all there, all around us, but we're too busy, too speedy, too engaged with the virtual worlds on our phones or tablets to appreciate the real world right under our noses.

And we seem to be permanently in a hurry. Always rushing to do the next thing on our never ending to do list – answer that email, post that photograph on Facebook or Instagram, write that report, attend the next meeting, check up on family, make sure the grocery order is checked out, plan meals for the week, get a wash on, weed the garden, lime plaster the middle room – the to do list literally does never end for most of us these days. So, given that none of us are ever going to get everything done, why don't we give ourselves a day off from it all once a week, a Sabbath. Time to just be, not worrying about the future, which we can't control – I mean, a global pandemic, hello, who saw that one coming – or regretting the past, which is beyond alteration. Take the time to be with family, with friends, or in nature. Take your time. But whatever you do, if you are with people, then be with them. Spending your time with folk constantly checking your phone is not being with people. In fact, while we're on the subject, turn off your phone for a day every week. I know, revolutionary. Let everyone who is likely to be in contact know, and then just turn off. Attention spans are reducing year on year. Phones, tablets, devices are attention thieves. You sit down for five minutes to glance at Facebook over a cup of tea, and an hour later you've gone down several worm holes and are still sat there. Be here now. Move, get outside, spend time with those you love, do things which bring you joy, make the most of your one wild exciting life – but make sure at least part of every day is spent outside. Doesn't have to be hours, five minutes sat outside with a cup of coffee is a great start. Sit, look, listen, be. Be present.

Maybe you don't have any outside space, maybe your nearest park is knee deep in dog poo or the haunt of drug dealers and pimps. There will be somewhere, we just need to look for it. I've lived here for over twenty years. On Thursday I went to get my Covid booster jab at our local doctors, thought I'd walk into town while waiting for Mike, discovered an entire park and set of walks that I had never realised were there. Nature and beauty are all around us if we just slow down, open our eyes, get outside and look. And the more people start looking and appreciating, the more of us who will be prepared to fight to defend our life giving, soul sustaining countryside.

The importance of story

Story is powerful, story is transformational, story changes lives. Presumably that's why Jesus chose to get his message across through the medium of story or parable. Just telling people what to do rarely works out well, it's not a sustainable model. The church has been trying it for over two thousand years now, with exponentially decreasing rates of success. Making people think, stimulating them, asking questions of them, telling them a story and leaving them to work it out for themselves – that's powerful, that works.

But it has also struck me as a result of this walk that the stories we tell ourselves have the power to bind us or to set us free. The stories we tell ourselves become the stories of our lives. What do I mean by this somewhat gnomic phrase? For more years than I care to remember I had told myself that I was fat, unfit, not at all sporty, couldn't do any exercise, should just stick to the life of the mind, that would be fine for me. Unsurprisingly, this became a self-fulfilling prophecy. The more I told myself this, the less physical activity I undertook, the fatter and more unfit I became, and so the prospect of even attempting to do anything vaguely exercise based became less and less attractive. And as we discovered in an earlier chapter, this is a story I'd been telling myself since school days, ignoring inconvenient evidence to the contrary such as the fact that I'd loved sports at primary school, loved to swim at any opportunity, loved to go for walks in the countryside, had taken up rowing at college and enjoyed it plus got around town by cycling, a form of physical exercise I believe.

Then along came the Amble and blew all that out of the water. My body was clearly capable of so much more than I'd allowed myself to believe. The story I'd been telling myself all these years was clearly a big fat lie. The good news was that there was still time to change, it wasn't quite too late, though I did leave it another eighteen months or so before the planets aligned again to point me at the person I needed to help me really begin to understand what my body was truly capable of and to push me to my limits and beyond.

But my point here is the power of the stories we tell ourselves. We treat them as gospel truth when really they are just stories. And we can change the narrative, we can turn it on its head. As I said in the body of the book, we have an old lizard part of our brains, the amygdala, always on the alert for any threats or dangers to us. It dates back to our cavemen days when the dangers were many and various. We still have dangers all around, but not ones the amygdala is programmed to look out for. Instead of telling us to lay off the fatty, sweet foods which surround us, the amygdala always fears famine – which would have been a common occurrence for our ancestors, but we have no need to lay down layers of fat against a slow down in the hunting season or a crop failure. Although maybe the current cost of living crisis and increased reliance on foodbanks will prove me wrong and the amygdala right . . . .

We are not our thoughts. We can change our patterns of thinking, the stories we tell ourselves, and if we change them, then we change our behaviour, we change our expectations, we change our lives.

Seven reflections, seven learning points, seven ways that the Amble has challenged and changed me. Made me stop and think and modify my behaviour, change the stories I tell myself. It hasn't happened overnight, I haven't done it alone, I've had help, and I'm not done yet. Always a work in progress, never the finished article, that's one of the things I've learned and am learning. And I hope to go on learning, challenging myself, stepping out of my comfort zone for however many weeks I've got left on this planet.

The question Marianna posed to all her friends and family at the beginning of this book was to ask everyone to reflect on their own lives and to consider whether they were achieving their dreams and ambitions? Thanks to the Amble, and to this book, I am.

Are you?

Acknowledgements

If it takes a village to raise a child, it feels pretty much the same is required to birth a book! There are so many people to thank for all their help and encouragement.

First and foremost to Mike, long suffering husband, without whom neither walk nor book would ever have happened.

To Mum and Dad, and the rest of the family who very much made me the person I am today.

To Cathy, Simon, Julian, Dave and Ruth for their company on various legs of the walk, but especially to Dave for all his advice before the walk, and particularly for all the wisdom he imparted during it. Very sadly, Dave died in March of 2022, pretty much of a broken heart so re-reading what I wrote on how he would cope with Ann's death is bittersweet now. They are both much missed.

To Sarah for her brilliant editing skills, which have made this a much better, more readable book than it would otherwise have been.

To Liz for her amazing cover art, and to her nephew, Martin Gray, for coming up with the title.

To my fabulous nieces, Bex, Hannah and Lydia who have all made major contributions each in their own way – and a special thanks to Lydia for the map of the walk.

To Ronya, for being my first ever reader, giving me such encouraging feedback, and for giving so generously of her time and skills to proofread and index the book. Not forgetting her husband Ray who did the final, final proof read!

To Dan and the team at Aspect Design, huge thanks for the brilliant design work – and for your patience with a rookie author.

To Revd Julie, and the rest of the benefice, who gave me so much support and encouragement and prayer.

To all those who donated to the two charities I was fundraising for – thank you, thank you, thank you for your kindness and generosity.

Finally, to Marianna, the best friend anyone could ever ask for. Her words and her life have been a big influence on my life, and I suspect, the lives of many others. And through this book, her memory and her words will live on, which I hope would have pleased and amused her.

Further Reading

These are all books which have inspired, challenged or enlightened me – usually all three!

Windswept, Annabel Abbs
Wanderers – A History of Women Walking, Kerri Andrews
Strong, Poorna Bell
Radical Confidence, Lisa Bilyeu
If Women Rose Rooted, Sharon Blackie
Hagitude, Sharon Blackie
Four Thousand Weeks, Oliver Burkeman
The Ribbons are for Fearlessness, Catrina Davies
How To Fail, Elizabeth Day
Coasting, Elise Downing
Untamed, Glennon Doyle
Big Magic, Elizabeth Gilbert
Runner, Lizzie Hawker
Leap In, Alexandra Heminsley
Rest is Resistance, Tricia Hersey
In Her Nature, Rachel Hewitt
Adventure Revolution, Belinda Kirk
Difficult Women – A History of Feminism in 11 Fights, Helen Lewis
The Electricity of Every Living Thing, Katherine May
Wintering, Katherine May

The Naked Hermit, Nick Mayhew-Smith
The Wisdom of Your Body, Hillary L. McBride
Becoming, Michelle Obama
Overwhelmed, Brigid Schulte
Stone Will Answer, Beatrice Searle
Wild, Cheryl Strayed
Solo, Jenny Tough
Move, Caroline Williams

Index